THE PRACTICE

THE PRACTICE OF VIRTUE

Classic and Contemporary Readings in Virtue Ethics

Edited by
Jennifer Welchman

Hackett Publishing Company, Inc.
Indianapolis/Cambridge

12 11 10 09 08 07 06   1 2 3 4 5 6 7

For further information, please address:

Hackett Publishing Company, Inc.
P.O. Box 44937
Indianapolis, IN 46244-0937

www.hackettpublishing.com

Cover design by Abigail Coyle
Text design by Chris Downey
Composition by Kim Arney Mulcahy
Printed at Edwards Brothers, Inc.

Library of Congress Cataloging-in-Publication Data

The practice of virtue : classic and contemporary readings
  in virtue ethics / edited by Jennifer Welchman.
      p. cm.
  Includes bibliographical references.
  ISBN 0-87220-810-9 — ISBN 0-87220-809-5 (pbk.)
  1. Ethics.   2. Virtue.   I. Welchman, Jennifer.

BJ1521.P73 2006
179'.9—dc22   2005057434

The paper used in this publication meets the minimum requirements of
American National Standard for Information Sciences—
Permanence of Paper for Printed Library Materials,
ANSI Z39.48-1984

CONTENTS

PREFACE

Virtue-centered theories of ethics have long competed with their principle-based counterparts in the Western philosophical tradition. After a century in which principle-based theories took precedence, virtue theories are again receiving attention. Demand for course material in virtue ethics is strong and growing, but has been difficult to meet due to the inadequate range of representative sources available in general introductory ethics readers and anthologies. *The Practice of Virtue* is designed to meet this challenge.

The Practice of Virtue offers readings from five classic sources that have played major roles in the development of Western virtue ethics and continue to influence contemporary discussion today: Aristotle, Seneca, Hutcheson, Hume, and Nietzsche. To bridge the gap between theory and practice, *The Practice of Virtue* also provides five specially commissioned essays on the application of the theories to practical problems in contemporary life. The essays by Rosalind Hursthouse, Julia Annas, Mark H. Waymack, Jacqueline Taylor, and Clancy W. Martin illustrate the ways virtue theories can be applied to questions such as how we should treat animals; set goals for ourselves; and approach issues in public policy, social practice, and business ethics.

Preparation of this text has been assisted by financial support from the University of Alberta; Leanne Kent and Angela Thachuk, research assistants; Deborah Wilkes, editor, Hackett Publishing; and the advice of colleagues too numerous to mention.

INTRODUCTION

What sort of person should I try to be? What consequences should I be pursuing? Which ways of acting are right? These are three fundamental questions that Western moral philosophies try to answer. The three main traditions in Western moral thought disagree about which of these three questions should be considered the most basic conceptually.

Some moral philosophers have argued that the most fundamental is the question of which consequences are best to pursue. Theories that take this approach are known as *consequentialist* ethical theories. According to consequentialist theorists, if we know what consequences are most worth pursuing, we can then determine which acts are right and what kind of people we should try to be. If, for example, we believe that the best consequence to pursue is the maximization of personal happiness, we can easily determine which acts are right and what sort of character to strive for. The right acts to perform will be those that maximize personal happiness and the right character traits to strive for will be those that help us promote the best consequences. Utilitarianism, one of the best-known forms of contemporary consequentialist ethics, proposes just this.

Others have argued that while it is natural and appropriate to want to promote our own and others' happiness by our actions, the question of *how* to act is more important than what we should act for. If, for example, we believe people have fundamental moral rights not to be treated in certain ways or we believe we owe it to our creator to live in accordance with divine commands, then we cannot determine which acts are right or wrong simply by looking at their consequences. We will need to ask ourselves whether or not a particular act would violate another's rights or the creator's commands. If it did, then the act would be wrong no matter how appealing the consequences. Similarly, with this approach, we will decide which character traits are virtues or vices in relation to our standards for right action. Character traits that help us to perform right acts are virtues, while those that promote wrongdoing are vices. Moral theories that adopt this general approach are called *deontological* theories (from the Greek word *deon*, meaning what is required, or our duty) because they claim that our duty to do what is right takes priority over achieving good consequences. The German philosopher Immanuel Kant has been the most important source for contemporary secular deontological ethical theories.

Through most of Western history, however, moral philosophers viewed the question of character as the most fundamental, an approach currently known as *virtue ethics*. According to this approach, it is premature to try to decide which consequences are worth acting for, or how we should treat other people, until we have first determined what sort of person any of us should try to be. For classical philosophers, such as Aristotle or Seneca, this means starting with the concept of *eudaimonia*, which is alternately translated as flourishing or happiness. What does a human being need to lead a flourishing or happy life? Some might say the answer is wealth, others power or social status, and still others health or physical well-being. Virtue theorists generally reject these suggestions because they believe none of these things are necessary or sufficient for personal flourishing since people do in fact lead flourishing and happy lives even if they lack both wealth and social status. Many even flourish despite chronic illness or injury. On the other hand, some people who are rich, socially influential, and in good health lead unhappy lives. Classical virtue theorists argued that this means the key to flourishing is not to be found in our external circumstances but within ourselves. Our flourishing is a function of our development as persons, specifically of the development of our character. The better our character, the more flourishing and happy our lives will be overall.

Classical virtue theorists also argued that a person who possesses strengths of character, or virtues—such as courage, generosity, justice, prudence, honesty, and compassion—is best equipped to tackle choices about what to do and what consequences to pursue. Virtuous people will not need rules to tell them not to harm others, to tell no lies, to stand up for the weak, or to help those in need, because their virtues already prompt them to behave accordingly. Thus, the right thing to do in any particular dilemma is whatever a virtuous person would choose to do—an act that expresses (or at least does not conflict with) the virtues that mark the virtuous person's character. Good objectives to act for are those that create a state of affairs in which virtuous action is promoted and not hindered.

WHY VIRTUE ETHICS? OBJECTIONS AND REPLIES

Virtue ethics is only one of three rival traditions in Western moral thought. Thus one can ask, Why adopt a virtue ethics approach? Aren't there important advantages to deontological and consequentialist systems that we will lose if we do?

First, both deontological and consequentialist approaches offer us principles of action to follow that allow us to determine precisely what we ought to do in moral dilemmas. Virtue ethics tells us to act as a virtuous person would. What will that mean in practice? It seems to mean that if we have a virtuous character we should do whatever we feel most strongly like doing. What if we are not very virtuous people? How will we know what a more virtuous person would feel like doing?

Perhaps we might find out what a more virtuous person would do by asking friends or colleagues whose character is better than our own. This raises a second question. How do we decide which person to ask? How do we recognize good character? Taking a deontological or consequentialist approach, we can judge a person's moral character by comparing their behavior with the appropriate set of principles. A good utilitarian is a person whose acts maximize happiness. A good Kantian is one who never acts in ways that violate the Categorical Imperative of Kantian moral theory. So if an individual consistently fails to maximize happiness or regularly violates the Categorical Imperative, we can conclude that he lacks good character. But in virtue ethics, the relation between character and action goes the other way. We define acts as right, and consequences as good, in terms of an individual's dispositions. However, dispositions are invisible. How then are we to evaluate another person's dispositions, if not by their results or their agreement with moral principles?

Third, although generosity, honesty, prudence, compassion, and justice are generally good characteristics to have, some would argue that this isn't always the case. Ordinary moral language may seem to bear this out. We call some people too generous for their own or others' good. Other people are criticized for being 'brutally honest.' Bleeding hearts take compassion to such an extreme we fear it may affect their judgment. "All work and no play," makes the prudent Jack a dull boy. One can simply have too much of any good thing; thus, even virtuous people may need principles to follow to ensure their judgment does not become distorted.

Fourth, different cultures seem to differ in the values they assign particular character traits. For example, a century ago in North American society, submissiveness to, and passive social dependence upon, men was highly valued in women. Today, a woman displaying the same degree of submissiveness would probably be said to suffer from low self-esteem, for which counseling would be recommended. It is now generally considered imprudent, even irresponsible, for a woman to rely passively upon others for her income or social position. Independence has come to be valued in both men and women. This suggests that recognition of traits as virtuous or vicious may be relative to cultural standards. If so, we could not look to theories of the virtues to provide universal moral standards that apply cross-culturally, of the sort deontological and consequentialist theories promise us.

Advocates of virtue ethics argue that the advantages claimed for principle-based alternatives are either mistaken or exaggerated. Principles of action do seem to offer us fairly precise decision-procedures for determining how to act, until we begin to apply them to concrete cases. Once we do, the usefulness of the recommended decision-procedures is immediately open to question. Broad universal principles, such as "never violate another person's autonomy," or "always act for the best consequences," are so abstract they may tell us little of value for resolving a problematic situation. How do we decide if another person is autonomous? Are all choices autonomous, or only some? Is a hastily made choice necessarily autonomous? What about people who seem to be autonomously choosing to violate others' autonomy? Can we either intervene or refrain without violating someone's autonomy? Or, if we take a consequentialist approach, we will have to ask ourselves, What is the best outcome in a given situation? What if others disagree, including the people whose interests we are trying to promote? Of course, deontological and consequentialist philosophers discuss these questions and offer much advice about how to apply their principles. The fact that we will need a great deal of theoretical guidance in applying their theories does not show that these approaches are wrong. However, it does show that it is an overstatement to say that principle-based theories all offer much simpler and more precise ways to make moral decisions.

Moreover, it is a mistake to suppose that virtue ethics has no place for rules. Virtues cannot be reduced to rules, because virtues are dispositions to respond to the world around us, and this responsiveness can take many forms. Take generosity, for example. Generosity is an active concern for the welfare of others, but the acts it will motivate one to perform will vary from case to case. Sometimes the generous thing to do will be to help someone resolve a problem, while at other times, the generous thing to do is just the opposite—to stand by and merely applaud their efforts to help themselves. While we cannot reduce a virtue like generosity to a universal rule, we can and do construct helpful rules of thumb about the kinds of behavior that are or are not compatible with virtue. Many of the moral rules taught to children are rules of just this sort; for example, "telling lies is dishonest," "bullying is cruel," "look before you leap," or "how would I feel if she did that to me?" Moral rules like these, derived from the virtues (sometimes called *v-rules* for short), do not provide universally applicable decision-procedures telling us just what to do in particular cases. Instead, they help us to interpret the situation as a virtuous person would, highlighting the features to which the just or generous, prudent or sympathetic person would focus upon were he or she in our shoes.

Thus, we do not have to be perfectly virtuous to know how to approach a moral dilemma nor are we forced to put off making decisions until a more virtuous person happens to offer advice. The v-rules in which we were educated usually provide all the guidance we need. They also help to answer the question of how we can identify individuals of exemplary character to turn to when we do want advice. The better a person's character, the more regularly and reliably their behavior will exemplify the sort of perceptiveness that the v-rules illustrate for us.

This brings us to the third worry: that people can be *too* virtuous in certain respects, with the result that their perceptions of a situation actually become distorted. The too-generous person seems blind to her own needs and legitimate interests. The brutally honest person seems unable to appreciate the effects of his honesty on others. The bleeding heart seems unable to appreciate the importance of balancing compassion against the need to cultivate personal responsibility. The ever-prudent Jack is dull because he represses the risk-taking, creative dispositions that add spice to life and personal relationships. Let us examine these claims more closely. What really seems to be going wrong in each case? Is it because these people possess the virtues of generosity, honesty, compassion, or prudence that they seem to go wrong? Or is it that they lack some other virtue that a more exemplary character would also possess? The blindness each sort of person exhibits to certain features of their situation suggests they have failed to develop other important virtues that would have given them better insight. The overly generous person may be lacking in an appropriate sense of self-worth, the brutally honest person in generosity, and so forth. Rather than being too virtuous, we might argue, these people are not virtuous enough. They lack key virtues that they need to develop.

What virtue ethics has to say about cultural relativism varies somewhat according to the particular theory being offered. However, for any theory, a certain amount of variation from culture to culture would be expected, even if the theorist holds that the virtues are precisely the same for every person wherever and whenever they live. This is because different physical and social environments present different challenges to, and opportunities for, the expression of virtuous dispositions. Thus the v-rules by which virtues are taught will differ also. "Look before you leap" or "don't count your chickens before they have hatched" may be helpful v-rules of prudence in one kind of physical environment (where cliffs and chickens are common) but useless in another (where cliffs and chickens are unknown). Isolated societies that rarely, if ever, experience attacks from other groups will have little need or opportunity to develop v-rules promoting courage under fire. "Respect your parents' values" is useful advice about the nature of loyalty in societies whose parents rear their own children, but pointless in societies in which children are reared by others.

Similarly, even if a theorist believes that the virtues are the same for all, that theorist can still accept that the relative importance of developing specific virtues to a high degree can also vary within and across societies. One could take the position that while no one can flourish unless they develop certain important or *cardinal* virtues, flourishing does not require that every individual develop every virtue to a particularly high degree. For example, benevolence, justice, courage, temperance, honesty, prudence, and loyalty are commonly held to be cardinal virtues essential for anyone to lead even a minimally flourishing life, let alone an admirable or exemplary one. However, this doesn't entail that each is equally important, whatever sort of life one leads. One can still grant that some are more crucial for the meritorious performance of particular social roles than others. Arguably, for example, it is more important that healthcare professionals be strongly motivated by benevolence than judges; more important for public officials to be motivated by justice than parents; more important that military officers be strongly motivated by courage and loyalty than financial planners, and so forth. (Of course this is conditional on the roles in question being themselves virtuous, i.e., roles a virtuous person could choose to perform. Some social roles—torturer, for example—would not pass this test.)

Returning to the objection then, cultural variation in the practice of virtues and the v-rules associated with them need not be seen as invalidating a virtue ethics approach. Nor does it indicate that moral praise or criticism is inherently relative to culture. It does mean we need to pay careful attention to the nature of the physical and social environment within which other cultures operate, and take these into account before we engage in evaluation. In the case of a woman, living over one hundred years ago, in social circumstances that offered her few opportunities to earn an acceptable living by her own means and censured independence in dealing with men, we could acknowledge that given those circumstances, dependence and submissiveness were not marks of deplorably low self-esteem, imprudence, or other vices. If endured for the good of others, her dependence and submissiveness might actually indicate great courage, benevolence, or loyalty. Nevertheless, we could still hold that the life she was constrained to lead was a less flourishing and happy life than she might have led had her opportunities for self-development been greater. We could also criticize the social arrangements that imposed those constraints as being incompatible with virtue.

Taking a virtue ethics approach need not force one to give up the idea that there may be one—and only one—set of virtues each and every individual ought to develop for a flourishing life and character. Neither does it require that one take such a view. Many opt for a more modest position: of the wide range of traits that can positively contribute to human flourishing, only a few cardinal virtues are necessary or essential. Others will take the yet more modest position that not even developing each of the cardinal virtues is absolutely necessary; some subset of these, combined with some subset of the lesser virtues, may under the right circumstances be sufficient. The more modest the position, of course, the more modest the legitimacy of cross-cultural assessments one may be entitled to make.

ADVANTAGES OF VIRTUE ETHICS

Assuming these replies are substantially correct, a virtue ethics approach is not at a disadvantage relative to principle-based alternatives. So, what are the advantages of virtue ethics?

First, we might point out that one reason we go to the trouble of constructing moral theories is to better understand moral life and its complexities. We cannot succeed in this objective if we misrepresent our subject matter. Some charge that this is precisely what principle-based accounts do.

As Edmund Pincoffs has remarked, principle-based ethical approaches seem to reduce morality and moral life to a series of quandaries with the result that being a good person, morally speaking, is being a person who is good at resolving moral puzzles by the conscientious application of appropriate moral principles or decision-procedures. This suggests that the only character trait of moral significance is conscientiousness. However, in daily life, we do not praise people's characters for their conscientiousness alone. We praise people for their possession of a host of other traits—loyalty, honesty, courage, and sympathy—that we take to be equally essential to leading a good life. A moral theory that assigns conscientiousness too central a place in its account of moral character will at best distort and at worst misrepresent these facts about moral life.

As Julia Annas will argue later in this book, another feature of morality that principle-based accounts may have difficulty capturing is our commonsense understanding of what is involved in good moral judgment. On a principle-based account, to be a good moral judge is ultimately to be good at applying a set of principles or decision-procedures to choices of actions, as if morality were something one could encompass in a technical manual. If this were correct, Annas argues, we would expect to find that in morality, as in music, mathematics, computer programming, and other technical fields, young people with a flair for the logic of technical systems could readily become acknowledged experts in the field. With morality, this does not seem to be the case. Age and experience of the world seem to be crucial requirements for good moral judgment. Virtue ethics approaches, which depict moral character as developing over time, are thus more in keeping with our commonsense understanding of how moral expertise is developed.

Defenders of principle-based approaches might reply as follows: the universal moral principles our theories provide are necessarily highly abstract and thus difficult to apply to particular cases without time and a good working knowledge of the world. This is why most such theories also provide secondary principles, derived from our universal first principles, telling us what to do when faced with special kinds of quandaries. As James Stuart Mill famously remarked: "it is a strange notion that the acknowledgment of a first principle is inconsistent with the admission of secondary one. To inform a traveler respecting the place of his ultimate destination is not to forbid the use of landmarks and direction posts on the way." It takes time and practice to master these secondary rules and thus it is not surprising that very young people are not particularly good moral judges.

A defender of virtue ethics will point out that when we look at particular secondary principles—for example, the sort one finds in professional ethical codes—more often than not they tell us more about what sort of person to be than about the acts one should perform. Codes for doctors and nurses require them to be benevolent, just, diligent, respectful of personal autonomy, trustworthy, and discrete. Codes for architects and engineers require them to care more for public safety than their own personal self-interest or their clients' wishes. If in practical life our secondary principles turn out to be injunctions to be virtuous, a virtue ethics explanation of what good moral judgment is and why it takes so much time and experience to develop seems simpler and more straightforward. Moral judgment is not essentially the application of a moral "technical manual" to life.

Finally, virtue ethics may seem to have an advantage over other approaches when it comes to the question of why we should care about morality in the first place. If morality is a form of code for evaluating acts or their consequences and following the code will oblige me to sacrifice my own interests, why should I bother? Virtue ethics can appeal to the traditional commonsense view that cultivating virtue is better for us personally because the virtues are important constituents of a good and flourishing life. Vices like injustice, greed, or cowardice may, in the short run, help us increase our wealth and social status or avoid risks to our health. However, as we have already observed, these are not sufficient for happiness. People can and often do fare quite well without them. Cardinal virtues, by contrast, are beneficial in themselves, even when they do not bring us wealth or other external goods. Here again, virtue ethics seems peculiarly well suited to the subject matter that philosophical ethical theories analyze: moral experience.

VARIETIES OF VIRTUE ETHICS

Virtue ethics is a tradition, not a theory. Many different theories of character and the virtues have contributed to this tradition. Five examples are presented in this text, selected from the works of Aristotle, Seneca, Hutcheson, Hume, and Nietzsche, paired with companion articles specially written for this book, discussing the application of these theories to issues in practical life. These are by no means the only important philosophical contributors to the Western tradition of virtue ethics. These five are notable both for their historical significance and for their continuing value as resources for contemporary philosophical debate.

The five classic theories are presented in chronological order, but it is not essential that they be studied in this way. While Aristotle's theory is and remains the single most influential theory in the tradition, newcomers to the field may well find Hutcheson's sentiment-based theory a more appealing example with which to start, as his identification of virtuous character with benevolence may more closely match popular conceptions of virtue with which students and many general readers are already familiar. From Hutcheson, one could work forward through Hume and Nietzsche, whose theories are in part responses to Hutcheson's.

One could then go back to the classical sources, Aristotle and Seneca.

Wherever one starts, one will find that important differences between the theories are traceable to differences in the authors' views of the best way to answer the question, What sort of person should I be?

Classical Theories: Aristotle and Seneca

Classical philosophers recommend that we take a naturalistic, functional approach to human nature, asking ourselves what sort of life our species is fitted to live, and what characteristics equip us to perform the functions essential to living this kind of life. Aristotle and the stoics agree that as a species, human beings are intensely social, interdependent creatures who crave social relationships for their own sake and who rely upon social cooperation to develop, live, and reproduce. However, unlike some social species whose natural desires and instincts oblige them to cooperate fully (ants, bees, and so on) our natural desire to live and work with others competes with an equally natural desire to satisfy purely personal objectives that may be incompatible with others' good or with social cooperation. Reason is the capacity with which we have been equipped to troubleshoot the problems our conflicting desires and impulses create.

Reason tells us that solving this problem of balancing our social and personal projects so that we can lead successful and fulfilling lives depends upon our development of a character whose predominant dispositions, social and nonsocial, operate in mutually reinforcing ways, disposing us to adopt goals for personal and social life that are mutually enhancing. Rationally speaking, then, the sort of character to aim for is one in which the expression of each of our predominant dispositions supports the expression of the others in our personal and social projects.

Dispositions of character are not the same as 'personality traits.' They are not predetermined features of our natures, inborn and essentially unalterable. If they were, it would be pointless to try to improve our lives by improving our dispositions. Dispositions are patterns of responsiveness to feelings, desires, and challenges that human beings develop over time, partly through social influences, partly by personal effort. In some respects, our dispositions are like our habits. However, while habits are tendencies to repeat the same *act* in the circumstances that trigger the habit, our dispositions are tendencies to respond with the same *concerns* or interests in circumstances that provide that disposition an outlet. So, for example, if I am a generous person, coming upon people in need doesn't trigger performance of the same action over and over again. Rather, if I am a generous person, recognizing people in need prompts my generous nature to look for appropriate outlets for action, although which particular act I will be disposed to perform as a result may never be the same twice. This is not the case with habits.

Dispositions can be helpful or harmful, attractive or unattractive, both to the person whose dispositions they are and for those around her. So although all virtues of character may be dispositions, not all dispositions can be virtues. Dispositions are virtues if they contribute directly to personal flourishing; e.g., benevolence, temperance, justice, courage, conviviality, and practical wisdom (or perceptiveness). Vices, by contrast, are dispositions that cause inner disharmony and interpersonal conflict; e.g., arrogance, coldness, vanity, and greed. In characters marred by vice, attempts to express one of our predominant dispositions can only succeed by frustrating the expression of others, making successful integration of one's social and personal life projects difficult or impossible.

Aristotle and Seneca agree that possession of a virtuous character is necessary for us to flourish as human beings and to lead rewarding lives. They disagree, however, on the question of whether possessing a virtuous character could ever be sufficient for a happy and rewarding life. Although their methods for studying human flourishing were very similar, their conceptions of human flourishing were less so. Aristotle argues that human flourishing is ideally the flourishing of our whole natures—rational, emotional, social, and purely physical—so he concluded that a certain amount of luck in the material and social circumstances of life is also necessary for happiness. Seneca and other stoics disagreed, arguing that a conception of *human* flourishing should focus more narrowly on dispositions uniquely distinctive of human beings. While we may welcome gifts of fortune that permit the satisfaction of desires or impulses that we share with lower animals, such as the desire for physical pleasure, these are by no means necessary for human flourishing.

Sentiment-based Accounts: Hutcheson and Hume

Classical philosophers evaluate individuals in terms of their characteristics as members of a particular species, just as we might evaluate a fish, a tree, or any other living thing as a good or bad example of its kind. For example, we would judge a trout without fins a bad example of a trout, because it is ill-equipped to function as trout must. Similarly, a duck that feared water could not function in the environment to which its species is adapted and would be a bad sort of duck, given the kind of creatures ducks are. Human beings who are irrational or who are cowardly, greedy, or unjust are flawed or bad examples of human beings, given the sort of creature human beings are. However, as we noted above, classical philosophers differed somewhat about which traits were most essential for becoming a good human being.

In the eighteenth century, new sentiment-based theories tried to avoid the problem of determining which human qualities are most essential to human nature by shifting their focus to our subjective experience. Instead of asking which characteristics any member of the human species ought to have to be a good example of humanity, they ask what dispositions do we in general find *preferable* based on our subjective experience of how different dispositions do, or do not, contribute to a happy and flourishing life.

From this starting point, Hutcheson argues that when we reflect on our own and others' dispositions, we find we naturally have a special feeling or sentiment of approval for dispositions such as benevolence, dispositions that motivate us to care about others' welfare. We also value dispositions that motivate us to work for our own good, such as prudence, diligence, and thrift. We approve the former for their own sake, while we approve of the latter, however, only for their instrumental value. Hutcheson calls our natural tendency or capacity to respond approvingly to benevolence our "moral sense." The moral virtues are the dispositions to which our moral sense gives its approval.

Hume's approach is similar, but when he analyzes our reflective responses to our own and others' dispositions, he arrives at a different conclusion. Hume argues that sympathy causes us to share in the pleasures and pains of others, so from sympathy or humanity we do, as Hutcheson argues, naturally and spontaneously approve of dispositions that motivate people to act for one another's good.

From sympathy, however, we also approve of dispositions that help an individual advance her own personal good. Thus we approve of prudence, thrift, and diligence as virtues in the same way we approve of social virtues like benevolence. Further, human beings naturally approve of some dispositions for their own sake, simply because we find them immediately agreeable, whether or not they promote their possessors' or others' welfare; for example, wit, good taste, and civility. So Hume will argue that these, too, may be considered moral virtues.

Perspectivism: Nietzsche

Nietzsche's approach is a radical reworking of aspects of both the classical and eighteenth-century approaches. He agreed with classical philosophers like Aristotle and the stoics that we evaluate human beings as examples ˌof the kind of creature we take humans to be. However, he combined this with sentiment-based approaches, arguing that what we take human beings to be or be capable of is always *relative* to a particular *perspective*, developed partly from our beliefs about the nature of our species, partly from subjective preferences, and very largely from social pressures. These perspectives become embedded in cultural traditions and thus perpetuate themselves over time. What commonsense morality will consider virtuous or vicious at any given time will be relative to the predominant perspective that culture takes on human nature.

To evaluate ourselves and our own personal development, we must take some perspective on human nature. In learning to see ourselves from our own culture's predominant perspectives, we gain invaluable training in self-assessment. Cultural perspectives are also limiting, however, in part because they tend to emphasize dispositions that help to stabilize social institutions (such as docility, modesty, self-control, and self-sacrifice) over traits that enhance personal growth and creativity (such as self-assertion, honesty, exuberance, and strength of will). If we are not to be enslaved by the perspective(s) customary in our culture, we must cultivate the dispositions that empower us to develop and pursue our own perspectives on human nature. By doing so, we not only enhance our own flourishing. We contribute to the ongoing flourishing of our culture by challenging received ideas about human nature and its possibilities and by pioneering new ones. Thus the cultivation of such self-empowering virtues is crucial if we and our cultural traditions are to avoid becoming decadent or moribund.

APPLYING VIRTUE ETHICS TO LIFE

We all apply our conceptions of good character when we evaluate individuals, acts, and policies. Sometimes we do this in very general terms, approving or criticizing individuals or policies for character traits we think everyone has equal reason to approve or condemn. Sometimes we do this in relation to the demands of particular social roles, commending or criticizing individuals (or policies) for traits they express (or seem likely to inculcate) that we think peculiarly important for that particular role. Thus, applying commonsense virtues and vices to practical moral life is something most of us can easily do.

Applying a theory of the virtues and vices with which we are not already thoroughly familiar may not be so easy, at least at first. It is nevertheless worth doing because our commonsense conceptions, as Nietzsche reminds us, may reflect social biases or historical circumstances in our culture's past that we would do well to move beyond. To move beyond the conceptions of human nature and virtue we have inherited requires reflective critical thinking—theorizing, in other words. Part of what is involved in understanding a moral theory is understanding how it works; how life would be different if one adopted it. So, a crucial part of learning any virtue theory is learning how to apply it. The essays in Part II of this book are intended to help readers gain this understanding by providing models for applying the theories presented in Part I to a variety of contemporary practical issues.

Rosalind Hursthouse shows us how moral issues involved in our treatment of animals and vulnerable human beings are transformed if we approach them from a virtue ethics perspective, stressing themes common to all five classic philosophies. Julia Annas addresses common concerns about the implications of adopting a stoic attitude to life, in particular what it will mean for our relations with others. Mark H. Waymack looks at how Hutcheson's approach will illuminate questions about the morality of adopting protectionist social legislation. Jacqueline Taylor discusses the problem of hate in society and how a Humean might respond. Finally, Clancy W. Martin discusses the significance of a Nietzschean approach for business ethics.

Following each essay in Part II are recommendations for further reading in recent philosophical literature on the application of these five varieties of virtue ethics to practical life.

SUGGESTIONS FOR FURTHER READING

A number of collections of articles on virtue ethics provide an excellent overview of the subject, together with discussions of historically important contributors (e.g., Aristotle, Hume, etc.). See for example: Steve Gardiner, ed., *Virtues Old and New* (Ithaca, NY: Cornell University Press, 2005); David Carr and Jan Steutel, eds., *Virtue Ethics and Moral Education* (New York: Routledge, 1999); Roger Crisp and Michael Slote, eds., *Virtue Ethics* (Oxford: Oxford University Press, 1997); Roger Crisp, ed., *How Should One Live?* (Oxford: Clarendon Press, 1996); Daniel Statman, *Virtue Ethics* (Edinburgh: Edinburgh University Press, 1997); Owen Flanagan and Amelie Oksenberg Rorty, eds., *Identity, Character and Morality* (Cambridge, MA: The MIT Press, 1990); Peter A. French, Theodore E. Uehling, and Howard K. Wettstein, eds., *Midwest Studies in Philosophy Volume 13. Ethical Theory: Character and Virtue* (Notre Dame, IN: University of Notre Dame Press, 1988); and Roger B. Kruschwitz and Robert C. Roberts, *The Virtues: Contemporary Essays on Moral Character* (Belmont, CA: Wadsworth, 1987).

For an engaging debate between contemporary representatives of virtue ethics and two rival traditions, see Marcia W. Baron, Philip Pettit, and Michael Slote, eds., *Three Methods of Ethics* (New York: Oxford University Press, 1997).

For readers with more background in the philosophical literature who are interested in contemporary studies of virtue ethics that focus on its theoretical prospects and problems, the following works are particularly recommended: Annette Baier, *Moral Prejudices* (Cambridge, MA: Harvard University Press, 1994); N.J.H. Dent, *The Moral Psychology of the Virtues* (Cambridge: Cambridge University Press, 1984); Julia Driver, *Uneasy Virtue* (New York: Cambridge University Press, 2001); Philippa Foot, *Virtues and Vices* (Oxford: Blackwell, 1978) and *Natural Goodness* (Oxford, Clarendon Press, 2001); William Galston, *Liberal Purposes* (New York: Cambridge University Press, 1991); Thomas Hurka, *Virtue, Vice, and Value* (Oxford: Oxford University Press, 2001); Rosalind Hursthouse, *On Virtue Ethics* (Oxford: Oxford University Press, 1999); Christine McKinnon, *Character, Virtue Theories, and the Vices* (Peterborough, Ontario: Broadview, 1999); Alasdair MacIntyre, *After Virtue,* 2nd ed. (Notre Dame, IN: University of Notre Dame Press, 1984); Edmund L. Pincoffs, *Quandaries and Virtues* (Lawrence: University Press of Kansas, 1986); Michael Slote, *Morals from Motives* (Oxford: Oxford University Press, 2001); Christine Swanton, *Virtue Ethics* (Oxford: Oxford University Press, 2003); and James D. Wallace, *Virtues and Vices* (Ithaca, NY: Cornell University Press, 1978).

PART I
CLASSIC VIRTUE THEORIES

Aristotle

INTRODUCTION

Aristotle was born in 384 B.C.E. in the small northern town of Stagira, in Macedonia. His father, Nicomachus, was court physician to Amyntas III, king of Macedonia, the grandfather of Alexander the Great. As a boy, Aristotle would probably have been instructed in rudiments of medical practice but whether because of his father's early death or his own lack of interest, Aristotle did not continue such studies after his father's death. His family was wealthy, so he could afford to follow his own tastes. In 367, in his late teens, he traveled to Athens, presumably to broaden his education. From his own writings, it is evident that he studied Plato's philosophy with great care. From other sources, it appears that he became a respected member of Plato's intellectual circle. Whether he actually taught in Plato's academy is not known, but if the anecdotes that have survived are anything to go by, Aristotle was notable for his extraordinarily wide-ranging intellectual interests, including subjects ranging from aesthetics to zoology. Plato is said to have teased him for his habitual reading and book collecting.

Aristotle left Athens shortly after Plato's death circa 348. Critics charged that he left because Plato's nephew Speusippus was chosen to succeed Plato as head of the Platonic Academy. Defenders suggest that his departure was due to a rise in anti-Macedonian feeling in the city. Whatever the reason, Aristotle moved to Assos in Atarneus, where the local ruler Hermias invited Aristotle and his fellow Academician Xenocrates to set up their own school. Aristotle married Hermias' niece, Pythias, who became the mother of his daughter Pythias and son Nicomachus. Three years later, he moved to Mytilene on the island of Lesbos, where according to tradition he developed his interest in empirical natural science. By 342, Aristotle had received an invitation from King Philip II of Macedon to return to Macedonia to become a tutor to the young Alexander. Aristotle remained at King Philip II's court for three years, after which he retired to family estates at Stagira.

In 335, Aristotle's old friend Xenocrates become the new head of the Platonic Academy and Aristotle returned to Athens. Though still respectful of Plato's teachings, Aristotle had moved beyond them in many areas, not least ethics. So instead of rejoining the Academy, he set up his own school, the Lyceum, nearby. He remained in Athens for twelve years, until another upsurge of anti-Macedonian feeling in 323. Aristotle removed to family estates on the island of Euboea. He died a year later.

Aristotle wrote and published extensively in his lifetime, but only fragments of his polished philosophical writings have survived. The texts we have, including the *Nicomachean Ethics,* were not written for publication. They appear to be lecture notes, collected and edited over many years, either for his own or his students' use. Unlike his published works, which were praised for their literary style, these texts are written in a compressed, economical fashion to illustrate the methods and arguments Aristotle thought most appropriate to solving the philosophical questions that interested him. In the *Nicomachean Ethics,* Aristotle's method is to consider rival conceptions of happiness, the good life, and the role of virtue, and then test them for their ability to explain or agree with commonsense opinion. Views that cannot account for commonsense beliefs arc to be rejected in favor of those that can, until we arrive at a consistent set of moral concepts and moral virtues that not only explains what the best life is but helps us to achieve it. As Aristotle says, with ethics, "the purpose of our examination is not [primarily] to know what virtue is but to become good."

Following this method, Aristotle eliminates the views of his old mentor, Plato, almost immediately. Plato had argued that what motivates us to live well and act well is knowledge of the good—in knowing the good we most nearly approach divine understanding and are at the same time the least likely to be tempted by false, inferior values such as pleasure or material wealth. Aristotle notes that while some agree, more do not. Some consider a life rich in material possessions to be the best life open to us, others a life rich in pleasure, still others prominent social status. Since Plato's account does not adequately explain how such erroneous views become entrenched, we need a new approach. Aristotle's suggestion is that we take a more holistic approach to human nature: we should ask what kind of creatures human beings are, and what our distinct mode of life is, before we try to determine which traits are essential for us to develop in an exemplary way. He will argue that the most essential are reason and the moral and intellectual virtues, especially practical wisdom.

People who are exemplary in these respects will be more successful than less accomplished individuals in most of their endeavors and so experience less frustration, pain, or disappointment. Thus, a virtuous life will usually prove a more pleasant and rewarding life. How *much* more rewarding will depend on how fortunate we are in obtaining the material goods necessary for carrying out our projects. Thus, the common view that wealth and social position make a difference to our realization of the best life is not mistaken, although the importance usually assigned to them is. Wealth and position are only good as *means* to other more important ends— the most crucial being our own self-development. The person of exemplary character is a person fitted to make the most of any situation. This is not only because the virtues are instrumentally valuable in helping us achieve our ends, but because the virtues are valuable in their own right. We are better for being virtuous, no matter what our circumstances.

Aristotle's famous "doctrine of the mean" is presented as a practical rubric for analyzing and assessing our personal development. At first, it may seem that Aristotle is simply suggesting that we should moderate our feelings and passions in order to moderate our losses and disappointments. On closer examination, however, it turns out to be quite the opposite. Its purpose is instead to help us perfect our characters. Excellence—not mediocrity—is the objective.

Nicomachean Ethics[1]

BOOK I
[HAPPINESS]

1 [ENDS AND GOODS]

Every craft and every line of inquiry, and likewise every action and decision, seems to seek some good; that is why some people were right to describe the good as what everything seeks. But the ends [that are sought] appear to differ; some are activities, and others are products apart from the activities. Wherever there are ends apart from the actions, the products are by nature better than the activities.

Since there are many actions, crafts, and sciences, the ends turn out to be many as well; for health is the end of medicine, a boat of boat building, victory of generalship, and wealth of household management. But some of these pursuits are subordinate to some one capacity; for instance, bridle making and every other science producing equipment for horses are subordinate to horsemanship, while this and every action in warfare are, in turn, subordinate to generalship, and in the same way other pursuits are subordinate to further ones. In all such cases, then, the ends of the ruling sciences are more choiceworthy than all the ends subordinate to them, since the lower ends are also pursued for the sake of the higher. Here it does not matter whether the ends of the actions are the activities themselves, or something apart from them, as in the sciences we have mentioned.

2 [THE HIGHEST GOOD AND POLITICAL SCIENCE]

Suppose, then, that the things achievable by action have some end that we wish for because of itself, and because of which we wish

---

1. The text for this selection is taken from Aristotle, *Nicomachean Ethics*, trans., with Introduction, Notes and Glossary, by Terence Irwin, 2nd ed. (Indianapolis: Hackett Publishing Company, 1999). Editorial notes have been added.

for the other things, and that we do not choose everything because
of something else—for if we do, it will go on without limit, so that
desire will prove to be empty and futile. Clearly, this end will be
the good, that is to say, the best good. Then does knowledge of this
good carry great weight for [our] way of life, and would it make us
better able, like archers who have a target to aim at, to hit the right
mark? If so, we should try to grasp, in outline at any rate, what the
good is, and which is its proper science or capacity.

It seems proper to the most controlling science—the highest ruling science. And this appears characteristic of political science. For
it is the one that prescribes which of the sciences ought to be studied in cities, and which ones each class in the city should learn, and
how far; indeed we see that even the most honored capacities—
generalship, household management, and rhetoric, for instance—
are subordinate to it. And since it uses the other sciences concerned
with action, and moreover legislates what must be done and what
avoided, its end will include the ends of the other sciences, and so
this will be the human good.

3 [THE METHOD OF POLITICAL SCIENCE]

Our discussion will be adequate if we make things perspicuous
enough to accord with the subject matter; for we would not seek
the same degree of exactness in all sorts of arguments alike, any
more than in the products of different crafts. Now, fine and just
things, which political science examines, differ and vary so much
as to seem to rest on convention only, not on nature. But [this is
not a good reason, since] goods also vary in the same way, because
they result in harm to many people—for some have been destroyed
because of their wealth, others because of their bravery. And so,
since this is our subject and these are our premises, we shall be satisfied to indicate the truth roughly and in outline; since our subject
and our premises are things that hold good usually [but not univer-
sally], we shall be satisfied to draw conclusions of the same sort.

Each of our claims, then, ought to be accepted in the same way
[as claiming to hold good usually]. For the educated person seeks
exactness in each area to the extent that the nature of the subject
allows; for apparently it is just as mistaken to demand demonstra-
tions from a rhetorician as to accept [merely] persuasive arguments

from a mathematician. Further, each person judges rightly what he knows, and is a good judge about that; hence the good judge in a given area is the person educated in that area, and the unqualifiedly good judge is the person educated in every area.

This is why a youth is not a suitable student of political science; for he lacks experience of the actions in life, which are the subject and premises of our arguments. Moreover, since he tends to follow his feelings, his study will be futile and useless; for the end [of political science] is action, not knowledge. It does not matter whether he is young in years or immature in character, since the deficiency does not depend on age, but results from following his feelings in his life and in a given pursuit; for an immature person, like an incontinent person, gets no benefit from his knowledge. But for those who accord with reason in forming their desires and in their actions, knowledge of political science will be of great benefit.

4 [COMMON BELIEFS]

Let us, then, begin again. Since every sort of knowledge and decision pursues some good, what is the good that we say political science seeks? What, [in other words,] is the highest of all the goods achievable in action? As far as its name goes, most people virtually agree; for both the many and the cultivated call it happiness, and they suppose that living well and doing well are the same as being happy. But they disagree about what happiness is, and the many do not give the same answer as the wise.

For the many think it is something obvious and evident—for instance, pleasure, wealth, or honor. Some take it to be one thing, others another. Indeed, the same person often changes his mind; for when he has fallen ill, he thinks happiness is health, and when he has fallen into poverty, he thinks it is wealth. And when they are conscious of their own ignorance, they admire anyone who speaks of something grand and above their heads. [Among the wise,] however, some used to think that besides these many goods there is some other good that exists in its own right and that causes all these goods to be goods.

Presumably, then, it is rather futile to examine all these beliefs, and it is enough to examine those that are most current or seem to have some argument for them. That is why we need to have been

brought up in fine habits if we are to be adequate students of fine
and just things, and of political questions generally. For we begin
from the [belief] that [something is true]; if this is apparent enough
to us, we can begin without also [knowing] why [it is true]. Someone who is well brought up has the beginnings, or can easily
acquire them. Someone who neither has them nor can acquire
them should listen to Hesiod: "He who grasps everything himself is
best of all; he is noble also who listens to one who has spoken well;
but he who neither grasps it himself nor takes to heart what he
hears from another is a useless man."[2]

5 [THE THREE LIVES]

But let us begin again from the point from which we digressed. For,
it would seem, people quite reasonably reach their conception of
the good, i.e., of happiness, from the lives [they lead]; for there are
roughly three most favored lives: the lives of gratification, of political activity, and, third, of study.

The many, the most vulgar, would seem to conceive the good
and happiness as pleasure, and hence they also like the life of gratification. In this they appear completely slavish, since the life they
decide on is a life for grazing animals. Still, they have some argument in their defense, since many in positions of power feel as Sardanapallus felt, [and also choose this life].[3]

The cultivated people, those active [in politics], conceive the
good as honor, since this is more or less the end [normally pursued]
in the political life. This, however, appears to be too superficial to
be what we are seeking; for it seems to depend more on those who
honor than on the one honored, whereas we intuitively believe that
the good is something of our own and hard to take from us. Fur-

---

2. Hesiod: an early Greek epic poet (possibly seventh century B.C.E.), best
known for his *Theogony* (on the genealogy of the gods) and *Works and
Days* (on the importance of justice and order in leading one's life). The reference is to the latter, *Works and Days*.

3. According to legend, Sardanapallus was an Assyrian king who so enjoyed
luxuriating in his wealth and privilege, he neglected his state duties. Beset
by invading armies, Sardanapallus set himself, his palace, and all his possession ablaze rather than lose them in defeat.

ther, it would seem, they pursue honor to convince themselves that they are good; at any rate, they seek to be honored by prudent people, among people who know them, and for virtue. It is clear, then, that—in their view at any rate—virtue is superior [to honor].

Perhaps, indeed, one might conceive virtue more than honor to be the end of the political life. However, this also is apparently too incomplete [to be the good]. For it seems possible for someone to possess virtue but be asleep or inactive throughout his life, and, moreover, to suffer the worst evils and misfortunes. If this is the sort of life he leads, no one would count him happy, except to defend a philosopher's paradox. Enough about this, since it has been adequately discussed in the popular works as well.[4]

The third life is the life of study, which we shall examine in what follows.[5]

The moneymaker's life is in a way forced on him [not chosen for itself]; and clearly wealth is not the good we are seeking, since it is [merely] useful, [choiceworthy only] for some other end.

7 [AN ACCOUNT OF THE HUMAN GOOD]

But let us return once again to the good we are looking for, and consider just what it could be. For it is apparently one thing in one action or craft, and another thing in another; for it is one thing in medicine, another in generalship, and so on for the rest. What, then, is the good of each action or craft? Surely it is that for the sake of which the other things are done; in medicine this is health, in generalship victory, in house-building a house, in another case something else, but in every action and decision it is the end, since it is for the sake of the end that everyone does the other actions.

---

4. The reference is to Aristotle's own published works, now lost.

5. The life of study, of contemplation of eternal truths, is characterized by Aristotle as the best life for those capable of it, because it most nearly resembles the life of the gods. It is thus superior to the life of practical virtue to which most of the *Nicomachean Ethics* is devoted. For those lacking theoretical tastes or abilities, however, the life of practical virtue will be the best life. Presumably, even those who aspire to the life of study will need to develop the practical virtues. For Aristotle's discussion, see Book 10, sections 6–8 of the complete text of *Nicomachean Ethics*.

And so, if there is some end of everything achievable in action, the good achievable in action will be this end; if there are more ends than one, [the good achievable in action] will be these ends.

Our argument, then, has followed a different route to reach the same conclusion. But we must try to make this still more perspicuous. Since there are apparently many ends, and we choose some of them (for instance, wealth, flutes, and, in general, instruments) because of something else, it is clear that not all ends are complete. But the best good is apparently something complete. And so, if only one end is complete, the good we are looking for will be this end; if more ends than one are complete, it will be the most complete end of these.

We say that an end pursued in its own right is more complete than an end pursued because of something else, and that an end that is never choiceworthy because of something else is more complete than ends that are choiceworthy both in their own right and because of this end. Hence an end that is always choiceworthy in its own right, never because of something else, is complete without qualification.

Now happiness, more than anything else, seems complete without qualification. For we always choose it because of itself, never because of something else. Honor, pleasure, understanding, and every virtue we certainly choose because of themselves, since we would choose each of them even if it had no further result; but we also choose them for the sake of happiness, supposing that through them we shall be happy. Happiness, by contrast, no one ever chooses for their sake, or for the sake of anything else at all.

The same conclusion [that happiness is complete] also appears to follow from self-sufficiency. For the complete good seems to be self-sufficient. What we count as self-sufficient is not what suffices for a solitary person by himself, living an isolated life, but what suffices also for parents, children, wife, and, in general, for friends and fellow citizens, since a human being is a naturally political [animal]. Here, however, we must impose some limit; for if we extend the good to parents' parents and children's children and to friends of friends, we shall go on without limit; but we must examine this another time. Anyhow, we regard something as self-sufficient when all by itself it makes a life choiceworthy and lacking nothing; and that is what we think happiness does.

Moreover, we think happiness is most choiceworthy of all goods, [since] it is not counted as one good among many. [If it were] counted as one among many, then, clearly, we think it would be more choiceworthy if the smallest of goods were added; for the good that is added becomes an extra quantity of goods, and the larger of two goods is always more choiceworthy. Happiness, then, is apparently something complete and self-sufficient, since it is the end of the things achievable in action.

But presumably the remark that the best good is happiness is apparently something [generally] agreed, and we still need a clearer statement of what the best good is. Perhaps, then, we shall find this if we first grasp the function of a human being. For just as the good, i.e., [doing] well, for a flautist, a sculptor, and every craftsman, and, in general, for whatever has a function and [characteristic] action, seems to depend on its function, the same seems to be true for a human being, if a human being has some function.

Then do the carpenter and the leather worker have their functions and actions, but has a human being no function? Is he by nature idle, without any function? Or, just as eye, hand, foot, and, in general, every [bodily] part apparently has its function, may we likewise ascribe to a human being some function apart from all of these? What, then, could this be? For living is apparently shared with plants, but what we are looking for is the special function of a human being; hence we should set aside the life of nutrition and growth. The life next in order is some sort of life of sense perception; but this too is apparently shared with horse, ox, and every animal.

The remaining possibility, then, is some sort of life of action of the [part of the soul] that has reason. One [part] of it has reason as obeying reason; the other has it as itself having reason and thinking. Moreover, life is also spoken of in two ways [as capacity and as activity], and we must take [a human being's special function to be] life as activity, since this seems to be called life more fully. We have found, then, that the human function is activity of the soul in accord with reason or requiring reason.

Now we say that the function of a [kind of thing]—of a harpist, for instance—is the same in kind as the function of an excellent individual of the kind—of an excellent harpist, for instance. And the same is true without qualification in every case, if we add to the function the superior achievement in accord with the virtue; for the function of a harpist is to play the harp, and the function of a good harpist is to play it well. Moreover, we take the human function to be a certain kind of life, and take this life to be activity and actions of the soul that involve reason; hence the function of the excellent man is to do this well and finely.

Now each function is completed well by being completed in accord with the virtue proper [to that kind of thing]. And so the human good proves to be activity of the soul in accord with virtue, and indeed with the best and most complete virtue, if there are more virtues than one. Moreover, in a complete life. For one swallow does not make a spring, nor does one day; nor, similarly, does one day or a short time make us blessed and happy.

This, then, is a sketch of the good; for, presumably, we must draw the outline first, and fill it in later. If the sketch is good, anyone, it seems, can advance and articulate it, and in such cases time discovers more, or is a good partner in discovery. That is also how the crafts have improved, since anyone can add what is lacking [in the outline]. We must also remember our previous remarks, so that we do not look for the same degree of exactness in all areas, but the degree that accords with a given subject matter and is proper to a given line of inquiry.

8 [DEFENSE OF THE ACCOUNT OF THE GOOD]

We should examine the principle, however, not only from the conclusion and premises [of a deduction], but also from what is said about it; for all the facts harmonize with a true account, whereas the truth soon clashes with a false one.

Goods are divided, then, into three types, some called external, some goods of the soul, others goods of the body. We say that the goods of the soul are goods most fully, and more than the others, and we take actions and activities of the soul to be [goods] of the soul. And so our account [of the good] is right, to judge by this belief anyhow—and it is an ancient belief, and accepted by philosophers.

Our account is also correct in saying that some sort of actions and activities are the end; for in that way the end turns out to be a good of the soul, not an external good. The belief that the happy person lives well and does well also agrees with our account, since we have virtually said that the end is a sort of living well and doing well.

Further, all the features that people look for in happiness appear to be true of the end described in our account. For to some people happiness seems to be virtue; to others prudence; to others some sort of wisdom; to others again it seems to be these, or one of these, involving pleasure or requiring it to be added; others add in external prosperity as well. Some of these views are traditional, held by many, while others are held by a few men who are widely esteemed. It is reasonable for each group not to be completely wrong, but to be correct on one point at least, or even on most points.

First, our account agrees with those who say happiness is virtue [in general] or some [particular] virtue; for activity in accord with virtue is proper to virtue. Presumably, though, it matters quite a bit whether we suppose that the best good consists in possessing or in using—that is to say, in a state or in an activity [that actualizes the state]. For someone may be in a state that achieves no good—if, for instance, he is asleep or inactive in some other way—but this cannot be true of the activity; for it will necessarily act and act well. And just as Olympic prizes are not for the finest and strongest, but for the contestants—since it is only these who win—the same is true in life; among the fine and good people, only those who act correctly win the prize.

Moreover, the life of these active people is also pleasant in itself. For being pleased is a condition of the soul, [and hence is included in the activity of the soul]. Further, each type of person finds pleasure in whatever he is called a lover of; a horse, for instance, pleases the horse-lover, a spectacle the lover of spectacles. Similarly, what is just pleases the lover of justice, and in general what accords with virtue pleases the lover of virtue.

Now the things that please most people conflict, because they are not pleasant by nature, whereas the things that please lovers of the fine are things pleasant by nature. Actions in accord with virtue are pleasant by nature, so that they both please lovers of the fine and are pleasant in their own right.

Hence these people's life does not need pleasure to be added [to virtuous activity] as some sort of extra decoration; rather, it has its pleasure within itself. For besides the reasons already given, someone who does not enjoy fine actions is not good; for no one would call a person just, for instance, if he did not enjoy doing just actions, or generous if he did not enjoy generous actions, and similarly for the other virtues. If this is so, actions in accord with the virtues are pleasant in their own right. Moreover, these actions are good and fine as well as pleasant; indeed, they are good, fine, and pleasant more than anything else is, since on this question the excellent person judges rightly, and his judgment agrees with what we have said. Happiness, then, is best, finest, and most pleasant, and the Delian inscription[6] is wrong to distinguish these things: "What is most just is finest; being healthy is most beneficial; but it is most pleasant to win our heart's desire." For all three features are found in the best activities, and we say happiness is these activities, or [rather] one of them, the best one.

Nonetheless, happiness evidently also needs external goods to be added, as we said, since we cannot, or cannot easily, do fine actions if we lack the resources. For, first of all, in many actions we use friends, wealth, and political power just as we use instruments. Further, deprivation of certain [externals]—for instance, good birth, good children, beauty—mars our blessedness. For we do not altogether have the character of happiness if we look utterly repulsive or are ill-born, solitary, or childless; and we have it even less, presumably, if our children or friends are totally bad, or were good but have died. And so, as we have said, happiness would seem to need this sort of prosperity added also. That is why some people identify happiness with good fortune, and others identify it with virtue.

9 [How Is Happiness Achieved?]

This also leads to a puzzle: Is happiness acquired by learning, or habituation, or by some other form of cultivation? Or is it the result of some divine fate, or even of fortune?

First, then, if the gods give any gift at all to human beings, it is reasonable for them to give us happiness more than any other human good, insofar as it is the best of human goods. Presumably, however, this question is more suitable for a different inquiry.

---

6. The inscription is "Delian" because it was on the Temple of Delos.

But even if it is not sent by the gods, but instead results from virtue and some sort of learning or cultivation, happiness appears to be one of the most divine things, since the prize and goal of virtue appears to be the best good, something divine and blessed. Moreover [if happiness comes in this way] it will be widely shared; for anyone who is not deformed [in his capacity] for virtue will be able to achieve happiness through some sort of learning and attention.

And since it is better to be happy in this way than because of fortune, it is reasonable for this to be the way [we become] happy. For whatever is natural is naturally in the finest state possible. The same is true of the products of crafts and of every other cause, especially the best cause; and it would be seriously inappropriate to entrust what is greatest and finest to fortune.

The answer to our question is also evident from our account. For we have said that happiness is a certain sort of activity of the soul in accord with virtue, [and hence not a result of fortune]. Of the other goods, some are necessary conditions of happiness, while others are naturally useful and cooperative as instruments [but are not parts of it]. Further, this conclusion agrees with our opening remarks. For we took the goal of political science to be the best good; and most of its attention is devoted to the character of the citizens, to make them good people who do fine actions.

It is not surprising, then, that we regard neither ox, nor horse, nor any other kind of animal as happy; for none of them can share in this sort of activity. For the same reason a child is not happy either, since his age prevents him from doing these sorts of actions. If he is called happy, he is being congratulated [simply] because of anticipated blessedness; for, as we have said, happiness requires both complete virtue and a complete life.

It needs a complete life because life includes many reversals of fortune, good and bad, and the most prosperous person may fall into a terrible disaster in old age, as the Trojan stories tell us about Priam.[7] If someone has suffered these sorts of misfortunes and comes to a miserable end, no one counts him happy.

---

7. According to legend, Priam was the last king of Troy. He lost thirteen sons and saw his city in ruins before being killed himself by the invading Greeks.

10 [CAN WE BE HAPPY DURING OUR LIFETIME?]

Then should we count no human being happy during his lifetime, but follow Solon's advice to wait to see the end?[8]

Let us grant that we must wait to see the end, and must then count someone blessed, not as now being blessed [during the time he is dead] but because he previously was blessed. Would it not be absurd, then, if, at the very time when he is happy, we refused to ascribe truly to him the happiness he has? Such refusal results from reluctance to call him happy during his lifetime, because of its ups and downs; for we suppose happiness is enduring and definitely not prone to fluctuate, but the same person's fortunes often turn to and fro. For clearly, if we take our cue from his fortunes, we shall often call him happy and then miserable again, thereby representing the happy person as a kind of chameleon, insecurely based.

But surely it is quite wrong to take our cue from someone's fortunes. For his doing well or badly does not rest on them. A human life, as we said, needs these added, but activities in accord with virtue control happiness, and the contrary activities control its contrary. Indeed, the present puzzle is further evidence for our account [of happiness]. For no human achievement has the stability of activities in accord with virtue, since these seem to be more enduring even than our knowledge of the sciences. Indeed, the most honorable among the virtues themselves are more enduring than the other virtues, because blessed people devote their lives to them more fully and more continually than to anything else—for this continual activity would seem to be the reason we do not forget them.

It follows, then, that the happy person has the [stability] we are looking for and keeps the character he has throughout his life. For always, or more than anything else, he will do and study the actions in accord with virtue, and will bear fortunes most finely, in every way and in all conditions appropriately, since he is truly "good, foursquare, and blameless."[9]

---

8. Solon (630–560 B.C.E.) was a famous Athenian statesman, who instituted civic reforms and a code of law that reduced the power of the traditional aristocracy and made the Athenian penal system considerably more humane.

9. A fragment from the work of Simonides, a famous lyric poet (sixth century B.C.E.), also discussed in Plato's dialogue, *Protagoras*.

Many events, however, are subject to fortune; some are minor, some major. Hence, minor strokes of good or ill fortune clearly will not carry any weight for his life. But many major strokes of good fortune will make it more blessed; for in themselves they naturally add adornment to it, and his use of them proves to be fine and excellent. Conversely, if he suffers many major misfortunes, they oppress and spoil his blessedness, since they involve pain and impede many activities. And yet, even here what is fine shines through, whenever someone bears many severe misfortunes with good temper, not because he feels no distress, but because he is noble and magnanimous.

If this is so, the happy person could never become miserable, but neither will he be blessed if he falls into misfortunes as bad as Priam's. Nor, however, will he be inconstant and prone to fluctuate, since he will neither be easily shaken from his happiness nor shaken by just any misfortunes.

12 [PRAISE AND HONOR]

Now that we have determined these points, let us consider whether happiness is something praiseworthy, or instead something honorable; for clearly it is not a capacity [which is neither praiseworthy nor honorable].

Whatever is praiseworthy appears to be praised for its character and its state in relation to something. We praise the just and the brave person, for instance, and in general the good person and virtue, because of their actions and achievements; and we praise the strong person, the good runner, and each of the others because he naturally has a certain character and is in a certain state in relation to something good and excellent. This is clear also from praises of the gods; for these praises appear ridiculous because they are referred to us, but they are referred to us because, as we said, praise depends on such a reference.

If praise is for these sorts of things, then clearly for the best things there is no praise, but something greater and better. And indeed this is how it appears. For the gods and the most godlike of men are [not praised, but] congratulated for their blessedness and happiness. The same is true of goods; for we never praise happiness, as we praise justice, but we count it blessed, as something better and more godlike [than anything that is praised]. Indeed, Eudoxus[10] seems to have used the right sort of argument in defending the supremacy of pleasure. By not praising pleasure, though it is a good, we indicate—so he thought—that it is superior to everything praiseworthy; [only] the god and the good have this superiority since the other goods are [praised] by reference to them. [Here he seems to have argued correctly.] For praise is given to virtue, since it makes us do fine actions; but celebrations are for achievements, either of body or of soul. But an exact treatment of this is presumably more proper for specialists in celebrations. For us, anyhow, it is clear from what has been said that happiness is something honorable and complete.

A further reason why this would seem to be correct is that happiness is a principle; for [the principle] is what we all aim at in all our other actions; and we take the principle and cause of goods to be something honorable and divine.

13 [INTRODUCTION TO THE VIRTUES]

Since happiness is a certain sort of activity of the soul in accord with complete virtue, we must examine virtue; for that will perhaps also be a way to study happiness better. It is clear that the virtue we must examine is human virtue, since we are also seeking the human good and human happiness. By human virtue we mean virtue of the soul, not of the body, since we also say that happiness is an activity of the soul. If this is so, it is clear that the politician must in some way know about the soul, just as someone setting out to heal the eyes must know about the whole body as well. This is all the more true to the extent that political science is better and more honorable than medicine; even among doctors, the cultivated ones devote a lot of effort to finding out about the body. Hence the politician as well [as the student of nature] must study the soul. But he must study it for his specific purpose, far enough for his inquiry

---

10. Eudoxus of Cnidus (fourth century B.C.E.), a noted astronomer and mathematician, who apparently advocated a hedonistic conception of moral good, identifying "good" with "pleasure."

[into virtue]; for a more exact treatment would presumably take more effort than his purpose requires.

[We] have discussed the soul sufficiently [for our purposes] in [our] popular works as well [as our less popular], and we should use this discussion. We have said, for instance, that one [part] of the soul is nonrational, while one has reason. Are these distinguished as parts of a body and everything divisible into parts are? Or are they two [only] in definition, and inseparable by nature, as the convex and the concave are in a surface? It does not matter for present purposes.

Consider the nonrational [part]. One [part] of it, i.e., the cause of nutrition and growth, would seem to be plantlike and shared [with all living things]; for we can ascribe this capacity of the soul to everything that is nourished, including embryos, and the same capacity to full-grown living things, since this is more reasonable than to ascribe another capacity to them. Hence the virtue of this capacity is apparently shared, not [specifically] human. For this part and this capacity more than others seem to be active in sleep, and here the good and the bad person are least distinct; hence happy people are said to be no better off than miserable people for half their lives. This lack of distinction is not surprising, since sleep is inactivity of the soul insofar as it is called excellent or base, unless to some small extent some movements penetrate [to our awareness], and in this way the decent person comes to have better images [in dreams] than just any random person has. Enough about this, however, and let us leave aside the nutritive part, since by nature it has no share in human virtue.

Another nature in the soul would also seem to be nonrational, though in a way it shares in reason. For in the continent and the incontinent person we praise their reason, that is to say, the [part] of the soul that has reason, because it exhorts them correctly and toward what is best; but they evidently also have in them some other [part] that is by nature something apart from reason, clashing and struggling with reason. For just as paralyzed parts of a body, when we decide to move them to the right, do the contrary and move off to the left, the same is true of the soul; for incontinent people have impulses in contrary directions. In bodies, admittedly, we see the part go astray, whereas we do not see it in the soul; nonetheless, presumably, we should suppose that the soul also has something apart from reason, countering and opposing reason. The [precise] way it is different does not matter.

However, this [part] as well [as the rational part] appears, as we said, to share in reason. At any rate, in the continent person it obeys reason; and in the temperate and the brave person it presumably listens still better to reason, since there it agrees with reason in everything. The nonrational [part], then, as well [as the whole soul] apparently has two parts. For while the plantlike [part] shares in reason not at all, the [part] with appetites and in general desires shares in reason in a way, insofar as it both listens to reason and obeys it. This is the way in which we are said to "listen to reason" from father or friends, as opposed to the way in which [we "give the reason"] in mathematics. The nonrational part also [obeys and] is persuaded in some way by reason, as is shown by correction, and by every sort of reproof and exhortation.

If, then, we ought to say that this [part] also has reason, then the [part] that has reason, as well [as the nonrational part], will have two parts. One will have reason fully, by having it within itself; the other will have reason by listening to reason as to a father.

The division between virtues accords with this difference. For some virtues are called virtues of thought, others virtues of character; wisdom, comprehension, and prudence are called virtues of thought, generosity and temperance virtues of character. For when we speak of someone's character we do not say that he is wise or has good comprehension, but that he is gentle or temperate. And yet, we also praise the wise person for his state, and the states that are praiseworthy are the ones we call virtues.

BOOK II
[VIRTUE OF CHARACTER]

1 [HOW A VIRTUE OF CHARACTER IS ACQUIRED]

Virtue, then, is of two sorts, virtue of thought and virtue of character. Virtue of thought arises and grows mostly from teaching; that is why it needs experience and time. Virtue of character [i.e., of thos] results from habit [ethos]; hence its name "ethical," slightly varied from "ethos." Hence it is also clear that none of the virtues of character arises in us naturally. For if something is by nature in one condition, habituation cannot bring it into another condition. A stone, for instance, by nature moves downwards, and habituation could not make it move upwards, not even if you threw it up ten thousand times to habituate it; nor could habituation make fire move downwards, or bring anything that is by nature in one condition into another condition. And so the virtues arise in us neither by nature nor against nature. Rather, we are by nature able to acquire them, and we are completed through habit.

Further, if something arises in us by nature, we first have the capacity for it, and later perform the activity. This is clear in the case of the senses; for we did not acquire them by frequent seeing or hearing, but we already had them when we exercised them, and did not get them by exercising them. Virtues, by contrast, we acquire, just as we acquire crafts, by having first activated them. For we learn a craft by producing the same product that we must produce when we have learned it; we become builders, for instance, by building, and we become harpists by playing the harp. Similarly, then, we become just by doing just actions, temperate by doing temperate actions, brave by doing brave actions. What goes on in cities is also evidence for this. For the legislator makes the citizens good by habituating them, and this is the wish of every legislator; if he fails to do it well he misses his goal. Correct habituation distinguishes a good political system from a bad one.

Further, the sources and means that develop each virtue also ruin it, just as they do in a craft. For playing the harp makes both good and bad harpists, and it is analogous in the case of builders and all the rest; for building well makes good builders, and building badly makes bad ones. Otherwise no teacher would be needed, but everyone would be born a good or a bad craftsman.

It is the same, then, with the virtues. For what we do in our dealings with other people makes some of us just, some unjust; what we do in terrifying situations, and the habits of fear or confidence that we acquire, make some of us brave and others cowardly. The same is true of situations involving appetites and anger; for one or another sort of conduct in these situations makes some temperate and mild, others intemperate and irascible. To sum it up in a single account: a state [of character] results from [the repetition of] similar activities. That is why we must perform the right activities, since differences in these imply corresponding differences in the states. It is not unimportant, then, to acquire one sort of habit or another, right from our youth. On the contrary, it is very important, indeed all-important.

2 [HABITUATION]

Our present discussion does not aim, as our others do, at study; for the purpose of our examination is not to know what virtue is, but to become good, since otherwise the inquiry would be of no benefit to us. And so we must examine the right ways of acting; for, as we have said, the actions also control the sorts of states we acquire.

First, then, actions should accord with the correct reason. That is a common [belief], and let us assume it. We shall discuss it later, and say what the correct reason is and how it is related to the other virtues. But let us take it as agreed in advance that every account of the actions we must do has to be stated in outline, not exactly. As we also said at the beginning, the type of accounts we demand should accord with the subject matter; and questions about actions and expediency, like questions about health, have no fixed answers. While this is the character of our general account, the account of particular cases is still more inexact. For these fall under no craft or profession; the agents themselves must consider in each case what the opportune action is, as doctors and navigators do. The account we offer, then, in our present inquiry is of this inexact sort; still, we must try to offer help.

First, then, we should observe that these sorts of states naturally tend to be ruined by excess and deficiency. We see this happen with strength and health—for we must use evident cases [such as these] as witnesses to things that are not evident. For both excessive and deficient exercise ruin bodily strength, and, similarly, too much or too little eating or drinking ruins health, whereas the proportionate amount produces, increases, and preserves it.

The same is true, then, of temperance, bravery, and the other virtues. For if, for instance, someone avoids and is afraid of everything, standing firm against nothing, he becomes cowardly; if he is afraid of nothing at all and goes to face everything, he becomes rash. Similarly, if he gratifies himself with every pleasure and abstains from none, he becomes intemperate; if he avoids them all, as boors do, he becomes some sort of insensible person. Temperance and bravery, then, are ruined by excess and deficiency, but preserved by the mean.

But these actions are not only the sources and causes both of the emergence and growth of virtues and of their ruin; the activities of the virtues [once we have acquired them] also consist in these same actions. For this is also true of more evident cases; strength, for instance, arises from eating a lot and from withstanding much hard labor, and it is the strong person who is most capable of these very actions. It is the same with the virtues. For abstaining from pleasures makes us become temperate, and once we have become temperate we are most capable of abstaining from pleasures. It is similar with bravery; habituation in disdain for frightening situations and in standing firm against them makes us become brave, and once we have become brave we shall be most capable of standing firm.

3 [The Importance of Pleasure and Pain]

But we must take someone's pleasure or pain following on his actions to be a sign of his state. For if someone who abstains from bodily pleasures enjoys the abstinence itself, he is temperate; if he is grieved by it, he is intemperate. Again, if he stands firm against terrifying situations and enjoys it, or at least does not find it painful, he is brave; if he finds it painful, he is cowardly. For virtue of character is about pleasures and pains. For pleasure causes us to do base actions, and pain causes us to abstain from fine ones. That is why we need to have had the appropriate upbringing—right from early youth, as Plato says—to make us find enjoyment or pain in the right things; for this is the correct education.

Further, virtues are concerned with actions and feelings; but every feeling and every action implies pleasure or pain; hence, for this reason too, virtue is about pleasures and pains. Corrective treatments also indicate this, since they use pleasures and pains; for correction is a form of medical treatment, and medical treatment naturally operates through contraries.

Further, as we said earlier, every state of soul is naturally related to and about whatever naturally makes it better or worse; and pleasures and pains make people base, from pursuing and avoiding the wrong ones, at the wrong time, in the wrong ways, or whatever other distinctions of that sort are needed in an account. These [bad effects of pleasure and pain] are the reason why people actually define the virtues as ways of being unaffected and undisturbed [by pleasures and pains]. They are wrong, however, because they speak of being unaffected without qualification, not of being unaffected in the right or wrong way, at the right or wrong time, and the added qualifications.

We assume, then, that virtue is the sort of state that does the best actions concerning pleasures and pains, and that vice is the contrary state. The following will also make it evident that virtue and vice are about the same things. For there are three objects of choice—fine, expedient, and pleasant—and three objects of avoidance—their contraries, shameful, harmful, and painful. About all these, then, the good person is correct and the bad person is in error, and especially about pleasure. For pleasure is shared with animals, and implied by every object of choice, since what is fine and what is expedient appear pleasant as well.

Further, pleasure grows up with all of us from infancy on. That is why it is hard to rub out this feeling that is dyed into our lives. We also estimate actions [as well as feelings]—some of us more, some less—by pleasure and pain. For this reason, our whole discussion must be about these; for good or bad enjoyment or pain is very important for our actions. Further, it is more difficult to fight pleasure than to fight spirit—and Heracleitus tells us [how difficult it is to fight spirit].[11] Now both craft and virtue are in every case about what is more difficult, since a good result is even better when it is more difficult. Hence, for this reason also, the whole discussion, for virtue and political science alike, must consider pleasures and pains; for if we use these well, we shall be good, and if badly, bad.

To sum up: Virtue is about pleasures and pains; the actions that are its sources also increase it or, if they are done badly, ruin it; and its activity is about the same actions as those that are its sources.

---

11. Heracleitus (sixth century B.C.E.): early philosopher and cosmologist who considered fire to be the essential element from which the other basic constituents of nature have evolved and into which they return through an ongoing cyclical process of transformation. The reference may to be to Heracleitus' book, which unfortunately has not survived.

4 [VIRTUOUS ACTIONS VERSUS VIRTUOUS CHARACTER]

Someone might be puzzled, however, about what we mean by saying that we become just by doing just actions and become temperate by doing temperate actions. For [one might suppose that] if we do grammatical or musical actions, we are grammarians or musicians, and, similarly, if we do just or temperate actions, we are thereby just or temperate. But surely actions are not enough, even in the case of crafts; for it is possible to produce a grammatical result by chance, or by following someone else's instructions. To be grammarians, then, we must both produce a grammatical result and produce it grammatically—that is to say, produce it in accord with the grammatical knowledge in us.

Moreover, in any case, what is true of crafts is not true of virtues. For the products of a craft determine by their own qualities whether they have been produced well; and so it suffices that they have the right qualities when they have been produced. But for actions in accord with the virtues to be done temperately or justly it does not suffice that they themselves have the right qualities. Rather, the agent must also be in the right state when he does them. First, he must know [that he is doing virtuous actions]; second, he must decide on them, and decide on them for themselves; and, third, he must also do them from a firm and unchanging state.

As conditions for having a craft, these three do not count, except for the bare knowing. As a condition for having a virtue, however, the knowing counts for nothing, or [rather] for only a little, whereas the other two conditions are very important, indeed all-important. And we achieve these other two conditions by the frequent doing of just and temperate actions. Hence actions are called just or temperate when they are the sort that a just or temperate person would do. But the just and temperate person is not the one who [merely] does these actions, but the one who also does them in the way in which just or temperate people do them.

It is right, then, to say that a person comes to be just from doing just actions and temperate from doing temperate actions; for no one has the least prospect of becoming good from failing to do them. The many, however, do not do these actions. They take refuge in arguments, thinking that they are doing philosophy, and that this is the way to become excellent people. They are like a sick person who listens attentively to the doctor, but acts on none of his instructions. Such a course of treatment will not improve the state of the sick person's body; nor will the many improve the state of their souls by this attitude to philosophy.

5 [VIRTUE OF CHARACTER: ITS GENUS]

Next we must examine what virtue is. Since there are three conditions arising in the soul—feelings, capacities, and states—virtue must be one of these. By feelings I mean appetite, anger, fear, confidence, envy, joy, love, hate, longing, jealousy, pity, and in general whatever implies pleasure or pain. By capacities I mean what we have when we are said to be capable of these feelings—capable of being angry, for instance, or of being afraid or of feeling pity. By states I mean what we have when we are well or badly off in relation to feelings. If, for instance, our feeling is too intense or slack, we are badly off in relation to anger, but if it is intermediate, we are well off; the same is true in the other cases.

First, then, neither virtues nor vices are feelings. For we are called excellent or base insofar as we have virtues or vices, not insofar as we have feelings. Further, we are neither praised nor blamed insofar as we have feelings; for we do not praise the angry or the frightened person, and do not blame the person who is simply angry, but only the person who is angry in a particular way. We are praised or blamed, however, insofar as we have virtues or vices. Further, we are angry and afraid without decision; but the virtues are decisions of some kind, or [rather] require decision. Besides, insofar as we have feelings, we are said to be moved; but insofar as we have virtues or vices, we are said to be in some condition rather than moved.

For these reasons the virtues are not capacities either; for we are neither called good nor called bad, nor are we praised or blamed, insofar as we are simply capable of feelings. Further, while we have capacities by nature, we do not become good or bad by nature; we have discussed this before.

If, then, the virtues are neither feelings nor capacities, the remaining possibility is that they are states. And so we have said what the genus of virtue is.

6 [Virtue of Character: Its Differentia]

It should be said, then, that every virtue causes its possessors to be in a good state and to perform their functions well. The virtue of eyes, for instance, makes the eyes and their functioning excellent, because it makes us see well; and similarly, the virtue of a horse makes the horse excellent, and thereby good at galloping, at carrying its rider, and at standing steady in the face of the enemy. If this is true in every case, the virtue of a human being will likewise be the state that makes a human being good and makes him perform his function well. We have already said how this will be true, and it will also be evident from our next remarks, if we consider the sort of nature that virtue has.

In everything continuous and divisible we can take more, less, and equal, and each of them either in the object itself or relative to us; and the equal is some intermediate between excess and deficiency. By the intermediate in the object I mean what is equidistant from each extremity; this is one and the same for all. But relative to us the intermediate is what is neither superfluous nor deficient; this is not one, and is not the same for all. If, for instance, ten are many and two are few, we take six as intermediate in the object, since it exceeds [two] and is exceeded [by ten] by an equal amount, [four]. This is what is intermediate by numerical proportion. But that is not how we must take the intermediate that is relative to us. For if ten pounds [of food], for instance, are a lot for someone to eat, and two pounds a little, it does not follow that the trainer will prescribe six, since this might also be either a little or a lot for the person who is to take it—for Milo [the athlete][12] a little, but for the beginner in gymnastics a lot; and the same is true for running and wrestling. In this way every scientific expert avoids excess and deficiency and seeks and chooses what is intermediate—but intermediate relative to us, not in the object.

This, then, is how each science produces its product well, by focusing on what is intermediate and making the product conform to that. This, indeed, is why people regularly comment on well-made

---

12. Milo of Croton (sixth century B.C.E.) was the most famous wrestler in antiquity. He is said to have won the championship in six successive Olympic Games and upon one occasion to have entered the stadium at Olympia carrying an ox.

products that nothing could be added or subtracted; they assume that excess or deficiency ruins a good [result], whereas the mean preserves it. Good craftsmen also, we say, focus on what is intermediate when they produce their product. And since virtue, like nature, is better and more exact than any craft, it will also aim at what is intermediate.

By virtue I mean virtue of character; for this is about feelings and actions, and these admit of excess, deficiency, and an intermediate condition. We can be afraid, for instance, or be confident, or have appetites, or get angry, or feel pity, and in general have pleasure or pain, both too much and too little, and in both ways not well. But having these feelings at the right times, about the right things, toward the right people, for the right end, and in the right way, is the intermediate and best condition, and this is proper to virtue. Similarly, actions also admit of excess, deficiency, and an intermediate condition.

Now virtue is about feelings and actions, in which excess and deficiency are in error and incur blame, whereas the intermediate condition is correct and wins praise, which are both proper to virtue. Virtue, then, is a mean, insofar as it aims at what is intermediate.

Moreover, there are many ways to be in error. . . . But there is only one way to be correct. That is why error is easy and correctness is difficult, since it is easy to miss the target and difficult to hit it. And so for this reason also excess and deficiency are proper to vice, the mean to virtue; "for we are noble in only one way, but bad in all sorts of ways."

Virtue, then, is a state that decides, consisting in a mean, the mean relative to us, which is defined by reference to reason, that is to say, to the reason by reference to which the prudent person would define it. It is a mean between two vices, one of excess and one of deficiency. It is a mean for this reason also: some vices miss what is right because they are deficient, others because they are excessive, in feelings or in actions, whereas virtue finds and chooses what is intermediate. That is why virtue, as far as its essence and the account stating what it is are concerned, is a mean, but, as far as the best [condition] and the good [result] are concerned, it is an extremity.

Now not every action or feeling admits of the mean. For the names of some automatically include baseness—for instance, spite, shamelessness, envy [among feelings], and adultery, theft, murder, among actions. For all of these and similar things are called by these names because they themselves, not their excesses or deficiencies, are base. Hence in doing these things we can never be correct, but must invariably be in error. We cannot do them well or not well—by committing adultery, for instance, with the right woman at the right time in the right way. On the contrary, it is true without qualification that to do any of them is to be in error.

[To think these admit of a mean], therefore, is like thinking that unjust or cowardly or intemperate action also admits of a mean, an excess and a deficiency. If it did, there would be a mean of excess, a mean of deficiency, an excess of excess and a deficiency of deficiency. On the contrary, just as there is no excess or deficiency of temperance or of bravery (since the intermediate is a sort of extreme), so also there is no mean of these vicious actions either, but whatever way anyone does them, he is in error. For in general there is no mean of excess or of deficiency, and no excess or deficiency of a mean.

7 [THE PARTICULAR VIRTUES OF CHARACTER]

However, we must not only state this general account but also apply it to the particular cases. For among accounts concerning actions, though the general ones are common to more cases, the specific ones are truer, since actions are about particular cases, and our account must accord with these. Let us, then, find these from the chart.[13]

First, then, in feelings of fear and confidence the mean is bravery. The excessively fearless person is nameless (indeed many cases are nameless), and the one who is excessively confident is rash. The one who is excessive in fear and deficient in confidence is cowardly.

In pleasures and pains—though not in all types, and in pains less than in pleasures—the mean is temperance and the excess intemperance. People deficient in pleasure are not often found, which is why they also lack even a name; let us call them insensible.

---

13. Here we have a tantalizing hint about Aristotle's pedagogical practice, suggesting he used a chart or table to illustrate the various virtues and associated vices in his lectures or discussions with students. No such chart is included in the text.

In giving and taking money the mean is generosity, the excess wastefulness and the deficiency ungenerosity. Here the vicious people have contrary excesses and defects; for the wasteful person is excessive in spending and deficient in taking, whereas the ungenerous person is excessive in taking and deficient in spending. At the moment we are speaking in outline and summary, and that is enough. . . . In questions of money there are also other conditions. Another mean is magnificence; for the magnificent person differs from the generous by being concerned with large matters, while the generous person is concerned with small. The excess is ostentation and vulgarity, and the deficiency is stinginess.

In honor and dishonor the mean is magnanimity, the excess something called a sort of vanity, and the deficiency pusillanimity. And just as we said that generosity differs from magnificence in its concern with small matters, similarly there is a virtue concerned with small honors, differing in the same way from magnanimity, which is concerned with great honors. For honor can be desired either in the right way or more or less than is right. If someone desires it to excess, he is called an honor-lover, and if his desire is deficient he is called indifferent to honor, but if he is intermediate he has no name. The corresponding conditions have no name either, except the condition of the honor-lover, which is called honor-loving. This is why people at the extremes lay claim to the intermediate area. Moreover, we also sometimes call the intermediate person an honor-lover, and sometimes call him indifferent to honor; and sometimes we praise the honor-lover, sometimes the person indifferent to honor.

Anger also admits of an excess, deficiency, and mean. These are all practically nameless; but since we call the intermediate person mild, let us call the mean mildness. Among the extreme people, let the excessive person be irascible, and his vice irascibility, and let the deficient person be a sort of inirascible person, and his deficiency inirascibility.

There are also three other means, somewhat similar to one another, but different. For they are all concerned with common dealings in conversations and actions, but differ insofar as one is concerned with truth-telling in these areas, the other two with sources of pleasure, some of which are found in amusement, and the others in daily life in general. Hence we should also discuss these states, so that we can better observe that in every case the

mean is praiseworthy, whereas the extremes are neither praiseworthy nor correct, but blameworthy. Most of these cases are also
nameless, and we must try, as in the other cases also, to supply
names ourselves, to make things clear and easy to follow.

In truth-telling, then, let us call the intermediate person truthful,
and the mean truthfulness; pretense that overstates will be boastful-
ness, and the person who has it boastful; pretense that understates
will be self-deprecation, and the person who has it self-deprecating.

In sources of pleasure in amusements let us call the intermediate
person witty, and the condition wit; the excess buffoonery and the
person who has it a buffoon; and the deficient person a sort of boor
and the state boorishness. In the other sources of pleasure, those in
daily life, let us call the person who is pleasant in the right way
friendly, and the mean state friendliness. If someone goes to excess
with no [ulterior] aim, he will be ingratiating; if he does it for his
own advantage, a flatterer. The deficient person, unpleasant in
everything, will be a sort of quarrelsome and ill-tempered person.

There are also means in feelings and about feelings. Shame, for
instance, is not a virtue, but the person prone to shame as well as
[the virtuous people we have described] receives praise. For here
also one person is called intermediate, and another—the person
excessively prone to shame, who is ashamed about everything—is
called excessive; the person who is deficient in shame or never feels
shame at all is said to have no sense of disgrace; and the intermediate one is called prone to shame.

Proper indignation is the mean between envy and spite; these
conditions are concerned with pleasure and pain at what happens
to our neighbors. For the properly indignant person feels pain
when someone does well undeservedly; the envious person exceeds
him by feeling pain when anyone does well, while the spiteful person is so deficient in feeling pain that he actually enjoys [other people's misfortunes].

We must consider justice after these. Since it is spoken of in
more than one way, we shall distinguish its two types and say how
each of them is a mean. Similarly, we must also consider the virtues
that belong to reason.[14]

---

14. The intellectual virtues are discussed at length in Book 6 of *Nicomachean Ethics*.

8 [RELATIONS BETWEEN MEAN AND EXTREME STATES]

Among these three conditions, then, two are vices—one of excess, one of deficiency—and one, the mean, is virtue. In a way, each of them is opposed to each of the others, since each extreme is contrary both to the intermediate condition and to the other extreme, while the intermediate is contrary to the extremes.

For, just as the equal is greater in comparison to the smaller, and smaller in comparison to the greater, so also the intermediate states are excessive in comparison to the deficiencies and deficient in comparison to the excesses—both in feelings and in actions. For the brave person, for instance, appears rash in comparison to the coward, and cowardly in comparison to the rash person; the temperate person appears intemperate in comparison to the insensible person, and insensible in comparison with the intemperate person; and the generous person appears wasteful in comparison to the ungenerous, and ungenerous in comparison to the wasteful person. That is why each of the extreme people tries to push the intermediate person to the other extreme, so that the coward, for instance, calls the brave person rash, and the rash person calls him a coward, and similarly in the other cases.

Since these conditions of soul are opposed to each other in these ways, the extremes are more contrary to each other than to the intermediate. For they are further from each other than from the intermediate, just as the large is further from the small, and the small from the large, than either is from the equal.

Further, sometimes one extreme—rashness or wastefulness, for instance—appears somewhat like the intermediate state, bravery or generosity. But the extremes are most unlike one another; and the things that are furthest apart from each other are defined as contraries. And so the things that are further apart are more contrary.

In some cases the deficiency, in others the excess, is more opposed to the intermediate condition. For instance, cowardice, the deficiency, not rashness, the excess, is more opposed to bravery, whereas intemperance, the excess, not insensibility, the deficiency, is more opposed to temperance.

This happens for two reasons: One reason is derived from the object itself. Since sometimes one extreme is closer and more similar to the intermediate condition, we oppose the contrary extreme, more than this closer one, to the intermediate condition. Since rashness, for instance, seems to be closer and more similar to bravery, and cowardice less similar, we oppose cowardice, more than rashness, to bravery; for what is further from the intermediate condition seems to be more contrary to it. This, then, is one reason, derived from the object itself. The other reason is derived from ourselves. For when we ourselves have some natural tendency to one extreme more than to the other, this extreme appears more opposed to the intermediate condition. Since, for instance, we have more of a natural tendency to pleasure, we drift more easily toward intemperance than toward orderliness. Hence we say that an extreme is more contrary if we naturally develop more in that direction; and this is why intemperance is more contrary to temperance, since it is the excess [of pleasure].

9 [How Can We Reach the Mean?]

We have said enough, then, to show that virtue of character is a mean and what sort of mean it is; that it is a mean between two vices, one of excess and one of deficiency; and that it is a mean because it aims at the intermediate condition in feelings and actions.

That is why it is also hard work to be excellent. For in each case it is hard work to find the intermediate; for instance, not everyone, but only one who knows, finds the midpoint in a circle. So also getting angry, or giving and spending money, is easy and everyone can do it; but doing it to the right person, in the right amount, at the right time, for the right end, and in the right way is no longer easy, nor can everyone do it. Hence doing these things well is rare, praiseworthy, and fine.

That is why anyone who aims at the intermediate condition must first of all steer clear of the more contrary extreme, following the advice that Calypso also gives: "Hold the ship outside the spray and surge."[15] For one extreme is more in error, the other less.

---

15. That is, to be sure of keeping one's boat off the rocks, stay so far away that one won't even feel the waves or spray thrown off them. The distance one maintains between one's self and danger may be excessive, but if one knows one has an inclination to go too far in some respect, the most practical way to develop control is to make a habit of erring on the side of caution. In Homer's *Odyssey*, Calypso was a nymph who unwisely did not follow such advice. She spent seven years in an ultimately unsuccessful attempt to seduce Odysseus, the poem's hero, away from his wife.

Since, therefore, it is hard to hit the intermediate extremely accurately, the second-best tack, as they say, is to take the lesser of the evils. We shall succeed best in this by the method we describe. We must also examine what we ourselves drift into easily. For different people have different natural tendencies toward different goals, and we shall come to know our own tendencies from the pleasure or pain that arises in us. We must drag ourselves off in the contrary direction; for if we pull far away from error, as they do in straightening bent wood, we shall reach the intermediate condition. And in everything we must beware above all of pleasure and its sources; for we are already biased in its favor when we come to judge it. Hence we must react to it as the elders reacted to Helen,[16] and on each occasion repeat what they said; for if we do this, and send it off, we shall be less in error.

In summary, then, if we do these things we shall best be able to reach the intermediate condition. But presumably this is difficult, especially in particular cases, since it is not easy to define the way we should be angry, with whom, about what, for how long. For sometimes, indeed, we ourselves praise deficient people and call them mild, and sometimes praise quarrelsome people and call them manly.

Still, we are not blamed if we deviate a little in excess or deficiency from doing well, but only if we deviate a long way, since then we are easily noticed. But how great and how serious a deviation receives blame is not easy to define in an account; for nothing else perceptible is easily defined either. Such things are among particulars, and the judgment depends on perception. This is enough, then, to make it clear that in every case the intermediate state is praised, but we must sometimes incline toward the excess, sometimes toward the deficiency; for that is the easiest way to hit the intermediate and good condition.

---

16. According to Homer, when a Greek invasion force demanded the return of Helen, whom the king's son, Paris, had stolen from her husband, Menelaus, the elders of Troy argued that she should be sent out of the city, for though her beauty was enticing, it was also, under the circumstances, a source of terrible danger.

BOOK III
[PRECONDITIONS OF VIRTUE]

1 [VOLUNTARY ACTION]

Virtue, then, is about feelings and actions. These receive praise or blame if they are voluntary, but pardon, sometimes even pity, if they are involuntary. Hence, presumably, in examining virtue we must define the voluntary and the involuntary. This is also useful to legislators, both for honors and for corrective treatments.

Now it seems that things coming about by force or because of ignorance are involuntary. What is forced has an external principle, the sort of principle in which the agent, or [rather] the victim, contributes nothing—if, for instance, a wind or people who have him in their control were to carry him off. But what about actions done because of fear of greater evils, or because of something fine? Suppose, for instance, a tyrant tells you to do something shameful, when he has control over your parents and children, and if you do it, they will live, but if not, they will die. These cases raise dispute about whether they are voluntary or involuntary.

However, the same sort [of unwelcome choice] is found in throwing cargo overboard in storms. For no one willingly throws cargo overboard, without qualification, but anyone with any sense throws it overboard to save himself and the others. These sorts of actions, then, are mixed, but they are more like voluntary actions. For at the time they are done they are choiceworthy, and the goal of an action accords with the specific occasion; hence we should also call the action voluntary or involuntary on the occasion when he does it. Now in fact he does it willingly. For in such actions he has within him the principle of moving the limbs that are the instruments [of the action]; but if the principle of the actions is in him, it is also up to him to do them or not to do them. Hence actions of this sort are voluntary, though presumably the actions without [the appropriate] qualification are involuntary, since no one would choose any such action in its own right.

For such [mixed] actions people are sometimes actually praised, whenever they endure something shameful or painful as the price of great and fine results. If they do the reverse, they are blamed; for it is a base person who endures what is most shameful for nothing

fine or for only some moderately fine result. In some cases there is
no praise, but there is pardon, whenever someone does a wrong
action because of conditions of a sort that overstrain human nature,
and that no one would endure. But presumably there are some
things we cannot be compelled to do. Rather than do them we
should suffer the most terrible consequences and accept death; for
the things that [allegedly] compelled Euripides' Alcmaeon to kill
his mother appear ridiculous.[17]

What sorts of things, then, should we say are forced? Perhaps
we should say that something is forced without qualification whenever its cause is external and the agent contributes nothing.

5 [Virtue and Vice Are in Our Power]

We have found, then, that we wish for the end, and deliberate and
decide about things that promote it; hence the actions concerned
with things that promote the end are in accord with decision and
are voluntary. The activities of the virtues are concerned with these
things [that promote the end].

Hence virtue is also up to us, and so also, in the same way, is
vice. For when acting is up to us, so is not acting, and when no is up
to us, so is yes. And so if acting, when it is fine, is up to us, not acting, when it is shameful, is also up to us; and if not acting, when it
is fine, is up to us, then acting, when it is shameful, is also up to us.
But if doing, and likewise not doing, fine or shameful actions is up
to us, and if, as we saw, [doing or not doing them] is [what it is] to
be a good or bad person, being decent or base is up to us. This does
not mean, however, that if he is unjust and wishes to stop, he will
thereby stop and be just. For neither does a sick person recover his
health [simply by wishing]; nonetheless, he is sick willingly, by living incontinently and disobeying the doctors, if that was how it
happened. At that time, then, he was free not to be sick, though no
longer free once he has let himself go, just as it was up to someone

---

17. According to legend, Alcmaeon's mother engineered his father's death,
so his father demanded that Alcmaeon kill her. Euripides' play, *Alcmaeon*,
has not survived, but presumably Euripides has Alcmaeon claim that duty
to his father compelled him to do as his father demanded. Aristotle treats
this as an exaggeration.

to throw a stone, since the principle was up to him, though he can no longer take it back once he has thrown it. Similarly, then, the person who is [now] unjust or intemperate was originally free not to acquire this character, so that he has it willingly, though once he has acquired the character, he is no longer free not to have it [now].

Now the virtues, as we say, are voluntary. For in fact we are ourselves in a way jointly responsible for our states of character, and the sort of character we have determines the sort of end we lay down. Hence the vices will also be voluntary, since the same is true of them.

SUGGESTIONS FOR FURTHER READING

The standard English translation of Aristotle's works is *The Complete Works of Aristotle: The Revised Oxford Translation*, 2 vols., ed. by J. Barnes (Princeton: Princeton University Press, 1984). For students and general readers, Terence H. Irwin's edition of the *Nicomachean Ethics*, 2nd ed., with Introduction, Notes, and Glossary (Indianapolis: Hackett Publishing Company, 1999) is highly recommended. Useful general introductions to Aristotle's philosophy include: J. A. Barnes, *A Very Short Introduction to Aristotle* (Oxford: Oxford University Press, 2000); Jonathan Barnes, ed., *The Cambridge Companion to Aristotle* (Cambridge: Cambridge University Press, 1995); and J. L. Ackrill, *Aristotle the Philosopher* (Oxford: Oxford University Press, 1981). For feminist commentaries on Aristotle, see Cynthia Freeland, ed., *Feminist Interpretations of Aristotle* (University Park: Pennsylvania University Press, 1998).

Gerard J. Hughes provides a very brief introduction to Aristotle's *Nicomachean Ethics* in *Aristotle on Ethics* (New York: Routledge, 2001). Also highly recommended are Sarah Broadie, *Ethics with Aristotle* (New York: Oxford University Press, 1991) and Nancy Sherman, *The Fabric of Character* (Oxford: Clarendon Press, 1989). Readers with a little more background will appreciate Richard Kraut, *Aristotle on the Human Good* (Oxford: Oxford University Press, 1989). For readers interested in Aristotle's relation to his contemporaries, see Julia Annas, *The Morality of Happiness* (New York: Oxford University Press, 1993) and Martha Craven Nussbaum, *Therapy of Desire: Theory and Practice in Hellenistic Ethics* (Princeton: Princeton University Press, 1994). For critical discussions of Aristotle's treatment of specific virtues, there are several excellent anthologies available, including Amélie O. Rorty, *Essays on Aristotle's Ethics* (Berkeley: University of California Press, 1981) and Nancy Sherman, *Aristotle's Ethics: Critical Essays* (Lanham, MD: Rowman and Littlefield, 1999). On the relation of Aristotle's ethics and political theory, see Fred Miller, "Aristotle: Ethics and Politics" in *The Blackwell Guide to Ancient Philosophy,* Christopher Shields, ed. (Malden, MA: Blackwell Publishing, 2003). Rosalind Hursthouse offers and defends a contemporary version of Aristotelian virtue ethics in her book, *On Virtue Ethics* (Oxford: Oxford University Press, 1999).

Seneca

INTRODUCTION

Lucius Annaeus Seneca was born circa 4 B.C.E. in Corduba, Spain to a wealthy family in the Equestrian order, a mid-ranking aristocratic order whose members usually pursued careers in commerce and finance, but to whom positions in government administration were increasingly becoming open. Seneca's father, Seneca the Elder, sent his three sons to Rome to be educated in rhetoric and legal oratory, to prepare them to take advantage of the new opportunities in public administration. Seneca's elder brother Novatus (later known as Gallio), to whom his essay, "On Happiness," is dedicated, later became governor of Achaea, but is now best known for being the official who refused to excise jurisdiction over St. Paul. Seneca would rise considerably higher politically—though not immediately. He suffered from severe asthma and in his early twenties he followed recommendations to move to Egypt for his health. He stayed with his aunt Marcia, the wife of the Roman Prefect. He apparently learned something of government administration while in their household, for when he returned to Rome about ten years later, his aunt and uncle used their influence to get him a political appointment as quaestor (financial officer) and, subsequently, enrollment in the Senate.

Seneca was soon highly regarded for his intelligence and oratory, so much so that he became the object of suspicious concern to both the Emperor Caligula and his successor, Claudius. Trumped-up charges were brought against Seneca in 41 and he was exiled to Corsica. Seneca spent much of the next eight years writing, producing a stream of poems, tragedies, and essays that were widely read and admired. His popularity and reputation for probity and good character, despite the earlier charges, is said to have convinced Agrippina, Claudius' second wife, that Seneca's reinstatement would win public favor. More likely, perhaps she wanted able advisors at the ready as she positioned her son, Nero, to succeed Claudius. In any case, Seneca was recalled and made tutor to Nero.

To judge from subsequent events, Seneca had no more effect on Nero's character than Aristotle had upon Alexander's.

Agrippina had Claudius poisoned in 54. For the following five years before the young Nero took personal control, Seneca and his colleague, Burrus, head of the Praetorian Guard, are said to have effectively directed the government. The historian, Tactius, credits the two for keeping government policy both just and judicious for as long as they were able to exercise influence. However, by 59, Nero was no longer as amenable to restraint, a fact he signaled by arranging Agrippina's murder. After Burrus died in 62, Seneca asked for leave to retire. Although for appearances' sake this was not immediately granted, Seneca was permitted to absent himself from Rome. Two years later it became official, but Seneca was not allowed to enjoy his retirement for long. In 65 he was implicated, probably falsely, in a plot to assassinate Nero. Seneca was ordered to commit suicide. He complied, dying in 65.

Seneca's contribution to moral philosophy was as one of stoicism's most elegant and influential exponents. Stoicism was a philosophical system originating in the third century B.C.E., shortly after the death of Aristotle. It took its name from the *stoa poikile* (or "painted colonade"), in Athens where its early founders, Zeno of Citium, Cleanthes, and Chrysippus would meet for lectures and discussions with their students and followers. The early stoics saw nature and all its parts, human and nonhuman, as a living entity, animated and ordered by a rational principle or *pneuma* ("breath" or "spirit") that pervades the whole. As organs of this living entity, things, animals, and persons could be evaluated objectively in terms of how well or poorly they fulfilled the functions specific to their type of entity. As rational, self-conscious beings, humans participate in nature's rational governance. Thus, we can use reason to order our lives as the divine reason orders the rest of nature. However, this power can be misused at our own cost. If we ignore and try to override nature's ends for the sake of purely subjective satisfactions, we risk avoidable suffering. Thus, the key to living a life of subjective contentment is to focus on living our lives in ways that are objectively good. To succeed we must "follow nature"; that is, attend carefully to nature's designs for our species.

Early stoic moral philosophers took Socrates as the model of how the man of ideal practical wisdom should lead his life. Human beings are naturally social creatures and thus, to follow nature, must act in accordance with their social impulses, working to form cooperative communities that allow their members to perfect their capacities for personal excellence to the extent each is able. Like Socrates, the wise man or "sage" will consider truly "good" or valuable only those things that contribute toward the individuals' self-realization; that is, wisdom and the intellectual and moral virtues. All other so-called goods, such as wealth, good looks, and political position are, objectively speaking, indifferent to one's self-development. Some are certainly to be preferred if they happen to come one's way, but none is essential for a good life.

Later Roman stoics, like Seneca, Epictetus, and Emperor Marcus Aurelius, continued to look to Socrates as the model of the ideal stoic sage, but unlike earlier stoics, focused primarily on the practical questions of how those of us who cannot hope to achieve such inner perfection may nevertheless lead morally decent and fulfilling lives in accordance with stoic principles. Thus Seneca's moral essays and his *Moral Letters to Lucilius* offer reflections on how best to respond to the challenges of business and professional life, personal and family crises, and turns of fortune good and bad. These essays and letters were enormously influential, not only on late classical moral philosophy but on the subsequent development of Western moral philosophy. This was partly because the Christian church borrowed liberally from stoicism, encouraging new generations to study stoic texts, but also because of the persuasive power of Seneca's prose. Seneca not only offers Lucilius instruction in stoic ethics, he freely discusses his own difficulties in living up to his principles. The advice he offers is clearly as much for his *own* benefit as his reader's. By opening up his own life to our critical examination, he shows us how to critically reflect upon our own— an essential first step toward stoic virtue.

On the Happy Life[1]

I. All people, dear brother Gallio,[2] want to live happy lives but, when it comes to discerning what it is that makes for a happy life, their vision is blurred. So difficult is it to achieve happiness that, once you have lost the track, the more energetically you press on the farther happiness recedes away from you. When the road takes you in the opposite direction, your own speed is the cause of your increasing distance from your destination.

In the first place, therefore, it is necessary to determine what is the result we wish to achieve. Then it is necessary to look around for the quickest route by which to travel there, with the ability to perceive in the course of the journey, provided it is direct, how much of the distance is extinguished each day and how much nearer we are to the goal to which we are impelled by a natural attraction.

For as long as we wander all over the place, following no guide but rather the roar and clamor of discordant voices calling to us from different directions, our short lifespan will be ground out in the midst of delusions; for life is short enough even if we spend it striving day and night for a healthy state of mind. Therefore it needs to be determined where we are headed and by what route; and it is necessary to have an experienced guide who has previously explored those regions we are planning to enter because our predicament is, in one respect, wholly unlike that faced by other travelers. They are prevented from going astray by their access to established roads and opportunities to ask the local inhabitants for directions; but in our case the most well-worn track and most crowded highway are the most deceptive.

---

1. The following selections from Seneca's *On the Happy Life* and *Moral Letters to Lucilius* were translated by Marcus Wilson.

2. The essay is addressed to Seneca's older brother Annaeus Novatus (who took the name Gallio). Like Seneca, he had a distinguished senatorial career that culminated in appointment as governor of the province of Achaia. When Seneca was implicated in an assassination plot against the Emperor Nero, Gallio, too, was obliged to commit suicide.

Nothing is more important to understand than that we must not, in the manner of sheep, follow the lead of the flock walking ahead of us, going where they go habitually, not where they need to go. Nothing entangles us in greater evils than our propensity to obey public opinion, to regard those things as best that are endorsed by the approval of the majority. Because we are surrounded by the example of so many others, we live our lives not according to reason but by imitation.

III. The life that is happy is in harmony with its own nature. This can only come about when the mind is in a healthy state and in permanent possession of its own sanity, robust and vigorous, capable of the noblest endurance, responsive to circumstances, concerned for the body and all that affects it but not to the point of anxiety, conscientious about the other accoutrements of life without being too enamored of any one thing, ready to make use of the gifts of fortune without being enslaved to them.

IV. You understand, even if I do not spell it out, that, once those things that irk or alarm us have been driven out, the result is lasting tranquility and freedom; and in place of pleasures that were paltry and ephemeral, there comes into being an overwhelming sense of joy, steady and invulnerable, a peace and concord of soul, and a sublimity that is also humane. For cruelty always arises out of weakness.

It is possible to define our idea of the good in different ways, which is to say that the same concept is able to be captured in different verbal formulations. Just as the same army on some occasions is spread out over a wide area and on others pulled back into a compact force or extends its center out into curving wings or is deployed with its front ranks in a straight line, yet its potency remains the same whatever its current formation and its motivation to stand in defense of the same cause remains the same, so also the definition of the highest good can sometimes be opened up and drawn out, at other times condensed and contracted into itself.

Therefore it will amount to the same thing if I say, "The highest good is a mind that takes delight in virtue and looks down on what is merely fortuitous," or, "It is an indomitable force of mind that, strengthened by experience, shows itself in action as calm, profoundly generous and concerned for the welfare of others." One could also define it like this: that we would call that person happy who counts nothing good or evil but a good or evil soul, who reveres the honorable, is content with virtue alone, who is neither overly exhilarated nor heartbroken by chance events, who is convinced there is no greater good than the good that is self-conferred, for whom true pleasure consists in the disdain of pleasures.

If you want to stretch it out further, it is possible to shift the same thought into one of several other forms while preserving intact its cogency. For what prevents us describing the happy life as the possession of a soul that is free and upright and undaunted and steadfast, standing beyond fear, beyond desire; a soul that treats integrity as the only good, lack of integrity as the only evil, and regards the remaining mass of things as having no significant value, adding nothing to the happy life and subtracting nothing from it, having no power to increase or detract from the highest good as they appear or vanish.

When a life is built on this foundation it is accompanied by constant cheerfulness, whether wished for or not, and a deep-rooted sense of elation stemming from deep within. It rejoices in what is its own and does not hanker after greater rewards than this interior satisfaction. Why should this not outweigh the trivial and frivolous and impermanent sensations of the frail body? On the day we lose our susceptibility to pleasure we lose our susceptibility to pain. You see how those who are possessed alternately by those most fickle and uncontrollable of tyrants, the pleasures and pains, are enslaved in an evil and poisonous system of servitude?

Therefore you must break out to liberty. The only thing that has power to grant this freedom is indifference to fortune. Then that incalculable good will arise, the serenity and majesty of a mind installed in a safe place and, with all delusions ousted, the grand and undying joy that attends the discovery of truth, as well as an ease and affability of soul; and the delight we discover in these comes not from the fact that they are goods but from the fact that they are born out of our own good.

IX. Someone may make the following objection. "The real motivation for your cultivating virtue is because you anticipate it will bring you pleasure." To begin with, if it is true that virtue carries with it pleasure, it does not follow that it is sought for this purpose. For virtue does not confer pleasure but confers pleasure in addition; it does not exert itself for pleasure, but its exertions, although directed at other ends, attain pleasure in the process.

In a field that has been ploughed for the sowing of some crop, certain flowers spring up here and there. The work was not undertaken for the sake of these little plants, although they are pleasing to the eye. A different purpose motivated the person planting the crop, and the flowers are an unintended byproduct. Similarly, pleasure is neither the reward nor cause of virtue, but a bonus. We do not embrace virtue because it delights us, but, if we embrace it, it also delights us.

The ultimate good of virtue resides in the perspicacity of choice and the perfected condition of a mind that has completed its proper journey and contained itself within its own bounds. With this the supreme good is accomplished and the mind needs nothing more. For there is nothing outside the whole nor is there any place farther than the end. Therefore you are mistaken when you ask what is it I hope to gain from striving for virtue. You are asking for something beyond the ultimate. Do you want to know what I want from virtue? Virtue itself. It has nothing better to give and is its own reward. Is this not a big enough reward for you? When I say to you, "The greatest good is the austerity and foresight and magnanimity and sanity and freedom and harmony and beauty of an unbreakable spirit," do you still want something more for which those qualities are just the means to another end? Why do you call my attention to pleasure? I want to know the proper good of the human being, not of the belly, in the magnitude of which even cattle and wild beasts surpass us.

XV. Someone else may ask, "Why can't virtue and pleasure be alloyed so that the highest good is realized when the same actions are both honorable and gratifying?" Because you cannot have any part of the honorable that is not itself honorable, and the supreme good will lose its integrity if it sees something in itself inconsistent with its finer quality.

Even the delight that arises from virtue, though it is a good thing, is no more a constituent part of the absolute good than happiness and serenity, which are also born out of the most exalted causes. For those things are goods but attendant upon the supreme good, not components of it.

The person who allies virtue with pleasure in a partnership, inevitably an unequal partnership, blunts all the force of the one by the fragility of the other, and sends under the yoke that freedom that cannot be defeated so long as it does not recognize anything as being more precious than itself. Such a person falls into a great enslavement by becoming dependent on fortune. The life that follows is worried, suspicious, fearful, ever-alarmed at chance occurrences, uncertain from one moment to the next.

You do not set virtue on solid and immovable foundations but order it to stand on shifting ground. What is so unstable as the reliance on chance events and the continual alteration of the human body and of things that affect the body? How can such a person obey god and accept whatever happens in a sound frame of mind and not complain of fate and react to misfortunes positively, when rocked by every little pinprick of pleasure or pain? Nor can those who incline to pleasure do a good job of protecting or liberating their country or standing up for their friends. So allow the supreme good to occupy a height from which no force can drag it down, a height beyond the reach of pain and hope and fear and anything else that would lessen its authority as the supreme good. Only virtue can stand on that height.

XVI. True happiness, therefore, is founded upon virtue. Of what will this virtue persuade you? That you should consider nothing either good or evil other than what is characterized by virtue or vice. Secondly, that you become immovable from the good and against evil so that, insofar as it is right to do so, you exemplify the divine.

What does virtue promise in return for this outlay? Huge advantages, equivalent even to those of the gods: you will be under no compulsion, you will not be in want of anything, you will be free, secure, unassailable; you will attempt nothing in vain, be excluded from nothing; everything will come out according to your judgment; no setbacks will occur, nothing contrary to your wishes or expectation.

"What are you saying? That virtue is sufficient for living a happy life?" Perfect and divine as virtue is, why would it not be sufficient, or, rather, superabundant? For what can be lacking for someone placed beyond all desires? What need is there of external things if you have gathered all your assets within yourself?[3] For

---

3. Recall what Seneca said at the outset; one needs a clear conception of one's goal if one is to improve one's life. Perfect virtue is that goal and for the stoic sage who achieves it, virtue is sufficient for happiness. Most of us will never attain it. Nevertheless, the quality of our lives hinges on the quality of our character.

those, however, who are still directing their steps in virtue's direction, even when well advanced, there is a need for a certain leniency on fortune's part as they struggle in the midst of human affairs until the time when they have untangled that knot and loosened every mortal bond. "So how are they any different?" Because some people are hobbled, some are fettered, some are spread-eagled on a rack. Those who have made progress toward betterment and lifted themselves higher drag a loosened chain. They are not yet free but are as good as free.[4]

XVII. One of those who yap at philosophy[5] may make a speech of their usual type: "So why do you talk more boldly than you live? Why do you lower your voice to a superior, consider money a necessary tool for life, get upset when you incur a loss, weep when you learn that your spouse or your friend is dead, have regard for your reputation, and allow yourself to be disturbed by slanders?

Why do you have more land in cultivation than your natural needs require? Why do your dinner parties not abide by your own recommendations? Why is your furniture polished? Why is the wine drunk at your house of a vintage older than yourself? Why is gold on display? Why have you planted trees that will provide you with nothing other than shade? How come your wife wears the price of a house hanging from her affluent ears? How come your servant boys are dressed in costly garments? How come at your place serving at table is raised to the level of an art, and the silver tableware is not set out haphazardly and instinctively but is skillfully arranged and you have a trained expert whose job it is to cut the meat?"

Add to this, if you wish: "Why do you own property overseas? Why more than you have visited? Why, to your disgrace, are you

---

4. If we are not yet fully virtuous, our state of character development will not as yet be sufficient for true happiness. Yet in pursuing virtue, we are already better off than those who do not recognize where true happiness is to be found.

5. Unlike early Greek stoics, such as Zeno, and the cynics, another Greek philosophical movement that held that nothing but virtue was necessary for happiness, Roman stoics like Seneca did not argue for the rejection of gifts of fortune, such as wealth, or social status. Critics argued that to fail to do so was hypocritical. In what follows, Seneca considers and replies to such charges.

either so uninterested that your few slaves are completely unknown to you or so extravagant that you have more slaves than your memory can recall?" Later I'll add to your invective and cast more aspersions on myself than you have thought of, but for now I'll reply as follows. I fall far short of sagacity and, to provide food for your malevolence, I will never be a perfect sage. Demand of me, therefore, not that I be on a par with the best but just somewhat better than the depraved. This is enough of an achievement for me, to subtract each day something from my vices and to castigate my failings.

I have not achieved soundness of mind, nor will I ever do so. I am setting out alleviations for my gout, not cures, and am content if the attacks are less frequent and less painful. But compared with the state of your feet, you cripples, I'm a sprinter. I do not say these things on behalf of myself—for I am sunk deep in every kind of vice—but on behalf of those who have improved themselves to some degree.

XXI. "Why is that follower of philosophy living the life of a wealthy man?[6] Why does he say riches need to be scorned and yet he possesses them, and thinks life needs to be scorned but he's still alive, and that health needs to be scorned and still he looks after himself very carefully and prefers to be in peak condition? He maintains exile is a word without substance, asking, 'What evil is there in a change of locality?' and yet, if allowed, he grows old in his homeland. He judges there to be no significant difference between a longer and a shorter lifespan but, if nothing prevents him, he prolongs his life and calmly thrives far into old age."

The philosopher says these things should be scorned not to make the point that he should not have them but that he should not be in a state of anxiety about them. He does not drive them from his presence but when they take their leave he sees them out without regret. Where more securely could fortune deposit its wealth than where it can be recovered without any complaint from the person giving it back.

---

6. Although the charges of hypocrisy discussed above were leveled generally at Roman stoics who did not reject worldly goods, here the text seems to become autobiographical. Seneca was himself very wealthy. His spending on behalf of his guests was lavish. And it was known that he had not endured his years of exile on Corsica wholly without complaint. Seneca's response thus seems personal as well as philosophical.

XXII. There can be no doubt that there is more scope in wealth than in poverty for the expression of a wise person's character, since in poverty there is only one type of virtue, not to be demeaned and ground down by it, but in wealth, moderation, generosity, responsibility, propriety, and nobility all have an open field in which to operate.

Wise people do not scorn themselves if they are short, although they'd like to be tall. If they are in poor health, thin in body or blind in one eye, they will prefer to be physically strong even though they are aware they have something in themselves that is stronger than the body. They will tolerate sickness but choose health.

Certain things, even though they are trivial in the larger context and can be taken away without damage to the primary good, nevertheless add something to the lasting joy that is born of virtue. Wealth encourages and enlivens the wise in the way a favorable wind affects the sailor it propels across the sea, or like a nice day in winter or a sunny spot in a cold place.

Where is the philosopher—I'm speaking of the stoics here, who think virtue is the only good—who does not agree that these things we refer to as "indifferent"[7] also contain some advantage, and that some of these are preferable to others. To a number of these a degree of respect is accorded, and in certain cases a considerable degree of respect. Make no mistake, therefore: wealth is one of the advantageous things.

"You must be trying to make a fool of me," you retort, "because wealth has the same importance for you as for me." Do you want to know how it does not have the same importance? If my wealth should melt away it would deprive me of nothing but itself, but if yours were to depart you would be stunned and feel you were deprived of what makes you yourself. With me, wealth has a certain place; in your case it has the highest place. In short, I own my wealth, your wealth owns you.

---

7. "Indifferent" was the stoics' technical term for "gifts of fortune," such as health, wealth, beauty, or social status. Stoics held that some indifferent things may rationally be preferred to others; e.g., those, like health, that are instrumentally valuable for pursuing a virtuous human life. However, strictly speaking, none are necessary either for virtue or happiness.

Moral Letters to Lucilius[8]

Letter 76

Everything is endowed with its own particular good. The abundance of its grapes and taste of its wine is what we appreciate in a vine; with a deer it is its speed. In pack animals you look for a strong back, since their only task is to transport freight. With dogs, keenness of scent is the prime quality of those whose task it is to track wild animals, swiftness of those that pursue the prey, aggression if their role is to bite and attack. In each thing that faculty should be considered best for which it is born, by which it is judged.

What is best in a human being? Reason. In this the human being surpasses the animals and comes close to the gods. Therefore perfected reason is our own particular good, because everything else we have in common with plants and animals. Someone is strong; so are lions. Someone is strikingly beautiful; so are peacocks. Another is a fast runner; so are horses. I am not saying that in all these abilities the human is eclipsed. I'm not looking to establish what is superior in human nature but what is unique. As humans we have body; so do trees. We have control of our own movement and direction; so do beasts and worms. We have a voice; but the sound made by dogs is much louder, the sound of the eagle is more high-pitched, that of the bull much deeper, and the song of the nightingale is sweeter and more supple.

What is peculiar to humanity? Reason. Right and perfected reason is the fulfillment of human well-being. So, if every thing is

---

8. In the last year of his life, probably while living in unofficial retirement outside of Rome, Seneca wrote (for publication) a series of 124 letters on moral and philosophical topics. He addressed them to a younger acquaintance, Lucilius Junior, a Roman civil servant working in Sicily, of whom little else is known. Varying considerably in length, the letters answer philosophical questions Lucilius had apparently posed and offer reflections on Seneca's own life, as well as more general issues in personal and public life. (Significant gaps between excerpts within any letter are indicated in the text.)

esteemed when it has realized its own particular good and has achieved the objective of its own nature, and the particular good of a human being is reason, if a person has perfected this, that person is considered worthy of esteem and has reached the summit of human nature. This perfected reason is called virtue and is identical with the honorable.

So that alone is good in a human being which is uniquely human. We are not investigating here what is good in general but what is good in the case of human beings. Given that there is nothing other than reason unique to human nature, this will be the only true good, but it is one that outweighs all others.

Therefore in the case of human beings, it is wholly beside the point how much land they have under plough, how much money they have invested, how many people pay their respects, how expensive are their couches or translucent their cups, but how good they are.

A person is good whose reason is well developed and right and fitted to what human nature wills. This is called virtue, this is what we refer to as the honorable and is the one and only human good. Since reason alone can perfect a human being, it is only perfected reason that brings happiness. Because it is the only true human good, it is the only source of true human fulfillment. We also talk of other things as goods which are enhanced and conserved by virtue; in other words, all virtue's works. But virtue itself is the only true good because there is no other good without it.

All our actions in every sphere of life are governed by the measuring of what is the honorable thing to do against what is despicable. It is to these values that our reasoning for or against an action is directed. I will spell out the implications of this. A good person who judges an action honorable will do it even if it will involve a lot of trouble, even if it will involve financial loss, even if it involves danger. Similarly, a good person will not do something despicable even if it would bring profit, even if it would bring pleasure, even if it would bring power. Nothing will be able to divert such a person from the honorable course or toward the despicable course.

If you were to admit the idea that there is some good beside what is honorable, no virtue would be left secure. For no virtue can be sustained if it has to pay homage to something beyond itself. If there is some such thing, it is inconsistent with reason from which the virtues come and with truth, which is nothing without reason. Any idea inconsistent with truth is false.

A good person, I'm sure you will agree, will feel the greatest respect for the gods. Such a person, therefore, would face any eventuality with a calmness of spirit, knowing that it happened in accordance with divine law by which everything in the universe is ordered. If this is so, there will be but one good recognized by the person, namely what is honorable. For it is part of the honorable to submit to the will of the gods, not to be incensed at the unexpected or to bemoan misfortune, but to accept fate patiently and comply with its mandates.

If you admit anything else to be a good besides the honorable, not only will craving for life persecute you but also the craving for life's paraphernalia, a situation that is intolerable, limitless, and unstable. Again, therefore, the only good is the honorable, which has bounds.

Letter 66

So it is Lucilius. Whatever true reason recommends is solid and imperishable. It uplifts and supports the mind so it remains always elevated. Those other things that popular opinion thoughtlessly values and treats as goods pump people up with empty pleasures. Likewise, the things people fear as if they were real evils stir them up with mental panic just as animals are spooked by the mere semblance of danger.

In neither case is there any foundation to the pleasure or distress of mind. The one does not warrant real joy nor the other real fear. Only reason is unalterable and capable of consistency of judgment. It is not the servant but the ruler of the senses. As two straight lines are equally straight, equally right, reason is equal to reason; and so also is virtue to virtue. Virtue is nothing other than right reason. All virtues are instances of reason. They are instances of reason if they are right. If they are right, they are also equal.

As is the case with reason, so is it also with actions. They too, therefore, are all equal. For in that they match reason they also match one another. Actions are equal among themselves, I maintain, insofar as they are honorable and right. But there are also great differences between actions as dictated by varying circumstances, which are sometimes open-ended, at others constrained, either in the public gaze or hidden in obscurity, affecting many other people or very few. Though circumstances are variable, whatever action is best is equal to any other best action; they are all honorable.

Analogously, all good persons are equal in respect of their goodness. Yet they have differences of age: one is older, another younger; of appearance: one is attractive, another ugly; of status: this one is rich, that one poor, this one popular, powerful, known to all the city and population, that one a nonentity to most people and obscure. But in respect of their goodness, they are equals.

About what is good and what is evil the senses are wholly unqualified to judge. They are ignorant of what is useful and what is useless. They cannot offer any opinion unless the thing is placed before them in the present. They cannot see ahead to the future or remember the past. As for consequences, they have no inkling. Yet it is from awareness of these consequences that the order and sequence of actions is interwoven and the unity of a life proceeding in a right direction is created. Therefore it falls to Reason to be the adjudicator of things good and things bad. To alien and extraneous things she assigns no value and treats those which are neither good nor evil as the most trivial and insignificant of trappings. All Reason's good is situated in the mind.

Of goods there is a group Reason thinks of as being in the first rank and with which she designedly associates herself, such as victory, good children, and public well-being. There is a second group that does not make itself known except in bad times, like enduring a painful illness or exile with composure. A third group is neutral, for these goods are no more in accordance with nature than contrary to nature, such as a modest way of walking or an orderly way of sitting. For to sit is no less in keeping with nature than to stand or go for a walk.

The first and second groups of goods are distinct. The first is aligned with nature: to find satisfaction in the affection of one's children or the security of one's homeland. The second group is at odds with nature: to show courage in withstanding torment or enduring thirst as some disease burns your body's organs.

"What's this?" someone will ask. "Can anything that is contrary to nature be a good?" Not at all; but that from which the good springs is sometimes contrary to nature. To be wounded, to have your flesh burnt off in a fire, to be crushed by ill health, these are against nature; but to beat such things with an undefeated spirit—that is to behave according to nature.[9]

To state my point briefly, the material from which good arises is sometimes against nature, but good itself never is. For no good is divorced from reason, and reason always conforms with nature.

What therefore is reason? Compliance with nature. What is the highest human good? It is to conduct oneself in harmony with nature's will.

Letter 95

Consider also this question, how we are to behave toward other human beings. How do we act? What principles can we give people to follow? That we should not shed human blood? It is surely an inadequate ideal to avoid harming those one has a duty to assist! What a great thing to pride ourselves on, that one member of the human race is civilized to another! Should we teach, then, that we must stretch out a helping hand to the shipwrecked, show the right road to the bewildered, share our bread with the starving? How long it would take to list everything item by item that ought either to be done for others or not done. I can more briefly impart a general principle to govern all our interactions with human beings.

---

9. Seneca is playing with several senses of "nature" in this letter. It is in our nature as animals to flee from what may damage us physically. However, because we are not merely animals but *rational* animals, it is also consistent with our nature to follow reason when it requires us to override animal impulse. Further, it is consistent with nature in a broader sense; i.e., nature as the universal order that determines our specific nature and the course of events in our world. In acting as reason directs, we act in accordance with our own nature and with the universal order of nature.

Everything that you see, everything human and divine, is one. We are all limbs of one all-encompassing body. Nature brought us into existence as creatures related to one another, forming us from the same elements for the same ends. She instilled in us reciprocal affection and made us innately sociable. She also invested us with a sense of fairness and justice. According to her law it is more deplorable to harm another than to be harmed. It is in obedience to her command that our hands are ready to assist those who need assistance.

That line of poetry should ever be in our hearts and on our lips: "I am human and I count nothing human as disconnected from me."[10] Let us possess what we possess as members of a community. Into it we were born. Our society is like an arch of stones that will collapse unless each stone lends its weight to the next, allowing the whole structure to support itself.

Letter 50

Harpaste is a female clown[11] belonging to my wife. You'll recall that we inherited the obligation to look after her under the terms of a will and she has continued to live in my house. I myself have little interest in whatever entertainment these freaks of nature afford. If ever I want to be amused by a fool I don't have far to look. I just laugh at myself.

Anyway, this clown has suddenly lost her eyesight. What I'm going to tell you is hard to believe, but it's true: she doesn't realize that she's gone blind and she keeps asking her attendant to change her room. She complains that the house is always too dark.

I think it will be obvious to you that the reason we smile at Harpaste's misunderstanding is that it is somehow typical of all of us. We do not recognize our own greed, our own passion for possessions. At least blind people generally look for a guide, but we wander about without anyone to show us the way and we say: "I'm

---

10. Seneca is quoting from the comedy *The Self-Tormentor*, a comedy by Roman playwright Terence (195–159 B.C.E.).

11. Harpaste was a "clown" or "fool"; i.e., a slave or servant kept for the amusement value of her appearance, speech, or mannerisms. Seneca would naturally disapprove of the practice for its exclusive focus on "indifferents" in assigning value to persons.

not driven by ambition; it's just that no one can survive in Rome any other way. I'm not extravagant; it's this city that costs so much to live in. The fact that I lose my temper, that I haven't settled down to any definite way of life, isn't a defect in me; youth is to blame for this." Why do we deceive ourselves? It is not our environment that is responsible for our failings. They are inside us, seated deep within our innermost being, and the reason it is so difficult to achieve a healthy state of mind is because we fail to recognize that it is we ourselves who are sick.

To learn the virtues is to unlearn the vices. As we aim to improve ourselves we should draw confidence from the fact that the possession of goodness, once it has been obtained, is a possession forever. Virtue can't be unlearned. This is because discordant things are only weakly fixed to their mismatched hosts. Consequently they can be detached and expelled. But things that arrive at their true home settle in for the long term. Virtue is in keeping with nature whereas the vices are antagonistic and hostile to it.

But while the virtues, once they have been welcomed in, do not leave and are easy to safeguard, nevertheless, establishing the initial contact with them is hard work because fear of the unfamiliar is typical of a feeble and irresolute mind. So the mind needs to be pushed into taking the first step. From then on the medicine is not bitter. It heartens at the same time as it cures. With other remedies the enjoyment comes after the return to health; philosophy, by contrast, is both therapeutic and sweet from the very first dose. Farewell.

SUGGESTIONS FOR FURTHER READING

There is no complete critical edition of Seneca's philosophical writings. Latin texts with (older) English translations are available from Harvard University Press, Loeb Classical Library series. Newer translations of selected essays can be found in various collections.

Stoic philosophers did not confine their interests to ethical problems, but also developed distinctive theories of nature, metaphysics, and logic. For overviews of classical stoicism, including stoic theories of nonethical subjects, featuring discussions of Seneca specifically or Roman stoicism generally, see J. M. Rist, *Stoic Philosophy* (Cambridge: Cambridge University Press, 1969); Brad Inwood, ed., *Cambridge Companion to the Stoics* (New York: Cambridge University Press, 2003); Katerina Ierodiakonou, ed., *Topics in Stoic Philosophy* (Oxford: Clarendon Press, 1999); and C. D. N. Costa, ed., *Seneca* (London: Routledge & K. Paul, 1974). On the influence of stoicism on the development of Christianity, see Richard Sorabji, *Emotion and Peace of Mind: From Stoic Agitation to Christian Temptation* (New York: Oxford University Press, 2000).

For an introduction focusing on stoic ethics in particular, see Tad Brennan, *The Stoic Life: Emotions, Duties, and Fate* (Oxford: Oxford University Press, 2005); Julia Annas, "My Station and Its Duties: Ideals and the Social Embeddedness of Virtue," *Proceedings of the Aristotelian Society* 102 (2002): 109–123. Two particularly good texts on the historical context in which stoic moral philosophy developed are Martha Craven Nussbaum, *Therapy of Desire: Theory and Practice in Hellenistic Ethics* (Princeton: Princeton University Press, 1994) and Julia Annas, *The Morality of Happiness* (New York: Oxford University Press 1993). Recently there has been a debate about the importance of rules in stoic ethics; this debate is helpfully reviewed in Stephen M. Gardiner, "Seneca's Virtuous Moral Rules," in *Virtue Ethics Old and New*, ed. by Stephen M. Gardiner (Ithaca, NY: Cornell University Press, 2005).

On Seneca's extraordinarily eventful life and career, see Miriam T. Griffin, *Seneca: A Philosopher in Politics* (Oxford: Clarendon Press, 1976).

Francis Hutcheson

INTRODUCTION

Francis Hutcheson was born August 8, 1694, in Northern Ireland, the son and grandson of Scottish Presbyterian ministers. As his family were dissenters from the Church of England, he was educated at dissenting schools prior to entering the University of Glasgow in 1711, at age 17. There he studied mathematics and natural philosophy. After pursuing his studies through the master's level, he stayed on to study theology. On completion of his studies, he entered the ministry and returned to Ireland. Hutcheson's scholarly abilities had already attracted notice and, in 1719, the Irish Presbyterian establishment in Dublin invited him to open a dissenting academy. The academy was successful and Hutcheson remained there for about eight years.

While in Dublin, Hutcheson became a member of the intellectual circle led by the Viscount Molesworth. This connection led to the publication of a series of philosophical letters attacking egoistic moral philosophies, letters in which Hutcheson worked out arguments that would subsequently appear much elaborated and developed in the first edition of his *Inquiry into the Original of Our Ideas of Beauty and Virtue* (1725). The *Inquiry* was followed by *An Essay on the Nature and Conduct of the Passions, with Illustrations on the Moral Sense* (1728). There were sporadic objections by conservative, more traditionally Calvinist Presbyterians to his depiction of human nature as inherently capable of unselfish and morally good action. However, his scholarly reputation was sufficient to win him the position of professor of moral philosophy at his alma mater, Glasgow University. He held the professorship from 1730 until his death in 1746.

Hutcheson became an extremely popular and successful lecturer, whose influence extended well beyond the precincts of his university. A seminal figure in what has become known as the Scottish Enlightenment, his students and correspondents included other notable figures in the movement, such as Adam Smith and David

Hume. Hutcheson's later works of moral philosophy included a text for university students, originally published in Latin, *A Short Introduction to Moral Philosophy* (1742, English translation 1747), and the posthumously published *A System of Moral Philosophy* (1755).

Hutcheson suggested his *Inquiry* was written to defend the Earl of Shaftesbury's assertion that we possess a "moral sense" that is the source of our conceptions of virtue. But the theory he worked out owes as much to Locke as to Shaftesbury, and departs substantially from each. Hutcheson accepts Locke's view that human knowledge is empirical in origin. All our ideas, including our ideas of good, are produced by our senses—external and internal. *External* senses provide ideas of objects outside us, which tell us either what those objects are like (ideas of the primary qualities of objects) or what active powers they have to affect our sensibilities in regular law-like ways (ideas of secondary and tertiary qualities of objects). *Internal* senses are mental capacities to receive ideas from reflecting upon the operation of our own minds, or upon our external ideas. Pleasure is one such inner, reflective sense, Locke argued, the love of which is our primary motive to action.

Hutcheson accepted Locke's general account of human knowledge but disagreed with his moral psychology. Hutcheson argues that we also possess other inner senses, including the sense of beauty and the moral sense, which he defines as mental "determinations" to take distinct forms of pleasure and pain in either the aesthetic qualities of our ideas of things (sense of beauty) or in our ideas of the character, motivations, and conduct of rational agents (moral sense). That we feel immediate, uncalculated approval upon observing a benevolent act, Hutcheson argues, is evidence of the existence of this inner, moral sensitivity. For we have this immediate response whenever we contemplate benevolent acts, whether those acts are directed toward ourselves or others, and whether or not the agent whose benevolence we approve is in a position to benefit us personally. Thus the moral sense is not simply an inclination to be pleased by whatever tends to our material advantage, or as Hutcheson puts it, our "natural" good. We approve benevolence in itself, as "good" in a distinct sense; that is, "morally good."

Because it is benevolence that we approve, and because our approval is stronger the freer of self-interest we take the agent's motivations to be, Hutcheson argues, we may conclude that while all benevolence is morally good, universal or public benevolence is morally superior to private benevolence. In application to actions, this means "that action is best, which procures the greatest happiness for the greatest numbers." This suggestion, together with the theory of moral rights Hutcheson develops from it, was an important source for utilitarian moral theory in the nineteenth century. It is important to remember, however, that Hutcheson himself was not a utilitarian. It is *not* the consequences of acts that make those acts or their agents morally good, but the *benevolence* that motivates them.

Hutcheson also departs significantly from the classical models on which Shaftesbury had drawn. Hutcheson does not view morality as an essentially personal project of self-perfection, as many classical philosophers seem to do. Nor is *eudaimonia* our motivation to develop and express virtuous dispositions. We are naturally disposed to benevolent concern for others and naturally disposed, on reflection, to approve our own and others' benevolence. Although benevolence is not always strong enough to outweigh the competing claims of self-interest, it is only the rare individual whose character is not significantly animated by it. The more typical vice of self-absorption in our own material concerns can be corrected by fostering reflection upon our characters so that our moral sense can fulfill its roles both of rewarding—and so reinforcing—benevolence, and of censuring its opposite.

An Inquiry into the Original
of Our Ideas of Beauty and Virtue[1]

THE PREFACE

There is no part of philosophy of more importance than a just
knowledge of human nature and its various powers and dispositions. Our late inquiries have been very much employed about our
understanding, and the several methods of obtaining truth. We
generally acknowledge that the importance of any truth is nothing
else than its moment, or efficacy to make men happy, or to give
them the greatest and most lasting pleasure; and wisdom denotes
only a capacity of pursuing this end by the best means. It must
surely then be of the greatest importance to have distinct conceptions of this end itself, as well as of the means necessary to obtain
it; that we may find out which are the greatest and most lasting
pleasures, and not employ our reason, after all our laborious
improvements of it, in trifling pursuits. It is to be feared indeed that
most of our studies, without this inquiry, will be of very little use to
us; for they seem to have scarce any other tendency than to lead us
into speculative knowledge itself. Nor are we distinctly told how it
is that knowledge or truth is pleasant to us.

    This consideration put the author of the following papers upon
inquiring into the various pleasures which human nature is capable
of receiving. We shall generally find in our modern philosophic
writings, nothing farther on this head, than some bare division of
them into sensible, and rational, and some trite commonplace
arguments to prove the latter more valuable than the former. Our
sensible pleasures are slightly passed over, and explained only by
some instances in tastes, smells, sounds, or such-like, which men of

---

1. The selection is from Hutcheson's *An Inquiry into the Original of Our
Ideas of Beauty and Virtue*, 4th ed. (London: D. Midwinter, A. Bettesworth,
C. Hitch, J. & J. Pemberton, R. Ware, C. Rivington, F. Clay, A. Ward, J. &
P. Knapton, T. Longman, R. Hett, and J. Wood, 1738). The spelling, font,
and occasionally the punctuation, have been modernized for the reader's
convenience. Editor's notes appear in brackets.

any tolerable reflection generally look upon as very trifling satisfactions. Our rational pleasures have had much the same kind of treatment. We are seldom taught any other notion of rational pleasure than that which we have upon reflecting on our possession or claim to those objects, which may be occasions of pleasure. Such objects we call advantageous; but advantage, or interest, cannot be distinctly conceived, till we know what those pleasures are which advantageous objects are apt to excite; and what senses or powers of perception we have with respect to such objects. We may perhaps find such an inquiry of more importance in morals, to prove what we call the reality of virtue, or that it is the surest happiness of the agent, than one would at first imagine.

In reflecting upon our external senses, we plainly see that our perceptions of pleasure or pain do not depend directly on our will. Objects do not please us, according as we incline they should. The presence of some objects necessarily pleases us, and the presence of others as necessarily displeases us. Nor can we, by our will, any otherwise procure pleasure, or avoid pain, than by procuring the former kind of objects, and avoiding the latter. By the very frame of our nature the one is made the occasion of delight, and the other of dissatisfaction.

The same observation will hold in all our other pleasures and pains. For there are many other sorts of objects, which please, or displease us as necessarily, as material objects do when they operate upon our organs of sense. There is scarcely any object which our minds are employed about, which is not thus constituted the necessary occasion of some pleasure or pain. Thus we find ourselves pleased with a regular form, a piece of architecture or painting, a composition of notes, a theorem, an action, an affection, a character. And we are conscious that this pleasure necessarily arises from the contemplation of the idea, which is then present to our minds, with all its circumstances, although some of these ideas have nothing of what we commonly call sensible perception in them; and in those which have, the pleasure arises from some uniformity, order, arrangement, imitation; and not from the simple ideas of color, or sound, or mode of extension separately considered.

These determinations to be pleased with any forms, or ideas which occur to our observation, the author chooses to call SENSES; distinguishing them from the powers which commonly go by that name, by calling our power of perceiving the beauty of regularity, order, harmony, an INTERNAL SENSE; and that determination to approve affections, actions, or characters of rational agents, which we call virtuous, he marks by the name of a MORAL SENSE.

His principle design is to show that human nature was not left quite indifferent in the affair of virtue, to form to itself observations concerning the advantage, or disadvantage of actions, and accordingly to regulate its conduct. The weakness of our reason, and the avocations arising from the infirmities and necessities of our nature, are so great, that very few men could ever have formed those long deductions of reason, which show some actions to be in the whole advantageous to the agent, and their contraries pernicious. The AUTHOR of nature has much better furnished us for a virtuous conduct than our moralists seem to imagine, by almost as quick and powerful instructions, as we have for the preservation of our bodies. He has given us strong affections to be the springs of each virtuous action; and made virtue a lovely form, that we might easily distinguish it from its contrary, and be made happy by the pursuit of it.

Treatise II: An Inquiry Concerning Moral Good and Evil

INTRODUCTION

The word MORAL GOODNESS, in this treatise, denotes our idea of *some quality apprehended in actions, which procures approbation, attended with desire of the agent's happiness.* MORAL EVIL denotes our idea of a *contrary quality, which excites condemnation or dislike.* Approbation and condemnation are probably simple ideas, which cannot be farther explained. We must be contented with these imperfect descriptions, until we discover whether we really have such ideas, and what general foundation there is in nature for this difference of actions, as morally good or evil.

These descriptions seem to contain a universally acknowledged difference of moral good and evil, from natural. All men who speak of moral good acknowledge that it procures approbation and good-will toward those we apprehend possessed of it; whereas natural good does not. In this matter men must consult their own breasts. How differently are they affected toward these they suppose possessed of honesty, faith, generosity, kindness; and those who are possessed of the natural goods, such as houses, lands, gardens, vineyards, health, strength, sagacity? We shall find that we necessarily love and approve the possessors of the former; but the possession of the latter procures no approbation or good-will at all toward the possessor, but often contrary affections of envy and hatred. In the same manner, whatever quality we apprehend to be morally evil, raises our dislike toward the person in whom we observe it, such as treachery, cruelty, ingratitude; whereas we heartily love, esteem, and pity many who are exposed to natural evils, such as pain, poverty, hunger, sickness, death.

Now the first question on this subject is, Whence arise these different ideas of actions?

Because we shall afterward frequently use the words *interest, advantage, natural good*, it is necessary here to fix their ideas. The pleasure in our sensible perceptions of any kind gives us our first idea of *natural good* or *happiness*; and then all objects which are apt to excite this pleasure are called *immediately good*. Those objects which may procure others immediately pleasant, are called *advantageous*: and we pursue both kinds from a view of *interest*, or from self-love.

Our sense of pleasure is antecedent to advantage or interest, and is the foundation of it. We do not perceive pleasure in objects, because it is our interest to do so; but objects or actions are advantageous, and are pursued or undertaken from interest, because we receive pleasure from them. Our perception of pleasure is necessary, and nothing is advantageous or naturally good to us, but what is apt to raise pleasure mediately, or immediately. Such objects as we know either from experience of sense, or reason, to be immediately or mediately advantageous, or apt to minister pleasure, we are said to pursue from self-interest, when our intention is only to enjoy this pleasure, which they have the power of exciting.

SECT I. OF THE MORAL SENSE BY WHICH WE PERCEIVE VIRTUE
AND VICE, AND APPROVE OR DISAPPROVE THEM IN OTHERS.

I. That the perceptions of moral good and evil are perfectly different from those of natural good or advantage, every one must convince himself by reflecting upon the different manner in which he finds himself affected when these objects occur to him. Had we no sense of good distinct from the advantage or interest arising from the external senses, and the perceptions of beauty and harmony; the sensations and affections toward a fruitful field, or commodious habitation, would be much the same with what we have toward a generous friend, or any noble character; for both are or may be advantageous to us: and we should no more admire any action, or love any person in a distant country, or age, whose influence could not extend to us, than we love the mountains of PERU, while we are unconcerned in the Spanish trade. We should have the same sentiments and affections toward inanimate beings, which we have toward rational agents, which yet every one knows to be false. Upon comparison, we say, why should we approve or love inanimate beings? They have no intention of good to us, or to any other person; their nature makes them fit for our uses, which they neither know nor study to serve. But it is not so with rational agents: they study the interest, and desire the happiness of other beings with whom they converse.

We are all then conscious of the difference between that *approbation* or perception of *moral excellence*, which benevolence excites toward the person in whom we observe it, and that opinion of natural goodness, which only raises desire of possession toward the good object. Now, what should make this difference, if all approbation, or sense of good be from prospect of advantage? Do not inanimate objects promote our advantage as well as benevolent persons, who do us offices of kindness and friendship? Should we not then have the same endearing approbation of both or only the same cold opinion of advantage in both? The reason why it is not so must be this, that we have a distinct perception of beauty or excellence in the kind affections of rational agents; whence we are determined to admire and love such characters and persons.

Suppose we reap the same advantage from two men, one of whom serves us from an ultimate desire of our happiness, or goodwill toward us; the other from views of self-interest, or by constraint: both are in this case equally beneficial or advantageous to us, and yet we shall have quite different sentiments of them. We must then certainly have other perceptions of moral actions than those of advantage: and that power of receiving these perceptions may be called a MORAL SENSE, since the definition agrees to it, *viz.*

a *determination of the mind, to receive any idea from the presence
of an object which occurs to us, independent of our will.*[2]

II. In our sentiments of actions which affect ourselves, there is
indeed a mixture of the ideas of *natural* and *moral* good, which
require some attention to separate them. But when we reflect upon
the actions which affect other persons only, we may observe the
moral ideas unmixed with those of natural good or evil. For let it be
here observed that those senses by which we perceive pleasure in
natural objects, whence they are constituted advantageous, could
never raise in us any desire of public good, but only of what was
good to ourselves in particular. Nor could they ever make us approve
an action merely because of its promoting the happiness of others.
And yet, as soon as any action is represented to us as flowing from
love, humanity, gratitude, compassion, a study of the good of others, and an ultimate desire of their happiness, although it were in
the most distant part of the world, or in some past age, we feel joy
within us, admire the lovely action, and praise its author. And on
the contrary, every action represented as flowing from ill-will, desire
of the misery of others without view to any prevalent good to the
public, or ingratitude, raises abhorrence and aversion.

It is true indeed that the actions we approve in others are generally imagined to tend to the natural good of mankind, or of some
parts of it. But whence this secret chain between each person and
mankind? How is my interest connected with the most distant parts
of it? And yet I must admire actions which show good-will toward
them, and love the author. Whence this love, compassion, indignation, and hatred toward even feigned characters, in the most distant
ages, and nations, according as they appear kind, faithful, compassionate, or of the opposite dispositions, toward their imaginary contemporaries? If there is no moral sense, which makes benevolent
actions appear beautiful; if all approbations be from the interest of
the approver, "What's HECUBA to us, or we to HECUBA?"[3]

IV. Some moralists,[4] who will rather twist self-love into a thousand shapes than allow any other principle of approbation than

---

2. See the Preface.

3. Tragedy of Hamlet.

4. [Chief among the moralists Hutcheson opposes here would be Thomas
Hobbes and Bernard Mandeville, each of whom had argued that human
beings are predominantly selfish.]

interest, may tell us that whatever profits one part without detriment to another, profits the whole, and then some small share will redound to each individual; that those actions which tend to the good of the whole, if universally performed, would most effectually secure to each individual his own happiness; and that consequently, we may approve such actions, from the opinion of their tending ultimately to our own advantage.

We need not trouble these gentlemen to show by their nice train of consequences, and influences of actions by way of precedent in particular instances, that we in this age reap any advantage from ORESTES' killing the treacherous AEGYSTHUS,[5] or from the actions of CODRUS or DECIUS.[6] Allow their reasonings to be perfectly good, they only prove that after long reflection and reasoning, we may find out some ground to judge certain actions advantageous to us, which every man admires as soon as he hears of them; and that too under a quite different conception.

V. This moral sense, either of our own actions, or of those of others, has this in common with our other senses, that however our desire of virtue may be counterbalanced by interest, our sentiment or perceptions of its beauty cannot; as it certainly might be, if the only ground of our approbation were views of advantage. Let us consider this both as to our own actions, and those of others.

A covetous man shall dislike any branch of trade, how useful soever it may be to the public, if there is no gain for himself in it; here is an aversion from interest. Propose a sufficient premium, and he shall be the first who sets about it, with full satisfaction in his own conduct. Now is it the same way with our sense of moral actions? Should any one advise us to wrong a minor, or orphan, or

---

5. [According to Homer, Orestes' act was thoroughly justified because Aegisthus had seduced his mother, murdered his father, Agamemnon, and plotted to kill Orestes, all in order to usurp the throne of Mycenae.]

6. [The reference is either to Publius Decius Mus, the Elder, or his son, Publius Decius Mus, the Younger. Each man died while leading the defense of Rome against successive invasions because each offered himself as a sacrifice to win the gods' favor and Rome's victory. According to legend, Codrus was the last king of Athens. Told that an oracle had declared that a Dorian invasion could not be repelled if his life were spared, Codrus disguised himself in ordinary clothes and attacked the Dorian forces single-handedly—to ensure his own death and thus the city's survival.]

to do an ungrateful action toward a benefactor; we at first view abhor it: assure us that is will be very advantageous to us, propose even a reward; our sense of the action is not altered. It is true, these motives may make us undertake it; but they have no more influence upon us to make us approve it, than a physician's advice has to make a nauseous potion pleasant to the taste, when we perhaps force ourselves to take it for the recovery of health.

Had we no notion of actions, beside our opinion of their advantage or disadvantage, could we ever choose an action as advantageous, which we are conscious is still evil?—as it too often happens in human affairs. Where would be the need of such high bribes to prevail with men to abandon the interests of a ruined party, or of tortures to force out the secrets of their friends? Is it so hard to convince men's understandings, if that be the only faculty we have to do with, that it is probably more advantageous to secure present gain, and avoid present evils, by joining with the prevalent party, than to wait for the remote possibility of future good, upon a revolution often improbable, and sometimes unexpected? And when men are overpersuaded by advantage, do they always approve their own conduct? Nay, how often is their remaining life odious, and shameful, in their own sense of it, as well as in that of others, to whom the base action was profitable?

If anyone becomes satisfied with his own conduct in such a case, upon what ground is it? How does he please himself, or vindicate his actions to others? Never by reflecting upon his private advantage, or alleging this to others as a vindication; but by gradually warping into the moral principles of his new party; for no party is without them. And thus men become pleased with their actions under some appearance of moral good, distinct from advantage.

It may perhaps be alleged that in those actions of our own which we call good, there is this constant advantage, superior to all others, which is the ground of our approbation, and the motive to them from self-love, *viz.*, that we suppose the DEITY will reward them. At present it is enough to observe, that many have high notions of honor, faith, generosity, justice, who have scarce any opinions about the DEITY, or any thoughts of future rewards; and abhor any thing which is treacherous, cruel, or unjust, without any regard to future punishments.

But farther, though these rewards and punishments may make my own actions appear advantageous to me, yet they would never make me approve, and love another person for the like actions, whose merit would not be imputed to me. Those actions are advantageous indeed to the agent; but his advantage is not my advantage: and self-love could never recommend to me actions as advantageous to others, or make me like the authors of them on that account.

VII. If what is said makes it appear, that we have some other amiable idea of actions than that of advantageous to ourselves, we may conclude, that this perception of moral good is not derived from custom, education, example, or study. These give us no new ideas: they might make us see private advantage in actions whose usefulness did not at first appear; or give us opinions of some tendency of actions to our detriment, by some nice deductions of reason, or by a rash prejudice, when upon the first view of the action we should have observed no such thing: but they never could have made us apprehend actions as amiable or odious, without any consideration of our own advantage.

VIII. We are not to imagine that this moral sense, more than the other senses, supposes any innate ideas, knowledge, or practical proposition: we mean by it only *a determination of our minds to receive the simple ideas of approbation or condemnation, from actions observed, antecedent to any opinions of advantage or loss to redound to ourselves from them*; even as we are pleased with a regular form, or a harmonious composition, without having any knowledge of mathematics, or seeing any advantage in that form or composition, different from the immediate pleasure.

SECT. II. CONCERNING THE IMMEDIATE MOTIVE
TO VIRTUOUS ACTIONS

The motives of human actions, or their immediate causes, would be best understood after considering the passions and affections; but here we shall only consider the springs of the actions which we call virtuous, as far as it is necessary to settle the general foundation of the moral sense.

I. Every action, which we apprehend as either morally good or evil, is always supposed to flow from some *affection* toward sensitive natures; and whatever we call VIRTUE or VICE, is either some such *affection*, or some *action* consequent upon it. Or it may perhaps be enough to make an action or omission appear vicious, if it argues the want of such affection toward rational agents, as we expect in characters counted morally good. All the actions counted religious in any country, are supposed, by those who count them so, to flow from some affections toward the DEITY; and whatever we call *social virtue*, we still suppose to flow from affections toward our fellow creatures: for in this all seem to agree, that external motions, when accompanied with no affections toward GOD or man, or evidencing no want of the expected affections toward either, can have no moral good or evil in them.

Ask, for instance, the most abstemious hermit if temperance of itself would be morally good, supposing it showed no obedience toward the DEITY, made us no fitter for devotion, or the service of mankind, or the search after truth, than luxury; and he will easily grant that it would be no moral good, though still it might be naturally good or advantageous to health: and mere courage, or contempt of danger, if we conceive it to have no regard to the defense of the innocent, or repairing of wrongs or self-interest, would only entitle its possessor to bedlam. When such sort of courage is sometimes admired, it is upon some secret apprehension of a good intention in the use of it, or as a natural ability capable of a useful application. Prudence, if it was only employed in promoting private interest, is never imagined to be a virtue: and justice, or observing a strict equality, if it has no regard to the good of mankind, the preservation of rights, and securing of peace, is a quality properer for its ordinary gestamen,[7] a beam and scales, than for a rational agent. So that these four qualities, commonly called cardinal virtues, obtain that name, because they are dispositions universally necessary to promote public good, and denote affections toward rational agents; otherwise there would appear no virtue in them.

III. As to the love of benevolence, the very name excludes self-interest. We never call that man benevolent, who is in fact useful to others, but at the same time only intends his own interest, without any ultimate desire of the good of others. If there be any benevolence at all, it must be disinterested; for the most useful action imaginable loses all appearance of benevolence, as soon as we discern that it only flowed from self-love, or interest.

---

7. [*Gestamen, -inis*, Latin, meaning a thing carried. In classical imagery, justice is depicted as a woman carrying a scale for balancing claims.]

But it must be here observed, that as all men have self-love, as well as benevolence, these two principles may jointly excite a man to the same action; and then they are to be considered as two forces impelling the same body to motion; sometimes they conspire, sometimes are indifferent to each other, and sometimes are in some degree opposite. Thus, if a man [should] have such strong benevolence, as would have produced an action without any views of self-interest; that such a man has also in view private advantage, along with public good, as the effect of his action, does no way diminish the benevolence of the action.

X. An honest farmer will tell you that he studies the preservation and happiness of his children, and loves them without any design of good to himself. But say some of our philosophers, "the happiness of their children gives parents pleasure, and their misery gives them pain; and therefore to obtain the former, and avoid the latter, they study, from self-love, the good of their children." Suppose several merchants joined in partnership of their whole effects; one of them is employed abroad in managing the stock of the company; his prosperity occasions gain to all, and his losses give them pain for their share in the loss: is this then the same kind of affection with that of parents to their children? Is there the same tender, personal regard? I fancy no parent will say so. In this case of merchants there is a plain conjunction of interest; but whence the conjunction of interest between the parent and child? Do the child's sensations give pleasure or pain to the parent? Is the parent hungry, thirsty, sick, when his children are so? No; but his naturally implanted desire of their good, and aversion to their misery, makes him be affected with joy or sorrow from their pleasures or pains. This desire then is antecedent to the conjunction of interest, and the cause of it, not the effect: it must then be disinterested. "No," says another sophist, "children are parts of ourselves, and in loving them we but love ourselves in them." A very good answer! Let us carry it as far as it will go. How are they parts of ourselves? Not as a leg or an arm: we are not conscious of their sensations. "But their bodies were formed from parts of ours." So is a fly, or a maggot, which may breed in any discharged blood or humour: very dear insects surely! There must be something else then which makes children parts of ourselves; and what is this but that affection, which NATURE determines us to have toward them? This love makes them part of ourselves, and therefore does

not flow from their being so before. This is indeed a good metaphor; and wherever we find a determination among several rational agents to mutual love, let each individual be looked upon as a
part of a great *whole*, or *system*, and concern himself in the public good of it.

Sect. III. The Sense of Virtue, and the Various Opinions About it, Reducible to One General Foundation. The Manner of Computing the Morality of Actions.

I. If we examine all the actions which are counted amiable any-
where, and inquire into the grounds upon which they are approved,
we shall find that in the opinion of the person who approves them,
they always appear as BENEVOLENT, or flowing from good-will to
others, and a study of their happiness, whether the approver be
one of the persons beloved, or profited, or not; so that all those
kind affections which incline us to make others happy, and all
actions supposed to flow from such affections, appear morally
good, if, while they are benevolent toward some persons, they be
not pernicious to others. Nor shall we find any thing amiable in
any action whatsoever, where there is no benevolence imagined;
nor in any disposition, or capacity, which is not supposed applicable to, and designed for, benevolent purposes. Nay, as was before
observed, the actions which in fact are exceedingly useful, shall
appear void of moral beauty, if we know they proceeded from no
kind intentions toward others; and yet an unsuccessful attempt at
kindness; or of promoting public good, shall appear as amiable as
the most successful, if it flowed from as strong benevolence.

III. Again, that we may see how benevolence is the foundation
of all apprehended excellence in social virtues, let us only observe
that amidst the diversity of sentiments on this head among various
sects, this is still allowed to be the way of deciding the controversy
about any disputed practice, *viz.* to inquire whether this conduct,
or the contrary, will most effectually promote the public good. The
morality is immediately adjusted, when the natural tendency, or
influence of the action upon the *universal natural good* of mankind, is agreed upon. That which produces more good than evil in
the whole is acknowledged good; and what does not, is counted
evil. In this case, we no other way regard the good of the actor, or

that of those who are thus inquiring, than as they make a part of the great system.

V. The actions which flow solely from self-love, and yet evidence no want of benevolence, having no hurtful effects upon others, seem perfectly indifferent in a moral sense, and neither raise the love or hatred of the observer. Our reason can indeed discover certain bounds, within which we may not only act from self-love, consistently with the good of the whole; but every mortal's acting thus within these bounds for his own good is absolutely necessary for the good of the whole; and the want of such self-love would be universally pernicious. Hence, he who pursues his own private good, with an intention also to concur with that constitution which tends to the good of the whole; and much more he who promotes his own good, with a direct view of making himself more capable of serving GOD, or doing good to mankind; acts not only innocently, but also honourably, and virtuously: for in both these cases, benevolence concurs with self-love to excite him to the action. And thus a neglect of our own good may be morally evil, and argue want of benevolence toward the whole. But when self-love breaks over the bounds above-mentioned, and leads us into actions detrimental to others, and to the whole; or makes us insensible of the generous kind affections; then it appears vicious, and is disapproved.

VI. Here we must also observe that every moral agent justly considers himself as a part of this rational system, which may be useful to the whole; so that he may be, in part, an object of his own benevolence. Nay, farther, as was hinted above, he may see that the preservation of the system requires every one to be innocently solicitous about himself. Hence he may conclude that an action which brings greater evil to the agent than good to others, however it may evidence strong benevolence, or a virtuous disposition in the agent, yet it must be founded upon a mistaken opinion of its tendency to public good, when it has no such tendency: so that a man who reasoned justly, and considered the whole, would not be led into it, were his benevolence ever so strong; nor would he recommend it to the practice of others.

VIII. In comparing the *moral qualities* of actions, in order to regulate our *election* among various actions proposed, or to find which of them has the greatest moral excellency, we are led by our moral sense of virtue to judge thus; that in equal degrees of happiness, expected to proceed from the action, the virtue is in proportion to the number of persons to whom the happiness shall extend; (and here the dignity, or moral importance of persons, may compensate numbers) and in equal numbers, the virtue is as the quantity of the happiness or natural good; or that the virtue is in a compound ratio of the quantity of good, and number of enjoyers. In the same manner, the moral evil, or vice, is as the degree of misery, and number of sufferers; so that *that action* is *best*, which procures the *greatest happiness* for the *greatest numbers*; and that worst, which, in like manner, occasions misery.

Again, when the consequences of actions are of a mixed nature, partly advantageous, and partly pernicious; that action is good, whose good effects preponderate the evil by being useful to many, and pernicious to few; and that evil, which is otherwise. Here also the moral importance of characters, or dignity of persons may compensate numbers; as may also the degrees of happiness or misery: for to procure an inconsiderable good to many, but an immense evil to few, may be evil; and an immense good to few may preponderate a small evil to many.

XI. To find a universal rule to compute the morality of any actions, with all their circumstances, when we judge of the actions done by ourselves, or by others, we must observe the following propositions or axioms.

1. The moral importance of any agent, or the quantity of public good he produces, is in a compound proportion of his benevolence and abilities. For 'tis plain that his good offices depend upon these two jointly. In like manner, the quantity of private good which any agent obtains for himself, is in a like compound proportion of his selfish principles, and his abilities. We speak here only of the external goods of this world, which one pursues from some selfish principles. For as to internal goods of the mind, these are most effectually obtained by the exercise of other affections than those called selfish, even those which carry the agent beyond himself toward the good of others.

2. In comparing the virtues of different agents, when the abilities are equal, the moments of public good are proportioned to the goodness of the temper, or the benevolence; and when the tempers are equal, the quantities of good are as the abilities.

3. The virtue then or goodness of temper is directly as the moment of good, when other circumstances are equal, and inversely as the abilities. That is to say, where the abilities are greatest, there is less virtue evidenced in any given moment of good produced.

4. But as the natural consequences of our actions are various, some good to ourselves, and evil to the public; and others evil to ourselves, and good to the public; or either useful both to ourselves and others, or pernicious to both; the entire spring of good actions is not always benevolence alone; or of evil, malice alone (nay, sedate malice is rarely found); but in most actions we must look upon self-love as another force, sometimes conspiring with benevolence, and assisting it, when we are excited by views of private interest, as well as public good; and sometimes opposing benevolence, when the good action is any way difficult or painful in the performance, or detrimental in its consequences to the agent.

These selfish motives . . . we may in general denote . . . by the word interest: which when it occurs with benevolence, in any action capable of increase or diminution, must produce a greater quantity of good than benevolence alone in the same abilities; and therefore when the moment of good, in an action partly intended for the good of the agent is but equal to the moment of good in the action of another agent, influenced only by benevolence, the former is less virtuous; and in this case the interest must be deducted to find the true effect of the benevolence or virtue. In the same manner, when interest is opposite to benevolence, and yet is surmounted by it; this interest must be added to the moment, to increase the virtue of the action, or the strength of the benevolence. By interest, in this last case, is understood all the advantage which the agent might have obtained by omitting the action, which is a negative motive to it; and this, when subtracted, becomes positive.

[5.] The fifth axiom only explains the external marks by which men must judge, who do not see into each other's hearts; for it may really happen in many cases that men may have benevolence sufficient to surmount any difficulty, and yet they may meet with none at all: and in that case, it is certain there is as much virtue in the agent, though he does not give such proof of it to his fellow-creatures, as if he had surmounted difficulties in his kind actions. And this too must be the case with the DEITY, to whom nothing is difficult.

Since then, in judging of the goodness of temper in any agent, the abilities must come into computation, as is above-mentioned, and none can act beyond their natural abilities; that must be the perfection of virtue, where the moment of good produced equals the ability, or when the being acts to the utmost of his power for the public good.

From the preceding reasonings we shall only draw this one inference, which seems the most joyful imaginable, even to the lowest rank of mankind, *viz.*, that no external circumstance of fortune, no involuntary disadvantages, can exclude any mortal from the most heroic virtue. For how small soever the moment of public good be, which any one can accomplish, yet if his abilities are proportionably small, the virtue may be as great as any whatsoever. Thus, not only the prince, the statesman, the general, are capable of true heroism, though these are the chief characters, whose fame is diffused through various nations and ages: but when we find in an honest trader, the kind friend, the faithful prudent adviser, the charitable and hospitable neighbor, the tender husband, and affectionate parent, the sedate yet cheerful companion, the generous assistant of merit, the cautious allayer of contention and debate, the promoter of love and good understanding among acquaintances; if we consider, that these were all the good offices which his station in the world gave him an opportunity of performing to mankind, we must judge this character really as amiable as those whose external splendor dazzles an injudicious world into an opinion, that they are the only heroes in virtue.

SECT. VII. A DEDUCTION OF SOME COMPLEX MORAL IDEAS; *VIZ.*,
OF OBLIGATION, AND RIGHT, PERFECT, AND EXTERNAL,
ALIENABLE, AND UNALIENABLE, FROM THIS MORAL SENSE.

V. Hence we may see the difference between *constraint* and *obligation*. There is indeed no difference between constraint, and the second sense of the word obligation, *viz.*, a constitution which makes an action eligible from self-interest, if we only mean external interest, distinct from the delightful consciousness which arises from the moral sense. The reader need scarcely be told that by constraint, we do not understand an external force moving our limbs without our consent; for in that case we are not agents at all; but that constraint which arises from the threatening and presenting some evil, in order to make us act in a certain manner. And yet there seems a universally acknowledged difference between even this sort of constraint and obligation. We never say, we are *obliged* to do an action which we count base, but we may be *constrained* to it: we never say that the divine laws, by their sanctions, constrain us, but oblige us; nor do we call obedience to the DEITY constraint, unless by a metaphor, though many own they are influenced by fear of punishments. And yet supposing an almighty evil being should require, under grievous penalties, treachery, cruelty, ingratitude, we would call this constraint. The difference is plainly this: when any sanctions cooperate with our moral sense, in exciting us to actions which we count morally good, we say we are obliged; but when sanctions of rewards or punishments oppose our moral sense, then we say we are bribed or constrained. In the former case we call the lawgiver good, as designing the public happiness; in the latter we call him evil, or unjust, for the supposed contrary intention. But were all our ideas of moral good or evil derived solely from opinions of private advantage or loss in actions, I see no possible difference which could be made in the meaning of these words.

VI. From this [moral] sense too we derive our ideas of RIGHTS. Whenever it appears to us, that *a faculty of doing, demanding, or possessing any thing, universally allowed in certain circumstances, would in the whole tend to the general good,* we say, that one in such circumstances has *a right to do, possess, or demand that thing.* And according as this tendency to the public good is greater or less, the right is greater or less.

The rights called *perfect* are of *such necessity to the public good, that the universal violation of them would make human life intolerable*; and it actually makes those miserable, whose rights are thus violated. On the contrary, to fulfill these rights in every instance tends to the public good, either directly, or by promoting the innocent advantage of a part. Hence it plainly follows, that to allow a violent defense, or prosecution of such rights, before civil government be constituted, cannot in any particular case be more detrimental to the public than the violation of them with impunity. And as to the general consequences, the universal use of force in a *state of nature*,[8] in pursuance of perfect rights, seems exceedingly advantageous to the whole, by making everyone dread any attempts against the perfect fights of others.

This is the moral effect which attends proper injury, or a violation of the perfect rights of others, *viz.*, a right to war, and all violence which is necessary to oblige the injurious to repair the damage, and give security against such offenses for the future. This is the sole foundation of the rights of punishing criminals, and of violent prosecutions of our rights, in a state of nature.

And these rights, naturally residing in the persons injured, or their voluntary or invited assistants to use force according to the judgments of indifferent arbitrators, being by the consent of the persons injured, transferred to the magistrate in a civil state, are the true foundation of his right of punishment. Instances of perfect rights are those to our lives; to the fruits of our labors; to demand performance of contracts upon valuable considerations, from men capable of performing them; to direct our own actions either for the public, or innocent private good, before we have submitted them to the direction of others in any measure: and many others of like nature.

Imperfect rights are *such as, when universally violated, would not necessarily make men miserable.* These rights tend to the improvement and increase of positive good in any society, but are not absolutely necessary to prevent universal misery. The violation of them only disappoints men of the happiness expected from the humanity or gratitude of others; but does not deprive men of any good which they had before. From this description it appears that a violent prosecution of such rights would generally occasion greater evil than the violation of them. Besides, the allowing of force in such cases would deprive men of the greatest pleasure of action of kindness, humanity, gratitude; which would cease to appear amia-

---

8. [State of nature: a situation in which no organized civil society exists. This means political obligations do not yet exist, so any obligations that do exist must be purely moral. Philosophers in the seventeenth and eighteenth centuries frequently used the idea of a prepolitical "state of nature" in thought experiments intended to test claims about the foundations of morality and politics.]

ble, when men could be constrained to perform them. Instances of imperfect rights are those which the poor have to the charity of the wealthy; which all men have to offices of no trouble or expense to the performer; which benefactors have to returns of gratitude, and such-like.

The violation of imperfect rights only argues a man to have such weak benevolence, as not to study advancing the positive good of others, when in the least opposite to his own: but the violation of perfect rights argues the injurious person to be positively evil or cruel; or at least so immoderately selfish as to be indifferent about the positive misery and ruin of others, when he imagines he can find his interest in it. In violating the former, we show a weak desire of public happiness, which every small view of private interest overbalances; but in violating the latter, we show ourselves so entirely negligent of the misery of others, that views of increasing our own good overcome all our compassion toward their sufferings. Now as the absence of good is more easily borne than the presence of misery; so our good wishes toward the positive good of others are weaker than our compassion toward their misery. He then who violates imperfect rights shows that his self-love overcomes only the desire of positive good to others; but he who violates perfect rights, betrays such a selfish desire of advancing his own positive good, as overcomes all compassion toward the misery of others.

Besides these two sorts of rights, there is a third called *external*; as when *the doing, possessing, or demanding of any thing, is really detrimental to the public in any particular instances, as being contrary to the imperfect right of another, but yet the universally denying men this faculty of doing, possessing, or demanding that thing, or of using force in pursuance of it, would do more mischief than all the evils to be feared from the use of this faculty.*

Instances of external rights are these; that of a wealthy miser to recall his loan from the most industrious poor tradesman at any time, that of demanding performance of a covenant too burdensome on one side; the right of a wealthy heir to refuse payment of any debts which were contracted by him under age. . . .

X. From the idea of right, as above explained, we must necessarily conclude, that there can be no right, or limitation of right, inconsistent with, or opposite to the greatest public good. And therefore in cases of extreme necessity, when the state cannot otherwise be preserved from ruin, it must certainly be just and good in limited governors, or in any other persons who can do it, to use the force of the state for its own preservation, beyond the limits fixed by the constitution, in some transitory acts, which are not to be made precedents. And on the other hand, when an equal necessity to avoid ruin requires it, the subjects may justly resume the powers ordinarily lodged in their governors, or may counteract them. This privilege of flagrant necessity we all allow in defense of the most perfect private rights: and if public rights are of more extensive importance, so are also public necessities. These necessities must be very grievous and flagrant, otherwise they can never overbalance the evils of violating a tolerable constitution, by an arbitrary act of power, on the one hand; or by an insurrection, or civil war, on the other. No person or state can be happy where they do not think their important rights are secure from cruelty, avarice, ambition, or caprice of their governors. Nor can any magistracy be safe, or effectual for the ends of its institution, where there are frequent terrors of insurrections. Whatever temporary acts therefore may be allowed in extraordinary cases; whatever may be lawful in the transitory act of a bold legislator, who without previous consent should rescue a slavish nation, and place their affairs so in the hands of a person or council, elected or limited by themselves, that they should soon have confidence in their own safety, and in the wisdom of the administration; yet, as to the fixed state which should ordinarily obtain in all communities, since no assumer of government can so demonstrate his superior wisdom or goodness to the satisfaction and security of the governed, as is necessary to their happiness; this must follow, that except when men, for their own interest, or out of public love, have by consent subjected their actions, or their goods, within certain limits to the disposal of others; no mortal can have a right from his superior wisdom, or goodness, or any other quality, to give laws to others without their consent, express or tacit; or to dispose of the fruits of their labors, or of any other right whatsoever. And therefore superior wisdom, or goodness, gives no right to men to govern others.

SUGGESTIONS FOR FURTHER READING

There is no critical edition of the works of Francis Hutcheson. However, there is a collection of facsimile reprints of his works, in seven volumes, prepared by Bernhard Fabian (Hildesheim: G. Olms,

1969–1971). Newer editions of specific works have begun to appear. Notable among these is Aaron Garrett's critical edition of Hutcheson's *An Essay on the Nature and Conduct of the Passions and Affections, with Illustrations on the Moral Sense* (Indianapolis: Liberty Fund, 2002).

On Hutcheson's life, the most comprehensive study remains W. R. Scott, *Francis Hutcheson: His Life, Teachings and Position in the History of Philosophy* (Cambridge: Cambridge University Press, 1900). Useful discussions of Hutcheson's place in the Scottish Enlightenment are to be found in D. D. Raphael, *The Moral Sense* (London: Oxford University Press, 1947); M. A. Stewart, ed., *Studies in the Philosophy of the Scottish Enlightenment* (Oxford: Clarendon Press, 1990); and Stephen Darwall, *The British Moralists and the Internal "Ought": 1640–1740* (Cambridge: Cambridge University Press, 1995). Darwall's book in particular is an indispensable study of the development of British moral philosophy in the period covered. On Hutcheson's theory of the sense of beauty, see Peter Kivy, *The Seventh Sense: Francis Hutcheson and Eighteenth-century British Aesthetics,* 2nd ed. (Oxford: Clarendon Press, 2003).

For discussions more specific to Hutcheson's ethics, see Joel Kupperman, "Francis Hutcheson, Morality and Nature," *History of Philosophy Quarterly* 2 (1985): 195–202; John D. Bishop, "Moral Motivation and the Development of Francis Hutcheson's Moral Philosophy," *Journal of the History of Ideas* 57 (1996): 277–295; and Mark Strasser, *Francis Hutcheson's Moral Theory: Its Form and Utility* (Wakefield, NH: Longwood Academic, 1990). On the relation of Hutcheson to Hume, see James Moore, "Hume and Hutcheson," in *Hume and Hume's Connexions,* M. A. Stewart and John Wright, eds. (University Park: Pennsylvania State University Press, 1995). Joan Tronto discusses Hutcheson as part of her background to contemporary care ethics in *Moral Boundaries: A Political Argument for an Ethic of Care* (New York: Routledge, 1993).

David Hume

David Hume was born in Edinburgh in 1711 and grew up on the family estate of Ninewells in nearby Berwick. As the younger son of a well-connected, but not wealthy, family, Hume was obliged to take up a profession to help support himself. He accompanied his older brother to Edinburgh University in 1722 to prepare himself for a career in law, following the example of his father and maternal grandfather. Hume, however, found literature, history, and philosophy more interesting than law, and opted instead to devote himself to literary pursuits. He was eventually persuaded to try a job with a shipping firm in Bristol, but gave it up within a year. Because the cost of living was lower in France, he moved to La Fleche and began writing what was to become his *Treatise of Human Nature,* published in 1739.

If Hume had hoped to make his literary or financial fortune from his book, he was badly disappointed. The first edition attracted no attention. His *Essays Moral and Political* (1741) initially fared little better. He sought professorships of philosophy at Edinburgh in 1744 and Glasgow in 1751, but failed to obtain either, in part because his accounts of human nature and morals were too skeptical of traditional religious and moral views to be acceptable. Family connections helped him to win appointments on military and diplomatic missions with General St. Clair (1746–1748). His experience and abilities led to further appointments as secretary at the British Embassy in Paris (1763–1766) and as undersecretary of state in London in 1767. He was also appointed librarian of the Advocates Library, Edinburgh (1752–1757), which though unpaid gave him the use of their extensive collection.

Hume did not neglect his philosophical pursuits during this period. Blaming the failure of his *Treatise* on poor exposition, he rewrote and republished the first section as *An Enquiry Concerning Human Understanding* (1748) and the third as *An Enquiry Concerning the Principles of Morals* (1751). He also produced his six-volume *History of England from the Invasion of Julius Caesar to the Revolution in 1688* (1754–1762), which was a commercial success. Financially comfortable at last, he retired from public life to Edinburgh, where he remained until his death in 1776.

Like Hutcheson, Hume held that virtues are character traits admired from the standpoint of a disinterested observer. But he differs from Hutcheson in important ways. First, unlike Hutcheson, Hume argues that benevolence is not the only disposition that disinterested human beings approve in one another. Because human beings are naturally sympathetic, we cannot help but approve benevolent concern for others. We also approve dispositions that tend toward a person's *own* good, such as discretion, prudence, and temperance. What is more, we approve character traits that are simply "immediately agreeable" (intrinsically valuable) either to the people who possess them (such as cheerfulness, tranquility, and self-esteem) or to the members of the person's social circle (wit, modesty, and social graciousness). Thus there are four distinct categories of virtues, Hume argues, not one.

Second, unlike Hutcheson, Hume argues that not all the dispositions we call virtues are *directly* approved from a disinterested standpoint. In some cases, approval arises *indirectly* as a result of education and habituation; for example, justice, fidelity, and chastity. Hume argues that we lack natural dispositions either to be, or to admire, just, faithful, or chaste persons. However, if our social environment is such that habitual respect for property, promises, and sexual mores is generally beneficial, then sympathy and self-interest will motivate us to develop such habits and to value them as virtues.

Hume's conception of virtue is thus more pluralistic than Hutcheson's, Aristotle's, or Seneca's, since any character trait may be viewed as a virtue provided that disinterested spectators can agree that the trait is useful or immediately agreeable either to its possessors or those with whom they interact. Critics have contended that Hume's conception is too pluralistic because it treats mere "social graces" and personal talents as moral virtues. In the last section of the reading, Hume will argue that if usage is anything to go by, his account is defensible, because it is consistent with the ways in which we express approval and disapproval of one another's character.

An Enquiry Concerning
the Principles of Morals[1]

SECTION I.—OF THE GENERAL PRINCIPLES OF MORALS

We shall endeavour to follow a very simple method: We shall anal-
yse that complication of mental qualities, which form what, in
common life, we call PERSONAL MERIT: We shall consider every
attribute of the mind, which renders a man an object either of
esteem and affection, or of hatred and contempt; every habit or
sentiment or faculty, which, if ascribed to any person, implies
either praise or blame, and may enter into any panegyric or satire
of his character and manners. The quick sensibility, which, on this
head, is so universal among mankind, gives a philosopher sufficient
assurance, that he can never be considerably mistaken in framing
the catalogue, or incur any danger of misplacing the objects of his
contemplation: He needs only enter into his own breast for a
moment, and consider whether or not he should desire to have this
or that quality ascribed to him, and whether such or such an impu-
tation would proceed from a friend or an enemy. The very nature
of language guides us almost infallibly in forming a judgment of
this nature; and as every tongue possesses one set of words which
are taken in a good sense, and another in the opposite, the least
acquaintance with the idiom suffices, without any reasoning, to
direct us in collecting and arranging the estimable or blameable
qualities of men. The only object of reasoning is to discover the circumstances on both sides, which are common to these qualities; to
observe that particular in which the estimable qualities agree on
the one hand, and the blameable on the other; and thence to reach
the foundation of ethics, and find those universal principles, from
which all censure or approbation is ultimately derived. As this is a
question of fact, not of abstract science, we can only expect suc-

---

1. [The selection is taken from David Hume, *An Enquiry Concerning the
Principles of Morals*, J. B. Schneewind, ed. (Indianapolis: Hackett Publishing Company, 1983). Editor's notes appear in brackets.]

cess, by following the experimental method, and deducing general maxims from a comparison of particular instances.

We shall begin our enquiry on this head by the consideration of social virtues, benevolence, and justice. The explication of them will probably give us an opening by which others may be accounted for.

Section II.—Of Benevolence.

Part I.

It may be esteemed, perhaps, a superfluous task to prove, that the benevolent or softer affections are ESTIMABLE; and wherever they appear, engage the approbation and good-will of mankind. The epithets *sociable, good-natured, humane, merciful, grateful, friendly, generous, beneficent,* or their equivalents, are known in all languages, and universally express the highest merit, which *human nature* is capable of attaining. Where these amiable qualities are attended with birth and power and eminent abilities, and display themselves in the good government or useful instruction of mankind, they seem even to raise the possessors of them above the rank of *human nature,* and make them approach in some measure to the divine. Exalted capacity, undaunted courage, prosperous success; these may only expose a hero or politician to the envy or ill-will of the public: But as soon as the praises are added of humane and beneficent; when instances are displayed of lenity, tenderness, or friendship: envy itself is silent, or joins the general voice of approbation and applause.

But I forget, that it is not my present business to recommend generosity and benevolence, or to paint, in their true colours, all the genuine charms of the social virtues. These, indeed, sufficiently engage every heart, on the first apprehension of them; and it is difficult to abstain from some sally of panegyric, as often as they occur in discourse or reasoning. But our object here being more the speculative, than the practical part of morals, it will suffice to remark, (what will readily, I believe, be allowed) that no qualities are more intitled to the general good-will and approbation of mankind than benevolence and humanity, friendship and gratitude, natural affection and public spirit, or whatever proceeds from a tender sympathy with others, and a generous concern for our kind and species. These, wherever they appear, seem to transfuse themselves, in a manner, into each beholder, and to call forth, in their own behalf, the same favourable and affectionate sentiments, which they exert on all around.

Part II.

WE may observe, that, in displaying the praises of any humane, beneficent man, there is one circumstance which never fails to be amply insisted on, namely, the happiness and satisfaction, derived to society from his intercourse and good offices. To his parents, we are apt to say, he endears himself by his pious attachment and duteous care, still more than by the connexions of nature. His children never feel his authority, but when employed for their advantage. With him, the ties of love are consolidated by benefi- cence and friendship. The ties of friendship approach, in a fond observance of each obliging office, to those of love and inclina- tion. His domestics and dependants have in him a sure resource; and no longer dread the power of fortune, but so far as she exer- cises it over him. From him the hungry receive food, the naked cloathing, the ignorant and slothful skill and industry. Like the sun, an inferior minister of providence, he cheers, invigorates, and *sustains* the surrounding world.

If confined to private life, the sphere of his activity is narrower; but his influence is all benign and gentle. If exalted into a higher station, mankind and posterity reap the fruit of his labours.

As these topics of praise never fail to be employed, and with success, where we would inspire esteem for any one; may it not thence be concluded, that the UTILITY, resulting from the social virtues, forms, at least, a *part* of their merit, and is one source of that approbation and regard so universally paid to them?

Upon the whole, then, it seems undeniable, *that* nothing can bestow more merit on any human creature than the sentiment of benevolence in an eminent degree; and *that* a *part*, at least, of its merit arises from its tendency to promote the interests of our spe- cies, and bestow happiness on human society. We carry our view into the salutary consequences of such a character and disposition; and whatever has so benign an influence, and forwards so desirable an end, is beheld with complacency and pleasure. The social vir- tues are never regarded without their beneficial tendencies, nor viewed as barren and unfruitful. The happiness of mankind, the order of society, the harmony of families, the mutual support of friends, are always considered as the result of their gentle dominion over the breasts of men.

How considerable a *part* of their merit we ought to ascribe to their utility, will better appear from future disquisitions;[2] as well as the reason, why this circumstance has such a command over our esteem and approbation.[3]

SECTION III.—OF JUSTICE.

Part I.

THAT Justice is useful to society, and consequently that *part* of its merit, at least, must arise from that consideration, it would be a superfluous undertaking to prove. That public utility is the *sole* origin of justice, and that reflections on the beneficial consequences of this virtue are the *sole* foundation of its merit; this proposition, being more curious and important, will better deserve our examination and enquiry.

Let us suppose, that nature has bestowed on the human race such profuse *abundance* of all *external* conveniencies, that, without any uncertainty in the event, without any care or industry on our part, every individual finds himself fully provided with whatever his most voracious appetites can want, or luxurious imagination wish or desire. His natural beauty, we shall suppose, surpasses all acquired ornaments: The perpetual clemency of the seasons renders useless all cloaths or covering: The raw herbage affords him the most delicious fare; the clear fountain, the richest beverage. No laborious occupation required: No tillage: No navigation. Music, poetry, and contemplation form his sole business: Conversation, mirth, and friendship his sole amusement.

It seems evident, that, in such a happy state, every other social virtue would flourish, and receive tenfold encrease; but the cautious, jealous virtue of justice would never once have been dreamed of. For what purpose make a partition of goods, where every one has already more than enough? Why give rise to property, where

---

2. Sect. 3rd and 4th. Of Justice: and Of Political Society.
3. Sect. 5th. Why Utility Pleases.

there cannot possibly be any injury? Why call this object *mine*, when, upon the seizing of it by another, I need but stretch out my hand to possess myself of what is equally valuable? Justice, in that case, being totally USELESS, would be an idle ceremonial, and could never possibly have place in the catalogue of virtues.

Again; suppose, that, though the necessities of human race continue the same as at present, yet the mind is so enlarged, and so replete with friendship and generosity, that every man has the utmost tenderness for every man, and feels no more concern for his own interest than for that of his fellows: It seems evident, that the USE of justice would, in this case, be suspended by such an extensive benevolence, nor would the divisions and barriers of property and obligation have ever been thought of. Why should I bind another, by a deed or promise, to do me any good office, when I know that he is already prompted, by the strongest inclination, to seek my happiness, and would, of himself, perform the desired service; except the hurt, he thereby receives, be greater than the benefit accruing to me? in which case, he knows, that, from my innate humanity and friendship, I should be the first to oppose myself to his imprudent generosity. Why raise landmarks between my neighbour's field and mine, when my heart has made no division between our interests; but shares all his joys and sorrows with the same force and vivacity as if originally my own? Every man, upon this supposition, being a second self to another, would trust all his interests to the discretion of every man; without jealousy, without partition, without distinction. And the whole human race would form only one family; where all would lie in common, and be used freely, without regard to property; but cautiously too, with as entire regard to the necessities of each individual, as if our own interests were most intimately concerned.

[Let] us reverse the foregoing suppositions; and carrying every thing to the opposite extreme, consider what would be the effect of these new situations. Suppose a society to fall into such want of all common necessaries, that the utmost frugality and industry cannot preserve the greater number from perishing, and the whole from extreme misery: It will readily, I believe, be admitted, that the strict laws of justice are suspended, in such a pressing emergence, and give place to the stronger motives of necessity and self-preservation. Is it any crime, after a shipwreck, to seize whatever means or instrument of safety one can lay hold of, without regard to former limitations of property? Or if a city besieged were perishing with hunger; can we imagine, that men will see any means of preservation before them, and lose their lives, from a scrupulous regard to what, in other situations, would be the rules of equity and justice? The USE and TENDENCY of that virtue is to procure happiness and security, by preserving order in society: But where the society is ready to perish from extreme necessity, no greater evil can be dreaded from violence and injustice; and every man may now provide for himself by all the means, which prudence can dictate, or humanity permit. The public, even in less urgent necessities, opens granaries, without the consent of proprietors; as justly supposing, that the authority of magistracy may, consistent with equity, extend so far: But were any number of men to assemble, without the tye of laws or civil jurisdiction; would an equal partition of bread in a famine, though effected by power and even violence, be regarded as criminal or injurious?

Were the human species so framed by nature as that each individual possessed within himself every faculty, requisite both for his own preservation and for the propagation of his kind: Were all society and intercourse cut off between man and man, by the primary intention of the supreme Creator: It seems evident, that so solitary a being would be as much incapable of justice, as of social discourse and conversation. Where mutual regards and forbearance serve to no manner of purpose, they would never direct the conduct of any reasonable man. The headlong course of the passions would be checked by no reflection on future consequences. And as each man is here supposed to love himself alone, and to depend only on himself and his own activity for safety and happiness, he would, on every occasion to the utmost of his power, challenge the preference above every other being, to none of which he is bound by any ties, either of nature or of interest.

But suppose the conjunction of the sexes to be established in nature, a family immediately arises; and particular rules being found requisite for its subsistence, these are immediately embraced; though without comprehending the rest of mankind within their prescriptions. Suppose, that several families unite together into one society, which is totally disjoined from all others, the rules, which preserve peace and order, enlarge themselves to the utmost extent of that society; but becoming then entirely useless, lose their force when carried one step farther. But again suppose, that several distinct societies maintain a kind of intercourse for mutual convenience and advantage, the boundaries of justice still grow larger, in proportion to the largeness of men's views, and the force of their mutual connexions. History, experience, reason sufficiently instruct us in this natural progress of human sentiments, and in the gradual enlargement of our regards to justice, in proportion as we become acquainted with the extensive utility of that virtue.

Thus we seem, upon the whole, to have attained a knowledge of the force of that principle here insisted on, and can determine what degree of esteem or moral approbation may result from reflections on public interest and utility. The necessity of justice to the support of society is the SOLE foundation of that virtue; and since no moral excellence is more highly esteemed, we may conclude, that this SOLE circumstance of usefulness has, in general, the strongest energy, and most entire command over our sentiments. It must, therefore, be the source of a considerable part of the merit ascribed to humanity, benevolence, friendship, public spirit, and other social virtues of that stamp; as it is the source of the moral approbation paid to fidelity, justice, veracity, integrity, and those other estimable and useful qualities and principles. It is entirely agreeable to the rules of philosophy, and even of common reason; where any principle has been found to have a great force and energy in one instance, to ascribe to it a like energy in all similar instances. This indeed is NEWTON's chief rule of philosophizing.[4]

SECTION V.—WHY UTILITY PLEASES.

Part I.

IT seems so natural a thought to ascribe to their utility the praise, which we bestow on the social virtues, that one would expect to meet with this principle every where in moral writers, as the chief foundation of their reasoning and enquiry. In common life, we may observe, that the circumstance of utility is always appealed to; nor is it supposed, that a greater eulogy can be given to any man, than to display his usefulness to the public, and enumerate the services, which he has performed to mankind and society. What praise, even of an inanimate form, if the regularity and elegance of its parts

---

4. Principia, lib. iii.

destroy not its fitness for any useful purpose! And how satisfactory an apology for any disproportion or seeming deformity, if we can show the necessity of that particular construction for the use intended! What wonder then, that a man, whose habits and conduct are hurtful to society, and dangerous or pernicious to every one who has an intercourse with him, should, on that account, be an object of disapprobation, and communicate to every spectator the strongest sentiment of disgust and hatred.[5]

From the apparent usefulness of the social virtues, it has readily been inferred by sceptics,[6] both ancient and modern, that all moral distinctions arise from education, and were, at first, invented, and afterward encouraged, by the art of politicians, in order to render men tractable, and subdue their natural ferocity and selfishness, which incapacitated them for society. This principle, indeed, of precept and education, must so far be owned to have a powerful influence, that it may frequently encrease or diminish, beyond their natural standard, the sentiments of approbation or dislike; and may even, in particular instances, create, without any natural principle, a new sentiment of this kind; as is evident in all superstitious practices and observances: But that *all* moral affection or dislike arises from this origin, will never surely be allowed by any judicious enquirer. Had nature made no such distinction, founded on

---

5. We ought not to imagine, because an inanimate object may be useful as well as a man, that therefore it ought also, according to this system, to merit the appellation of *virtuous*. The sentiments, excited by utility, are, in the two cases, very different; and the one is mixed with affection, esteem, approbation, &c. and not the other. In like manner, an inanimate object may have good colour and proportions as well as a human figure. But can we ever be in love with the former? There are a numerous set of passions and sentiments, of which thinking rational beings are, by the original constitution of nature, the only proper objects: And though the very same qualities be transferred to an insensible, inanimate being, they will not excite the same sentiments. The beneficial qualities of herbs and minerals are, indeed, sometimes called their *virtues*; but this is an effect of the caprice of language, which ought not to be regarded in reasoning. . . .

6. [The modern "skeptics" Hume has in mind would certainly include the English philosophers Thomas Hobbes (1588–1679) and Bernard Mandeville (1670–1733), who were both notorious for arguing that humans are predominantly egoistic creatures who accept political and moral restraints only to the extent beneficial to their own long-term self-interest.]

the original constitution of the mind, the words, *honourable* and *shameful, lovely* and *odious, noble* and *despicable,* had never had place in any language; nor could politicians, had they invented these terms, ever have been able to render them intelligible, or make them convey any idea to the audience. So that nothing can be more superficial than this paradox of the sceptics; and it were well, if, in the abstruser studies of logic and metaphysics, we could as easily obviate the cavils of that sect, as in the practical and more intelligible sciences of politics and morals.

The social virtues must, therefore, be allowed to have a natural beauty and amiableness, which, at first, antecedent to all precept or education, recommends them to the esteem of uninstructed mankind, and engages their affections. And as the public utility of these virtues is the chief circumstance, whence they derive their merit, it follows, that the end, which they have a tendency to promote, must be some way agreeable to us, and take hold of some natural affection. It must please, either from considerations of self-interest, or from more generous motives and regards.

It has often been asserted, that, as every man has a strong connexion with society, and perceives the impossibility of his solitary subsistence, he becomes, on that account, favourable to all those habits or principles, which promote order in society, and insure to him the quiet possession of so inestimable a blessing. As much as we value our own happiness and welfare, as much must we applaud the practice of justice and humanity, by which alone the social confederacy can be maintained, and every man reap the fruits of mutual protection and assistance.

We frequently bestow praise on virtuous actions, performed in very distant ages and remote countries; where the utmost subtilty of imagination would not discover any appearance of self-interest, or find any connexion of our present happiness and security with events so widely separated from us.

It is but a weak subterfuge, when pressed by these facts and arguments, to say, that we transport ourselves, by the force of imagination, into distant ages and countries, and consider the advantage, which we should have reaped from these characters, had we been contemporaries, and had any commerce with the persons. It is not conceivable, how a *real* sentiment or passion can ever arise from a known *imaginary* interest; especially when our *real* interest is still kept in view, and is often acknowledged to be entirely distinct from the imaginary, and even sometimes opposite to it.

Usefulness is agreeable, and engages our approbation. This is a matter of fact, confirmed by daily observation. But, *useful?* For what? For some body's interest, surely. Whose interest then? Not our own only: For our approbation frequently extends farther. It must, therefore, be the interest of those, who are served by the character or action approved of; and these we may conclude, however remote, are not totally indifferent to us. By opening up this principle, we shall discover one great source of moral distinctions.

Part II.

SELF-LOVE is a principle in human nature of such extensive energy, and the interest of each individual is, in general, so closely connected with that of the community, that those philosophers were excusable, who fancied, that all our concern for the public might be resolved into a concern for our own happiness and preservation. They saw every moment, instances of approbation or blame, satisfaction or displeasure toward characters and actions; they denominated the objects of these sentiments, *virtues,* or *vices;* they observed, that the former had a tendency to encrease the happiness, and the latter the misery of man-kind; they asked, whether it were possible that we could have any general concern for society, or any disinterested resentment of the welfare or injury of others; they found it simpler to consider all these sentiments as modifications of self-love; and they discovered a pretence, at least, for this unity of principle, in that close union of interest, which is so observable between the public and each individual.

But notwithstanding this frequent confusion of interests, it is easy to attain what natural philosophers, after lord BACON,[7] have affected to call the *experimentum crucis,* or that experiment, which points out the right way in any doubt or ambiguity. We have found instances, in which private interest was separate from public; in which it was even contrary: And yet we observed the moral

---

7. [Francis Bacon (1561–1626): English statesman and philosopher who argued that the natural sciences should rely upon inductive empirical methods of investigation instead of attempting to deduce natural laws from the analysis of concepts.]

sentiment to continue, notwithstanding this disjunction of interests. And wherever these distinct interests sensibly concurred, we always found a sensible encrease of the sentiment, and a more warm affection to virtue, and detestation of vice, or what we properly call *gratitude* and *revenge*. Compelled by these instances, we must renounce the theory, which accounts for every moral sentiment by the principle of self-love. We must adopt a more public affection, and allow, that the interests of society are not, even on their own account, entirely indifferent to us. Usefulness is only a tendency to a certain end; and it is a contradiction in terms, that any thing pleases as means to an end, where the end itself no wise affects us. If usefulness, therefore, be a source of moral sentiment, and if this usefulness be not always considered with a reference to self; it follows, that every thing, which contributes to the happiness of society, recommends itself directly to our approbation and goodwill. Here is a principle, which accounts, in great part, for the origin of morality: And what need we seek for abstruse and remote systems, when there occurs one so obvious and natural?[8]

A statesman or patriot, who serves our own country, in our own time, has always a more passionate regard paid to him, than one whose beneficial influence operated on distant ages or remote nations; where the good, resulting from his generous humanity, being less connected with us, seems more obscure, and affects us with a less lively sympathy. We may own the merit to be equally great, though our sentiments are not raised to an equal height, in both cases. The judgment here corrects the inequalities of our inter-

---

8. It is needless to push our researches so far as to ask, why we have humanity or a fellow-feeling with others. It is sufficient, that this is experienced to be a principle in human nature. We must stop somewhere in our examination of causes; and there are, in every science, some general principles, beyond which we cannot hope to find any principle more general. No man is absolutely indifferent to the happiness and misery of others. The first has a natural tendency to give pleasure; the second, pain. This every one may find in himself. It is not probable, that these principles can be resolved into principles more simple and universal, whatever attempts may have been made to that purpose. But if it were possible, it belongs not to the present subject; and we may here safely consider these principles as original: Happy, if we can render all the consequences sufficiently plain and perspicuous!

nal emotions and perceptions; in like manner, as it preserves us from error, in the several variations of images, presented to our external senses. The same object, at a double distance, really throws on the eye a picture of but half the bulk; yet we imagine that it appears of the same size in both situations; because we know, that, on our approach to it, its image would expand on the eye, and that the difference consists not in the object itself, but in our position with regard to it. And, indeed, without such a correction of appearances, both in internal and external sentiment, men could never think or talk steadily on any subject; while their fluctuating situations produce a continual variation on objects, and throw them into such different and contrary lights and positions.[9]

The more we converse with mankind, and the greater social intercourse we maintain, the more shall we be familiarized to these general preferences and distinctions, without which our conversation and discourse could scarcely be rendered intelligible to each other. Every man's interest is peculiar to himself, and the aversions and desires, which result from it, cannot be supposed to affect others in a like degree. General language, therefore, being formed for general use, must be moulded on some more general views, and must affix the epithets of praise or blame, in conformity to sentiments, which arise from the general interests of the community. And if these sentiments, in most men, be not so strong as those, which have a reference to private good; yet still they must make some distinction, even

---

9. For a like reason, the tendencies of actions and characters, not their real accidental consequences, are alone regarded in our determinations or general judgments; though in our real feeling or sentiment, we cannot help paying greater regard to one whose station, joined to virtue, renders him really useful to society, than to one, who exerts the social virtues only in good intentions and benevolent affections. Separating the character from the fortune, by an easy and necessary effort of thought, we pronounce these persons alike, and give them the same general praise. The judgment corrects or endeavours to correct the appearance: But is not able entirely to prevail over sentiment.

Why is this peach-tree said to be better than that other; but because it produces more or better fruit? And would not the same praise be given it, though snails or vermin had destroyed the peaches, before they came to full maturity? In morals too, is not *the tree known by the fruit?* And cannot we easily distinguish between nature and accident, in the one case as well as in the other?

in persons the most depraved and selfish; and must attach the notion of good to a beneficent conduct, and of evil to the contrary. Sympathy, we shall allow, is much fainter than our concern for ourselves, and sympathy with persons remote from us, much fainter than that with persons near and contiguous; but for this very reason, it is necessary for us, in our calm judgments and discourse concerning the characters of men, to neglect all these differences, and render our sentiments more public and social. Besides, that we ourselves often change our situation in this particular, we every day meet with persons, who are in a situation different from us, and who could never converse with us, were we to remain constantly in that position and point of view, which is peculiar to ourselves. The intercourse of sentiments, therefore, in society and conversation, makes us form some general unalterable standard, by which we may approve or disapprove of characters and manners. And though the heart takes not part with those general notions, nor regulates all its love and hatred, by the universal, abstract differences of vice and virtue, without regard to self, or the persons with whom we are more intimately connected; yet have these moral differences a considerable influence, and being sufficient, at least, for discourse, serve all our purposes in company, in the pulpit, on the theatre, and in the schools.[10]

Thus, in whatever light we take this subject, the merit, ascribed to the social virtues, appears still uniform, and arises chiefly from that regard, which the natural sentiment of benevolence engages us to pay to the interests of mankind and society. If we consider the principles of the human make, such as they appear to daily experience and observation, we must, *à priori*,[11] conclude it impossible for such a

---

10. It is wisely ordained by nature, that private connexions should commonly prevail over universal views and considerations; otherwise our affections and actions would be dissipated and lost, for want of a proper limited object. Thus a small benefit done to ourselves, or our near friends, excites more lively sentiments of love and approbation than a great benefit done to a distant commonwealth: But still we know here, as in all the senses, to correct these inequalities by reflection, and retain a general standard of vice and virtue, founded chiefly on general usefulness.

11. [That is, reasoning "prior to" or "independent of" empirical investigation, working strictly from the concepts involved. Hume is pointing out that if we accept the ordinary classification of humanity as a social species, we must deduce that humans are not wholly egoistic.]

creature as man to be totally indifferent to the well- or ill-being of his fellow-creatures, and not readily, of himself, to pronounce, where nothing gives him any particular byass, that what promotes their happiness is good, what tends to their misery is evil, without any farther regard or consideration. Here then are the faint rudiments, at least, or outlines, of a *general* distinction between actions; and in proportion as the humanity of the person is supposed to encrease, his connexion with those who are injured or benefited, and his lively conception of their misery or happiness; his consequent censure or approbation acquires proportionable vigour. There is no necessity, that a generous action, barely mentioned in an old history or remote gazette, should communicate any strong feelings of applause and admiration. Virtue, placed at such a distance, is liked a fixed star, which, though to the eye of reason, it may appear as luminous as the sun in his meridian, is so infinitely removed, as to affect the senses, neither with light nor heat. Bring this virtue nearer, by our acquaintance or connexion with the persons, or even by an eloquent recital of the case; our hearts are immediately caught, our sympathy enlivened, and our cool approbation converted into the warmest sentiments of friendship and regard. These seem necessary and infallible consequences of the general principles of human nature, as discovered in common life and practice.

Again; reverse these views and reasonings: Consider the matter *à posteriori*;[12] and weighing the consequences, enquire if the merit of social virtue be not, in a great measure, derived from the feelings of humanity, with which it affects the spectators. It appears to be matter of fact, that the circumstance of *utility*, in all subjects, is a source of praise and approbation: That it is constantly appealed to in all moral decisions concerning the merit and demerit of actions: That it is the *sole* source of that high regard paid to justice, fidelity, honour, allegiance, and chastity: That it is inseparable from all the other social virtues, humanity, generosity, charity, affability, lenity, mercy, and moderation: And, in a word, that it is a foundation of the chief part of morals, which has a reference to mankind and our fellow-creatures.

---

12. [That is, reasoning only "after" empirical investigation (in contrast to *à priori* reasoning.) Hume is suggesting here that investigation of the psychological mechanisms involved in human behavior supports his claim that we are motivated by sympathy or humanity to act for others' welfare.]

It appears also, that in our general approbation of characters and manners, the useful tendency of the social virtues moves us not by any regards to self-interest, but has an influence much more universal and extensive. It appears, that a tendency to public good, and to the promoting of peace, harmony, and order in society, does always, by affecting the benevolent principles of our frame, engage us on the side of the social virtues. And it appears, as an additional confirmation, that these principles of humanity and sympathy enter so deeply into all our sentiments, and have so powerful an influence, as may enable them to excite the strongest censure and applause. The present theory is the simple result of all these inferences, each of which seems founded on uniform experience and observation.

Were it doubtful, whether there were any such principle in our nature as humanity or a concern for others, yet when we see, in numberless instances, that whatever has a tendency to promote the interests of society, is so highly approved of, we ought thence to learn the force of the benevolent principle; since it is impossible for any thing to please as means to an end, where the end is totally indifferent. On the other hand, were it doubtful, whether there were, implanted in our nature, any general principle of moral blame and approbation, yet when we see, in numberless instances, the influence of humanity, we ought thence to conclude, that it is impossible, but that every thing, which promotes the interest of society, must communicate pleasure, and what is pernicious give uneasiness. But when these different reflections and observations concur in establishing the same conclusion, must they not bestow an undisputed evidence upon it?

Section IX—Conclusion.

Part I.

It may justly appear surprising, that any man, in so late an age, should find it requisite to prove, by elaborate reasoning, that PERSONAL MERIT consists altogether in the possession of mental qualities, *useful* or *agreeable* to the *person himself* or to *others*. It might be expected, that this principle would have occurred even to the first rude, unpractised enquirers concerning morals, and been received from its own evidence, without any argument or disputation. Whatever is valuable in any kind, so naturally classes itself under the division of *useful* or *agreeable*, the *utile* or the *dulce*, that it is not easy to imagine, why we should ever seek farther, or consider the question as a matter of nice research or enquiry. And as every thing useful or agreeable must possess these qualities with regard either to the *person himself* or to *others*, the compleat delineation or description of merit seems to be performed as naturally as a shadow is cast by the sun, or an image is reflected upon water.

But however the case may have fared with philosophy; in common life, these principles are still implicitly maintained, nor is any other topic of praise or blame ever recurred to, when we employ any panegyric or satire, any applause or censure of human action and behaviour. If we observe men, in every intercourse of business or pleasure, in every discourse and conversation; we shall find them no where, except in the schools, at any loss upon this subject. What so natural, for instance, as the following dialogue? You are very happy, we shall suppose one to say, addressing himself to another, that you have given your daughter to CLEANTHES. He is a man of honour and humanity. Every one, who has any intercourse with him, is sure of *fair* and *kind* treatment.[13] I congratulate you too, says another on the promising expectations of this son-in-law; whose assiduous application to the study of the laws, whose quick penetration and early knowledge both of men and business, prognosticate the greatest honours and advancement.[14] You surprise me, replies a third, when you talk of CLEANTHES as a man of business and application. I met him lately in a circle of the gayest company, and he was the very life and soul of our conversation: So much wit with good manners; so much gallantry without affectation; so much ingenious knowledge so genteelly delivered, I have never before observed in any one.[15] You would admire him still more, says a fourth, if you knew him more familiarly. That cheerfulness, which

---

13. Qualities useful to others.

14. Qualities useful to the person himself. Section VI. [For Hume's discussion of particular examples of such virtues, including discretion, industry, and strength of mind, see Section 6 of the full text.]

15. Qualities immediately agreeable to others. Section VIII. [For Hume's discussion of particular examples of such virtues, including politeness, wit, modesty, decency, and cleanliness, see Section 8 of the full text.]

you might remark in him, is not a sudden flash struck out by company: It runs through the whole tenor of his life, and preserves a perpetual serenity on his countenance, and tranquility in his soul. He has met with severe trials, misfortunes as well as dangers; and by his greatness of mind, was still superior to all of them.[16] The image, gentlemen, which you have here delineated of CLEANTHES cry'd I, is that of accomplished merit. Each of you has given a stroke of the pencil to his figure; and you have unawares exceeded all the pictures drawn by GRATIAN or CASTIGLIONE.[17] A philosopher might select his character as a model of perfect virtue.

And as every quality, which is useful or agreeable to ourselves or others, is, in common life, allowed to be a part of personal merit; so no other will ever be received, where men judge of things by their natural, unprejudiced reason, without the delusive glosses of superstition and false religion. Celibacy, fasting, penance, mortification, self-denial, humility, silence, solitude, and the whole train of monkish virtues; for what reason they are every where rejected by men of sense, but because they serve to no manner of purpose; neither advance a man's fortune in the world, nor render him a more valuable member of society; neither qualify him for the entertainment of company, nor increase his power of self-enjoyment? We observe, on the contrary, that they cross all these desirable ends; stupefy the understanding and harden the heart, obscure the fancy and sour the temper. We justly, therefore, transfer them to the opposite column, and place them in the catalogue of vices.

Avarice, ambition, vanity, and all the passions vulgarly, though improperly, comprised under the denomination of *self-love*, are here excluded from our theory concerning the origin of morals, not because they are too weak, but because they have not a proper

---

16. Qualities immediately agreeable to the person himself. Section VII. [For Hume's discussion of particular examples of such virtues, including cheerfulness, greatness of mind or dignity, courage, tranquility, benevolence, and delicacy of taste, see Section 7 of the full text.]

17. ["Gratian" probably refers to Baltasar Gracián y Morales (1601–1658), Spanish author of texts on character and manners, whose *El Discreto* (*The Compleat Gentleman*) was widely read in England. The Italian diplomat and writer Baldassare Castiglione (1478–1529) was the author of probably the most widely read European book on courtly manners up to Hume's day, *Il Cortegiano* (*The Courtier*).]

direction, for that purpose. The notion of moral implies some sentiment common to all mankind, which recommends the same object to general approbation, and make every man, or most men, agree in the same opinion or decision concerning it. It also implies some sentiment, so universal and comprehensive as to extend to all mankind, and render the actions and conduct, even of the persons the most remote, an object of applause or censure, according as they agree or disagree with that rule of right which is established.

When a man denominates another his *enemy*, his *rival*, his *antagonist*, his *adversary*, he is understood to speak the language of self-love, and to express sentiments, peculiar to himself, and arising from his particular circumstances and situation, But when he bestows on any man the epithets of *vicious* or *odious* or *depraved*, he then speaks another language, and expresses sentiments, in which, he expects, all his audience are to concur with him. He must therefore depart from his private and particular situation, and must chuse a point of view, common to him with others: He must move some universal principles of the human frame, and touch a string, to which all mankind have an accord and symphony. If he mean, therefore, to express, that this man possesses qualities, whose tendency is pernicious to society, he has chosen this common point of view, and has touched the principle of humanity, in which every man, in some degree, concurs. And though this affection of humanity may not generally be esteemed so strong as vanity or ambition, yet, being common to all men, it can alone be the foundation of morals, or of any general system of blame or praise. One man's ambition is not another's ambition; nor will the same events or object satisfy both; But the humanity of one man is the humanity of every one; and the same object touches this passion in all creatures.

What more, therefore, can we ask to distinguish the sentiments, dependent on humanity, from those connected with any other passion, or to satisfy us, why the former are the origin of morals, not the latter? Whatever conduct gains my approbation, by touching my humanity, procures also the applause of all mankind, by affecting the same principle in them: But what serves my avarice or ambition pleases these passions in me alone, and affects not the avarice and ambition of the rest of mankind. There is no circumstance of conduct in any man, provided it have a beneficial tendency, that is not agreeable to my humanity, however remote the person: But every man, so far removed as neither to cross nor serve my avarice and ambition, is regarded as wholly indifferent by those passions. The distinction, therefore, between these species of sentiment being so great and evident, language must soon be moulded upon it, and must invent a peculiar set of terms, in order to express those universal sentiments of censure or approbation, which arise from humanity, or from views of general usefulness and its contrary. VIRTUE and VICE become then known: Morals are recognized: Certain general ideas are framed of human conduct and behaviour: Such measures are expected from men, in such situations: This action is determined to be conformable to our abstract rule; that other, contrary. And by such universal principles are the particular sentiments of self-love frequently controuled and limited.[18]

Part II.

HAVING expressed the moral *approbation* attending merit or virtue, there remains nothing, but briefly to consider our interested *obligation* to it, and to enquire, whether every man, who has any regard to his own happiness and welfare, will not best find his account in the practice of every moral duty.

That the virtues which are immediately *useful* or *agreeable* to the person possessed of them, are desirable in a view to self-interest, it would surely be superfluous to prove. Moralists, indeed, may spare themselves all the pains, which they often take in recommending these duties. To what purpose collect arguments to evince, that temperance is advantageous, and the excesses of pleasure hurtful?

---

18. It seems certain, both from reason and experience, that a rude, untaught savage regulates chiefly his love and hatred by the ideas of private utility and injury, and has but faint conceptions of a general rule or system of behaviour. The man who stands opposite to him in battle, he hates heartily, not only for the present moment, which is almost unavoidable, but for ever after; nor is he satisfied without the most extreme punishment and vengeance. But we, accustomed to society, and to more enlarged reflections, consider, that this man is serving his own country and community; that any man, in the same situation, would do the same; that we ourselves, in like circumstances, observe a like conduct; that, in general, human society is best supported on such maxims: And by these suppositions and views, we correct, in some measure, our ruder and narrower passions.

When it appears, that these excesses are only denominated such, because they are hurtful; and that, if unlimited use of strong liquors, for instance, no more impaired health or the faculties of mind and body than the use of air or water, it would not be a whit more vicious or blameable.

It seems equally superfluous to prove, that the *companionable* virtues of good manners and wit, decency and genteelness, are more desirable than the contrary qualities. Vanity alone, without any other consideration, is a sufficient motive to make us wish for the possession of these accomplishments. No man was ever willingly deficient in this particular. All our failures here proceed from bad education, want of capacity, or a perverse and unpliable disposition. Would you have your company coveted, admired, followed; rather than hated, despised, avoided? Can any one seriously deliberate in the case? As no enjoyment is sincere, without some reference to company and society; so no society can be agreeable, or even tolerable, where a man feels his presence unwelcome, and discovers all around him symptoms of disgust and aversion.

Treating vice with the greatest candour, and making it all possible concessions, we must acknowledge, that there is not, in any instance, the smallest pretext for giving it the preference above virtue, with a view to self-interest; except, perhaps, in the case of justice, where a man, taking things in a certain light, may often seem to be a loser by his integrity. And though it is allowed, that, without a regard to property, no society could subsist; yet, according to the imperfect way in which human affairs are conducted, a sensible knave, in particular incidents, may think, that an act of iniquity or infidelity will make a considerable addition to his fortune, without causing any considerable breach in the social union and confederacy. That *honesty is the best policy*, may be a good general rule; but is liable to many exceptions: And he, it may, perhaps, be thought, conducts himself with most wisdom, who observes the general rule, and takes advantage of all the exceptions.

I must confess, that, if a man think, that this reasoning much requires an answer, it will be a little difficult to find any, which will to him appear satisfactory and convincing. If his heart rebel not against such pernicious maxims, if he feel no reluctance to the thoughts of villany or baseness, he has indeed lost a considerable motive to virtue; and we may expect, that his practice will be answerable to his speculation. But in all ingenuous natures, the antipathy to treachery and roguery is too strong to be counterbalanced by any views of profit or pecuniary advantage. Inward peace of mind, consciousness of integrity, a satisfactory review of our own conduct; these are circumstances very requisite to happiness, and will be cherished and cultivated by every honest man, who feels the importance of them.

Such a one has, besides, the frequent satisfaction of seeing knaves, with all their pretended cunning and abilities, betrayed by their own maxims; and while they purpose to cheat with moderation and secrecy, a tempting incident occurs, nature is frail, and they give into the snare; whence they can never extricate themselves, without a total loss of reputation, and the forfeiture of all future trust and confidence with mankind.

But were they ever so secret and successful, the honest man, if he has any tincture of philosophy, or even common observation and reflection, will discover that they themselves are, in the end, the greatest dupes, and have sacrificed the invaluable enjoyment of a character, with themselves at least, for the acquisition of worthless toys and gewgaws.

APPENDIX IV.—OF SOME VERBAL DISPUTES.

NOTHING is more usual than for philosophers to encroach upon the province of grammarians; and to engage in disputes of words, while they imagine, that they are handling controversies of the deepest importance and concern. It was in order to avoid altercations so frivolous and endless, that I endeavoured to state with the utmost caution the object of our present enquiry; and proposed simply to collect on the one hand, a list of those mental qualities which are the object of love or esteem, and form a part of personal merit, and on the other hand, a catalogue of those qualities, which are the object of censure or reproach, and which detract from the character of the person, possessed of them; subjoining some reflections concerning the origin of these sentiments of praise or blame. On all occasions, where there might arise the least hesitation, I avoided the terms *virtue* and *vice*; because some of those qualities, which I classed among the objects of praise, receive, in the ENGLISH language, the appellation of *talents*, rather than of virtues; as some of the blameable or censurable qualities are often called *defects*, rather than vices. It may now, perhaps, be expected, that, before we conclude this moral enquiry, we should exactly separate the one from the other; should mark the precise boundaries of virtues and talents, vices and defects; and should explain the reason and origin of that distinction. But in order to excuse myself from this undertaking, which would, at last, prove only a grammatical enquiry, I shall subjoin the four following reflections, which shall contain all that I intend to say on the present subject.

First, I do not find, that in the ENGLISH, or any other modern tongue, the boundaries are exactly fixed between virtues and talents, vices and defects, or that a precise definition can be given of the one as contradistinguished from the other. Were we to say, for instance, that the esteemable qualities alone, which are voluntary, are entitled to the appellation of virtues; we should soon recollect the qualities of courage, equanimity, patience, self-command; with many others, which almost every language classes under this appellation, though they depend little or not at all on our choice. Should we affirm, that the qualities alone, which prompt us to act our part in society, are entitled to that honourable distinction; it must immediately occur, that these are indeed the most valuable qualities, and are commonly denominated the *social* virtues; but that this very epithet supposes, that there are also virtues of another species. Should we lay hold of the distinction between *intellectual* and *moral* endowments, and affirm the last alone to be the real and genuine virtues, because they alone lead to action; we should find, that many of those qualities, usually called intellectual virtues, such as prudence, penetration, discernment, discretion, had also a considerable influence on conduct. The distinction between the *heart* and the *head* may also be adopted: The qualities of the first may be defined such as in their immediate exertion are accompanied with a feeling or sentiment; and these alone may be called the genuine virtues. But industry, frugality, temperance, secrecy, perseverance, and many other laudable powers or habits, generally stiled virtues, are exerted without any immediate sentiment in the person possessed of them; and are only known to him by their effects. It is fortunate, amidst all this seeming perplexity, that the question, being merely verbal, cannot possibly be of any importance. A moral, philosophical discourse needs not enter into all these caprices of language, which are so variable in different dialects, and in different ages of the same dialect. But on the whole, it seems to me, that, though it is always allowed, that there are virtues of many different kinds, yet, when a man is called *virtuous,* or is denominated a man of virtue, we chiefly regard his social qualities, which are, indeed, the most valuable. It is, at the same time, certain, that any remarkable defect in courage, temperance, economy, industry, understanding, dignity of mind, would bereave even a very good-natured, honest man of this honourable appellation. Who did ever say, except by way of irony, that such a one was a man of great virtue, but an egregious blockhead?

But, *secondly,* it is no wonder that languages should not be very precise in marking the boundaries between virtues and talents, vices and defects; since there is so little distinction made in our internal estimation of them.

It is hard to tell, whether you hurt a man's character most by calling him a knave or a coward, and whether a beastly glutton or drunkard be not as odious and contemptible, as a selfish, ungenerous miser. Give me my choice, and I would rather, for my own happiness and self-enjoyment, have a friendly, humane heart, than possess all the other virtues of DEMONSTHENES and PHILIP united.[19]

What is it then we can here dispute about? If sense and courage, temperance and industry, wisdom and knowledge confessedly form a considerable part of *personal merit:* if a man, possessed of these qualities, is both better satisfied with himself, and better entitled to the goodwill, esteem, and services of others, than one entirely destitute of them; if, in short, the *sentiments* are similar, which arise from these endowments and from the social virtues; is there any reason for being so extremely scrupulous about a *word,* or disputing whether they be entitled to the denomination of virtues?

This leads to the *third* reflection, which we proposed to make, to wit, that the ancient moralists, the best models, made no mate-

---

19. [Demosthenes (fourth century B.C.E.), Athenian statesman and orator, was considered the greatest public speaker of his era. His oratory was instrumental in rallying Greek opposition to the efforts of his contemporary, King Philip of Macedon (father of Alexander the Great), to gain control of the Greek peninsula. Philip was a clever political and military strategist, whose oratory is said to have impressed visiting Greeks, including Demosthenes himself.]

rial distinction among the different species of mental endowments and defects, but treated all alike under the appellation of virtues and vices, and made them indiscriminately the object of their moral reasonings.

SUGGESTIONS FOR FURTHER READING

Oxford University Press is in the process of publishing a new critical edition of Hume's major philosophical works, but relatively few volumes have appeared as yet. *The Philosophical Works of David Hume*, four volumes, edited by T. H. Green and T. H. Grose (London: Longman, Green, 1874–1875), remains the only reasonably complete collection available. However, good critical editions of Hume's major ethical writings, designed both for students and for specialists, are readily available from a number of sources.

On Hume's life, see Ernest C. Mossner's *The Life of David Hume*, 2nd ed. (Oxford: Clarendon Press, 1980). For good general introductions to Hume's philosophy, see Barry Stroud, *Hume* (London: Routledge, 1977), Terence Penelhum, *Hume* (London: Macmillan, 1975), and David Fate Norton, ed., *The Cambridge Companion to Hume* (Cambridge: Cambridge University Press, 1993) (a second expanded edition is currently in preparation).

On Hume's moral theory, James Ballie's short, accessible introduction, *Hume on Morality* (London: Routledge, 2000), is a good place to start. Annette Baier's *A Progress of the Sentiments: Reflections on Hume's "Treatise"* (Cambridge: Harvard University Press, 1991), though focused on Hume's *Treatise* rather than the *Enquiry*, is a valuable study of the moral psychology that underlies both works. Edmund Pincoffs offers a contemporary neo-Humean virtue theory in Part II of his *Quandaries and Virtues: Against Reductivism in Ethics* (Lawrence: University of Kansas Press, 1986). For recent feminist work on Hume, see Anne Jaap Jacobson, ed., *Feminist Interpretations of David Hume* (University Park: Pennsylvania University Press, 2000).

For readers interested in the relation of Hume's work to his contemporaries, see James Feiser, "Hume's Wide View of the Virtues: An Analysis of His Early Critics," *Hume Studies* 24 (1998): 295–311, and Stephen Darwall, *The British Moralists and the Internal*

"Ought": 1670–1740 (Cambridge: Cambridge University Press, 1995). On the relation of Hume to Hutcheson, see James Moore, "Hume and Hutcheson," in *Hume and Hume's Connexions*, M. A. Stewart and John Wright, eds. (University Park: Pennsylvania State University Press, 1995).

Friedrich Nietzsche

Friedrich Nietzsche was born in 1844 in Röcken, Prussia, where his father was a Lutheran pastor. In 1849, when Nietzsche was three, his father died and the family moved to Naumberg where Nietzsche attended a private school. He was successful there, subsequently earning a scholarship to the prestigious Schulpforta, one of Germany's leading Protestant boarding schools. He excelled in the largely classical studies offered at the school. In 1864, his family sent him to the University of Bonn to study theology and classical philology to prepare him to follow his father and grandfather into the Lutheran clergy. Neither the university nor his putative career path suited Nietzsche, however. In 1865, he transferred to the University of Leipzig to concentrate on classical philology.

A brilliant student, Nietzsche was granted his doctorate by Leipzig without the usual examinations or thesis, and the University of Basel in Switzerland offered him the professorship of classical philology. Shortly after taking up his position, he took a leave to volunteer as a medical orderly in the Franco-Prussian War. Unfortunately, Nietzsche contracted dysentery, diphtheria, and, possibly, syphilis. Although he survived, he never fully recovered his health. He lived the rest of his working life as a semi-invalid, obliged to take extended sick leaves from his position at Basel. He finally resigned in 1879, supporting himself with a small pension from Basel and family resources. Though he wrote and published extensively, his writings were poorly received in his lifetime and he made little from his publications.

Though his resignation from Basel did not help his finances, it did have the advantage of freeing him to concentrate on what had long since become his primary interest—philosophy. Nietzsche had become acquainted with the philosophy of Schopenhauer while at Leipzig and was subsequently a member of Richard Wagner's inner circle, although he ultimately rejected both men's views. His first book, *The Birth of Tragedy from the Spirit of Music* (1872), was a speculative rather than an analytical philological investigation of ancient tragedy in which Nietzsche attempted to demonstrate the value of a historically informed genealogical approach to philosophical issues, such as the aesthetics of tragedy. Now widely recognized as a classic, this highly original interdisciplinary treatise impressed neither philologists nor philosophers on its first appearance. Subsequent works produced during his years at Basel, *Unfashionable Observations* (1873–1876) and *Human, all too Human* (1878–1880), were similarly largely ignored by both audiences.

Freed from his university duties, Nietzsche's productivity increased extraordinarily and he produced eight major works between 1883 and 1888, including *Thus Spoke Zarathustra* (1883–1885), *Beyond Good and Evil* (1886), *On the Genealogy of Morality* (1887), *The Case of Wagner* (1888), *Twilight of the Idols* (1895), *The Antichrist* (1895), *Nietzsche Contra Wagner* (1888), and *Ecce Homo* (1908). In 1889, Nietzsche suffered a mental collapse, probably due to a syphilis infection (then an incurable condition). He survived eleven more years but without ever regaining his sanity. This was in some ways merciful, as in the years prior to his death in 1900, his sister Elisabeth Förster-Nietzsche, wife of a leading figure in German racist and anti-Semitic circles, sought to repackage Nietzsche's critical assessments of contemporary approaches to morality, religion, and culture as arguments for the national and racial purification later championed by the nationalist–socialist movement. A skeptic about absolute values and an opponent of any form of absolutism, including anti-Semitism, Nietzsche would have been horrified had he been able to appreciate his sister's abuse of his philosophical legacy.

Nietzsche called himself an "immoralist." Early readers took this to mean that Nietzsche was opposed to moral values generally, but this is not the case. Instead, Nietzsche opposed what he took to be false and misleading representations of moral values, specifically theories of values that treated moral values, virtues, and principles as absolute, objective realities to which human beings were obliged to conform. Our values arise in response to the human situation. Desiring survival and the means of survival, we evaluate ourselves and our circumstances in relation to our objectives. Although the situation is the same for all, different perspectives have arisen on how humans beings may best respond to the challenges our situation presents. Unless we are prepared to critically reflect upon the perspectives we inherit from our culture, Nietzsche thought, we risk becoming servants of systems of values that are inappropriate for or false to our natures. Only individuals who have reflected upon and accepted their own values for themselves possess values and characters that are truly, authentically their own.

In the selections that follow, Nietzsche adopts what he calls a genealogical approach to morality to help understand how certain value perspectives have become dominant in Western European thought, but this is not strictly or only a historical genealogy—the same developmental process replays itself in every age and every individual's moral development. Most crucial for our purposes are the "master" and "slave" perspectives—the former, an individual, virtue-based approach that celebrates self-development and self-assertion, and the latter, a reaction against the first, an obligation-based perspective that celebrates self-restraint and self-subordination to the interests of one's group. Though both perspectives have contributed to our moral outlooks in important ways, Nietzsche holds, the latter has too frequently prevailed, with the result that mediocrity and conformity come to be valued above nobler, "master" virtues such as courage, insight, solitude (self-sufficiency), and sympathy. This we must oppose because the latter are essential to any creative enterprise, most especially the one that concerns us most—the creative enterprise of self-development.

On the Genealogy of Morality[1]

First Treatise: "Good and Evil," "Good and Bad"

1. —These English psychologists whom we also have to thank for the only attempts so far to produce a history of the genesis of morality—they themselves are no small riddle for us; I confess, in fact, that precisely as riddles in the flesh they have something substantial over their books—*they themselves are interesting!* These English psychologists—what do they actually want? One finds them, whether voluntarily or involuntarily, always at the same task, namely of pushing the *partie honteuse*[2] of our inner world into the foreground and of seeking that which is actually effective, leading, decisive for our development, precisely where the intellectual pride of man would least of all *wish* to find it (for example in the *vis inertia*[3] habit or in forgetfulness or in a blind and accidental interlacing and mechanism of ideas or in anything purely passive, automatic, reflexive, molecular, and fundamentally mindless). . . But I am told that they are simply old, cold, boring frogs who creep and hop around on human beings, into human beings, as if they were really in their element there, namely in a *swamp*. I resist this, still more, I don't believe it; and if one is permitted to wish where one cannot know, then I wish from my heart that the reverse may be the case with them—that these explorers and microscopists of the soul are basically brave, magnanimous, and proud animals who know how to keep a rein on their hearts as well as their pain and have trained themselves to sacrifice all desirability to truth, to

---

1. [This selection is from Friedrich Nietzsche, *On the Genealogy of Morality*, trans., with an introduction and notes by Maudemarie Clark and Alan J. Swensen (Indianapolis: Hackett Publishing Company, 1998).]

2. *Partie honteuse*: shameful part. (In the plural, this expression is the equivalent of the English "private parts.")

3. *Vis inertia*: force of activity. In Newtonian physics, this term denotes the resistance offered by matter to any force tending to alter its state of rest or motion.

every truth, even plain, harsh, ugly, unpleasant, unchristian, immoral truth . . . For there are such truths—

2. Hats off then to whatever good spirits may be at work in these historians of morality! Unfortunately, however, it is certain that they lack the *historical spirit* itself. . . . As is simply the age-old practice among philosophers, they all think *essentially* ahistorically; of this there is no doubt. The ineptitude of their moral genealogy is exposed right at the beginning, where it is a matter of determining the origins of the concept and judgment "good." "Originally"—so they decree—"unegoistic actions were praised and called good from the perspective of those to whom they were rendered, hence for whom they were *useful;* later one *forgot* this origin of the praise and, simply because unegoistic actions were *as a matter of habit* always praised as good, one also felt them to be good—as if they were something good in themselves." . . . Now in the first place it is obvious to me that the actual genesis of the concept "good" is sought and fixed in the wrong place by this theory: the judgment "good" does *not* stem from those to whom "goodness" is rendered! Rather it was "the good" themselves, that is the noble, powerful, higher-ranking, and high-minded who felt and ranked themselves and their doings as good, which is to say, as of the first rank, in contrast to everything base, low-minded, common, and vulgar. Out of this *pathos of distance* they first took for themselves the right to create values, to coin names for values. [T]*hat* is the origin of the opposition "good" and "bad." . . . (We should allow ourselves to comprehend the origin of language itself as an expression of power on the part of those who rule: they say "this *is* such and such," they seal each thing and happening with a sound and thus, as it were, take possession of it.) It is because of this origin that from the outset the word "good" does *not* necessarily attach itself to "unegoistic" actions—as is the superstition of those genealogists of morality. On the contrary, only when aristocratic value judgments begin to *decline* does this entire opposition "egoistic," "unegoistic" impose itself more and more on the human conscience—to make use of my language, it is *the herd instinct* that finally finds a voice (also *words*) in this opposition. And even then it takes a long time until this instinct becomes dominant to such an extent that moral valuation in effect gets caught and stuck at that opposition (as is the case in present day Europe: today the prejudice that takes "moral," "unegoistic,"

"*désintéressé*"[4] to be concepts of equal value already rules with the force of an "*idée fixe*"[5] and sickness in the head).

4. —The pointer to the *right* path was given to me by the question: what do the terms coined for "good" in the various languages actually mean from an etymological viewpoint? Here I found that they all lead back to the *same conceptual transformation*—that everywhere the basic concept is "noble," "aristocratic" in the sense related to the estates, out of which "good" in the sense of "noble of soul," "high-natured of soul," "privileged of soul" necessarily develops: a development that always runs parallel to that other one which makes "common," "vulgar," "base" pass over finally into the concept "bad." The most eloquent example of the latter is the German word "*schlecht*" [bad] itself: which is identical with "*schlicht*" [plain, simple]—compare "*schlechtweg*," "*schlechterdings*" [simply or downright]—and originally designated the plain, the common man, as yet without a suspecting sideward glance, simply in opposition to the noble one. Around the time of the Thirty-Years' War, in other words late enough, this sense shifts into the one now commonly used:—With respect to morality's genealogy this appears to me to be an *essential* insight; that it is only now being discovered is due to the inhibiting influence that democratic prejudice exercises in the modern world with regard to all questions of origins.

5. With no regard to *our* problem—which can for good reasons be called a *quiet* problem and which addresses itself selectively to but few ears—it is of no small interest to discover that often in those words and roots that designate "good" that main nuance still shimmers through with respect to which nobles felt themselves to be humans of a higher rank. To be sure, they may name themselves in the most frequent cases simply after their superiority in power (as "the powerful," "the lords," "the commanders") or after the most visible distinguishing mark of this superiority, for example as "the rich," "the possessors," (that is the sense of *arya;*[6] and likewise in Iranian and Slavic). But also after a *typical character trait*: and this is the case which concerns us here. They call themselves for example

---

4. *Désintéressé*: disinterested, unselfish, selfless.

5. *Idée fixe*: obsession. Literally: a fixed idea.

6. *Arya:* (Sanskrit) noble.

"the truthful"—led by the Greek nobility, whose mouthpiece is the Megarian poet Theognis. The word coined for this, *esthlos,*[7] means according to its root one who *is,* who possesses reality, who is real, who is true; then, with a subjective turn, the true one as the truthful one: in this phase of the concept's transformation it becomes the by- and catchword of the nobility and passes over completely into the sense of "aristocratic," as that which distinguishes from the *lying* common man as Theognis understands and depicts him—until finally, after the demise of the nobility, the word remains as the term for *noblesse* of soul and becomes as it were ripe and sweet. In the word *kakos*[8] as well as in *deilos*[9] (the plebeian in contrast to the *agathos*[10]), cowardliness is underscored: perhaps this gives a hint in which direction one should seek the etymological origins of *agathos,* which can be interpreted in many ways. In the Latin *malus*[11] (beside which I place *melas*[12]), the common man could be charac- terized as the dark-colored, above all as the black-haired ("*hic niger est*[13]—"), as the pre-Aryan occupant of Italian soil, who by his color stood out most clearly from the blonds who had become the rulers, namely the Aryan conqueror-race; at any rate Gaelic offered me an exactly corresponding case—*fin*[14](for example in the name Fin-Gal), the distinguishing word of the nobility, in the end, the good, noble, pure one, originally the blond-headed one, in contrast to the dark, black-haired original inhabitants. Our German "*gut*" [good] itself: wasn't it supposed to mean "the godly one," the man "of godly race"? And to be identical with the name for the nation (originally for the nobility) of the Goths? The reasons for this sup- position do not belong here.—

6. To this rule that the concept of superiority in politics always resolves itself into a concept of superiority of soul, it is not immedi- ately an exception (although it provides occasion for exceptions)

---

7. *Esthlos:* good, brave, noble.

8. *Kakos:* bad, ugly, ill-born, base, cowardly, ignoble.

9. *Deilos:* cowardly, worthless, low-born, miserable, wretched.

10. *Agathos:* good, well-born, noble, brave, capable.

11. *Malus:* bad, evil.

12. *Melas:* black, dark.

13. *Hic niger est:* he is black. Horace's *Satires,* I. 4, line 85.

14. *Fin:* (Gaelic) white, bright.

when the highest caste is at the same time the *priestly* caste and hence prefers for its collective name a predicate that recalls its priestly function. Here, for example, "pure" and "impure" stand opposite each other for the first time as marks of distinction among the estates; and here, too, one later finds the development of a "good" and a "bad" in a sense no longer related to the estates. Incidentally, let one beware from the outset of taking these concepts "pure" and "impure" too seriously, too broadly, or even too symbolically: rather all of earlier humanity's concepts were initially understood in a coarse, crude, superficial, narrow, straightforward, and above all *unsymbolic* manner, to an extant that we can hardly imagine. The "pure one" is from the beginning simply a human being who washes himself, who forbids himself certain foods that bring about skin diseases, who doesn't sleep with the dirty women of the baser people, who abhors blood—nothing more, at least not much more! On the other hand the entire nature of an essentially priestly aristocracy admittedly makes clear why it was precisely here that the valuation opposites could so soon become internalized and heightened in a dangerous manner.

7. —One will already have guessed how easily the priestly manner of valuation can branch off from the knightly-aristocratic and then develop into its opposite; this process is especially given an impetus every time the priestly caste and the warrior caste confront each other jealously and are unable to agree on a price. The knightly-aristocratic value judgments have as their presupposition a powerful physicality, a blossoming, rich, even overflowing health, together with that which is required for its preservation: war, adventure, the hunt, dance, athletic contests, and in general everything which includes strong, free, cheerful-hearted activity. The priestly-noble manner of valuation—as we have seen—has other presuppositions: too bad for it when it comes to war! Priests are, as is well known, the *most evil enemies*—why is that? Because they are the most powerless. Out of their powerlessness their hate grows into something enormous and uncanny, into something most spiritual and most poisonous. The truly great haters in the history of the world have always been priests, also the most ingenious haters:—compared with the spirit of priestly revenge all the rest of spirit taken together hardly merits consideration. Human history would be much too stupid an affair without the spirit that has entered into it through the powerless:—let us turn right to the

greatest example. Of all that has been done on earth against "the noble," "the mighty," "the lords," "the power-holders," nothing is worthy of mention in comparison with that which the *Jews* have done against them: the Jews, that priestly people who in the end were only able to obtain satisfaction from their enemies and conquerors through a radical revaluation of their values, that is, through an act of *spiritual revenge*. This was the only way that suited a priestly people, the people of the most suppressed priestly desire for revenge. It was the Jews who in opposition to the aristocratic value equation (good = noble = powerful = beautiful = happy = beloved of God) dared its inversion, with fear-inspiring consistency, and held it fast with teeth of the most unfathomable hate (the hate of powerlessness), namely: "the miserable alone are the good; the poor, powerless, lowly alone are the good; the suffering, deprived, sick, ugly are also the only pious, the only blessed in God, for them alone is there blessedness,—whereas you, you noble and powerful ones, you are in all eternity the evil, the cruel, the lustful, the insatiable, the godless, you will eternally be the wretched, accursed, and damned!"—We know *who* inherited this Jewish revaluation . . . In connection with the enormous and immeasurably doom-laden initiative provided by the Jews with this most fundamental of all declarations of war, I call attention to the proposition which I arrived at on another occasion ("Beyond Good and Evil" section 195)—namely, that with the Jews *the slave revolt in morality* begins: that revolt which has a two-thousand-year history behind it and which has only moved out of our sight today because it—has been victorious . . .

10. The slave revolt in morality begins when *ressentiment* itself becomes creative and gives birth to values: the *ressentiment* of beings denied the true reaction, that of the deed, who recover their losses only through an imaginary revenge. Whereas all noble morality grows out of a triumphant yes-saying to oneself, from the outset slave morality says "no" to an "outside," to a "different," to a "not-self": and *this* "no" is its creative deed. This reversal of the value-establishing glance—this *necessary* direction toward the outside instead of back onto oneself—belongs to the very nature of *ressentiment*: in order to come into being, slave-morality always needs an opposite and external world; it needs, psychologically speaking, external stimuli in order to be able to act at all,—its action is, from the ground up, reaction. The reverse is the case with the noble

manner of valuation: it acts and grows spontaneously, it seeks out its opposite only in order to say "yes" to itself still more gratefully and more jubilantly—its negative concept "low" "common" "bad" is only an after-birth, a pale contrast-image in relation to its positive basic concept, saturated through and through with life and passion: "we noble ones, we good ones, we beautiful ones, we happy ones!" When the noble manner of valuation lays a hand on reality and sins against it, this occurs relative to the sphere with which it is *not* sufficiently acquainted, indeed against a real knowledge of which it rigidly defends itself: in some cases it forms a wrong idea of the sphere it holds in contempt, that of the common man, of the lower people; on the other hand, consider that the affect of contempt, of looking down on, of the superior glance—assuming that it does *falsify* the image of the one held in contempt—will in any case fall far short of the falsification with which the suppressed hate, the revenge of the powerless, lays a hand on its opponent—in effigy, of course. Indeed there is too much carelessness in contempt, too much taking-lightly, too much looking away and impatience mixed in, even too much of a feeling of cheer in oneself, for it to be capable of transforming its object into a real caricature and monster. Do not fail to hear the almost benevolent nuances that, for example, the Greek nobility places in all words by which it distinguishes the lower people from itself; how they are mixed with and sugared by a kind of pity, considerateness, leniency to the point that almost all words that apply to the common man ultimately survive as expressions for "unhappy" "pitiful"—and how, on the other hand, to the Greek ear "bad" "low" "unhappy" have never ceased to end on the same note, with a tone color in which "unhappy" predominates: this as inheritance of the old, nobler aristocratic manner of valuation that does not deny itself even in its contempt. The "well-born" simply *felt* themselves to be the "happy"; they did not first have to construct their happiness artificially by looking at their enemies, to talk themselves into it, to *lie themselves into it* (as all human beings of *ressentiment* tend to do); and as full human beings, overloaded with power and therefore *necessarily* active, they likewise did not know how to separate activity out from happiness,—for them being active is of necessity included in happiness (whence *eu prattein*[15] takes its origins)—all of

---

15. *Eu prattein*: to do well, to fare well, or to do good.

this very much in opposition to "happiness" on the level of the powerless, oppressed, those festering with poisonous and hostile feelings, in whom it essentially appears as narcotic, anesthetic, calm, peace, "Sabbath," relaxation of mind and stretching of limbs, in short, *passively*. While the noble human being lives with himself in confidence and openness *(gennaios*[16] "noble-born" underscores the nuance "sincere" and probably also "naive") the human being of *ressentiment* is neither sincere, nor naive, nor honest and frank with himself. His soul *looks obliquely* at things; his spirit loves hiding places, secret passages and backdoors, everything hidden strikes him as *his* world, *his* security, *his* balm; he knows all about being silent, not forgetting, waiting, belittling oneself for the moment, humbling oneself. A race of such human beings of *ressentiment* in the end necessarily becomes *more prudent* than any noble race, it will also honor prudence in an entirely different measure: namely as a primary condition of existence. With noble human beings, in contrast, prudence is likely to have a refined aftertaste of luxury and sophistication about it:—here it is not nearly as essential as the complete functional reliability of the regulating *unconscious* instincts or even a certain imprudence, for example the gallant making-straight-for-it, be it toward danger, be it toward the enemy, or that impassioned suddenness of anger, love, reverence, gratitude, and revenge by which noble souls in all ages have recognized each other. For the *ressentiment* of the noble human being, when it appears in him, runs its course and exhausts itself in an immediate reaction, therefore it does not *poison*—on the other hand it does not appear at all in countless cases where it is unavoidable in all the weak and powerless. To be unable for any length of time to take his enemies, his accidents, his *misdeeds* themselves seriously—that is the sign of strong, full natures in which there is an excess of formative, reconstructive, healing power that also makes one forget (a good example of this from the modern world is Mirabeau, who had no memory for insults and base deeds committed against him and who was only unable to forgive because he—forgot). Such a human is simply able to shake off with a single shrug a collection of worms that in others would dig itself in; here alone is also possible—assuming that it is at all possible on earth—the true "*love* of one's enemies." What great reverence for

---

16. *Gennaios*: high-born, noble, high-minded.

his enemies a noble human being has!—and such reverence is already a bridge to love . . . After all, he demands his enemy for himself, as his distinction; he can stand no other enemy than one in whom there is nothing to hold in contempt and *a very great deal* to honor! On the other hand, imagine "the enemy" as the human being of *ressentiment* conceives of him—and precisely here is his deed, his creation: he has conceived of "the evil enemy," "*the evil one,*" and this indeed as the basic concept, starting from which he now also thinks up, as reaction and counterpart, a "good one" . . . himself! . . .

11. Precisely the reverse, therefore, of the case of the noble one, who conceives the basic concept "good" in advance and spontaneously, starting from himself that is, and from there first creates for himself an idea of "bad"! This "bad" of noble origin and that "evil" out of the brewing cauldron of unsatiated hate—the first, an after-creation, something on the side, a complementary color; the second, in contrast, the original, the beginning, the true *deed* in the conception of a slave morality—how differently the two words "bad" and "evil" stand there, seemingly set in opposition to the same concept "good"! But it is *not* the same concept "good": on the contrary, just ask yourself *who* is actually "evil" in the sense of the morality of *ressentiment.* To answer in all strictness: *precisely the "good one"* of the other morality, precisely the noble, the powerful, the ruling one, only recolored, only reinterpreted, only reseen through the poisonous eye of *ressentiment.* There is one point we wish to deny least of all here: whoever encounters those "good ones" only as enemies encounters nothing but *evil enemies,* and the same humans who are kept so strictly within limits *inter pares,*[17] by mores, worship, custom, gratitude, still more by mutual surveillance, by jealousy, and who on the other hand in their conduct toward each other prove themselves so inventive in consideration, self-control, tact, loyalty, pride, and friendship,—they are not much better than uncaged beasts of prey toward the outside world, where that which is foreign, the foreign world, begins. There they enjoy freedom from all social constraint; in the wilderness they recover the losses incurred through the tension that comes from a long enclosure and fencing-in within the peace of the community; they step *back* into the innocence of the beast-of-prey conscience, as

---

17. *Inter pares:* among equals; here, "among themselves."

jubilant monsters, who perhaps walk away from a hideous succession of murder, arson, rape, torture with such high spirits and equanimity that it seems as if they have only played a student prank, convinced that for years to come the poets will again have something to sing and to praise. At the base of all these noble races one cannot fail to recognize the beast of prey, the splendid *blond beast* who roams about lusting after booty and victory; from time to time this hidden base needs to discharge itself, the animal must get out, must go back into the wilderness: Roman, Arab, Germanic, Japanese nobility, Homeric heroes, Scandinavian Vikings—in this need they are all alike. It is the noble races who have left the concept "barbarian" in all their tracks wherever they have gone; indeed from within their highest culture a consciousness of this betrays itself and even a pride in it (for example when Pericles says to his Athenians in that famous funeral oration, "to every land and sea our boldness has broken a path, everywhere setting up unperishing monuments in good *and bad*"). This "boldness" of noble races— mad, absurd, sudden in its expression; the unpredictable, in their enterprises even the improbable—Pericles singles out for distinction the *rhathymia*[18] of the Athenians—their indifference and contempt toward all security, body, life, comfort; their appalling light-heartedness and depth of desire in all destruction, in all delights of victory and of cruelty—all was summed up for those who suffered from it in the image of the "barbarian," of the "evil enemy," for example the "Goth," the "Vandal." Assuming it were true, that which is now in any case believed as "truth," that the *meaning of all culture* is simply to breed a tame and civilized animal, a *domestic animal*, out of the beast of prey "man," then one would have to regard all those instincts of reaction and *ressentiment*, with the help of which the noble dynasties together with their ideals were finally brought to ruin and overwhelmed, as the actual *tools of culture*; which is admittedly not to say that the *bearers* of these instincts themselves at the same time also represent culture. On the contrary, the opposite would not simply be probable—no! today it is *obvious!* These bearers of the oppressing and retaliation-craving instincts, the descendants of all European and non-European slavery, of all pre-Aryan population in particular—they represent the

---

18. *Rhathymia*: easiness of temper; indifference, rashness. Thucydides 2.39.

regression of humankind! These "tools of culture" are a disgrace to humanity, and rather something that raises a suspicion, a counter-argument against "culture" in general! It may be entirely justifiable if one cannot escape one's fear of the blond beast at the base of all noble races and is on guard: but who would not a hundred times sooner fear if he might at the same time admire, than *not* fear but be unable to escape the disgusting sight of the deformed, reduced, atrophied, poisoned? And is that not *our* doom? What causes *our* aversion to "man"?—for we *suffer* from man, there is no doubt.— *Not* fear; rather that we have nothing left to fear in man; that the worm "man" is in the foreground and teeming; that the "tame man," this hopelessly mediocre and uninspiring being, has already learned to feel himself as the goal and pinnacle, as the meaning of history, as "higher man"—indeed that he has a certain right to feel this way, insofar as he feels himself distanced from the profusion of the deformed, sickly, tired, worn-out of which Europe today is beginning to stink; hence as something that is at least relatively well formed, at least still capable of living, that at least says "yes" to life . . .

12. —At this point I will not suppress a sigh and a final confidence. What is it that I in particular find utterly unbearable? That with which I cannot cope alone, that causes me to suffocate and languish? Bad air! Bad air! That something deformed comes near me; that I should have to smell the entrails of a deformed soul! . . . How much can one not otherwise bear of distress, deprivation, foul weather, infirmity, drudgery, isolation? Basically one deals with everything else, born as one is to a subterranean and fighting existence; again and again one reaches the light, again and again one experiences one's golden hour of victory,—and then one stands there as one was born, unbreakable, tensed, ready for something new, something still more difficult, more distant, like a bow that any distress simply pulls tauter still.—But from time to time grant me—assuming that there are heavenly patronesses beyond good and evil—a glimpse, grant me just one glimpse of something perfect, completely formed, happy, powerful, triumphant, in which there is still something to fear! Of a human being who justifies man *himself;* a human being who is a stroke of luck, completing and redeeming man, and for whose sake one may hold fast to *belief in man*! . . . For things stand thus: the reduction and equalization of the European human conceals *our* greatest danger, for this sight

makes tired . . . We see today nothing that wishes to become greater, we sense that things are still going downhill, downhill—into something thinner, more good-natured, more prudent, more comfortable, more mediocre, more apathetic, more Chinese, more Christian—man, there is no doubt, is becoming ever "better" . . . Precisely here lies Europe's doom—with the fear of man we have also forfeited the love of him, the reverence toward him, the hope for him, indeed the will to him. The sight of man now makes tired—what is nihilism today if it is not *that?* . . . We are tired of *man* . . .

13. —But let us come back: the problem of the *other* origin of "good," of the good one as conceived by the man of *ressentiment,* demands its conclusion.—That the lambs feel anger toward the great birds of prey does not strike us as odd: but that is no reason for holding it against the great birds of prey that they snatch up little lambs for themselves. And when the lambs say among themselves "these birds of prey are evil; and whoever is as little as possible a bird of prey but rather its opposite, a lamb,—isn't he good?" there is nothing to criticize in this setting up of an ideal, even if the birds of prey should look on this a little mockingly and perhaps say to themselves: "*we* do not feel any anger toward them, these good lambs, as a matter of fact, we love them: nothing is more tasty than a tender lamb."—To demand of strength that it *not* express itself as strength, that it *not* be a desire to overwhelm, a desire to cast down, a desire to become lord, a thirst for enemies and resistances and triumphs, is just as nonsensical as to demand of weakness that it express itself as strength. A quantum of power is just such a quantum of drive, will, effect—more precisely, it is nothing other than this very driving, willing, effecting, and only through the seduction of language (and the basic errors of reason petrified therein), which understands and misunderstands all effecting as conditioned by an effecting something, by a "subject," can it appear otherwise. For just as common people separate the lightning from its flash and take the latter as a *doing,* as an effect of a subject called lightning, so popular morality also separates strength from the expressions of strength as if there were behind the strong an indifferent substratum that is free to express strength—or not to. But there is no such substratum; there is no "being" behind the doing, effecting, becoming; "the doer" is simply fabricated into the doing—the doing is everything. Common

people basically double the doing when they have the lightning flash; this is a doing-doing: the same happening is posited first as cause and then once again as its effect. Natural scientists do no better when they say "force moves, force causes," and so on—our entire science, despite all its coolness, its freedom from affect, still stands under the seduction of language and has not gotten rid of the changelings slipped over on it, the "subjects" (the atom, for example, is such a changeling, likewise the Kantian "thing in itself"): small wonder if the suppressed, hiddenly glowing affects of revenge and hate exploit this belief and basically even uphold no other belief more ardently than this one, that *the strong one is free* to be weak, and the bird of prey to be a lamb:—they thereby gain for themselves the right to hold the bird of prey *accountable* for being a bird of prey . . . When out of the vengeful cunning of powerlessness the oppressed, downtrodden, violated say to themselves: "let us be different from the evil ones, namely good! And good is what everyone is who does not do violence, who injures no one, who doesn't attack, who doesn't retaliate, who leaves vengeance to God, who keeps himself concealed, as we do, who avoids all evil, and in general demands very little of life, like us, the patient, humble, righteous"—it means, when listened to coldly and without prejudice, actually nothing more than: "we weak ones are simply weak; it is good if we do nothing *for which we are not strong enough*"—but this harsh matter of fact, this prudence of the lowest order, which even insects have (presumably playing dead when in great danger in order not to do "too much"), has, thanks to that counterfeiting and self-deception of powerlessness, clothed itself in the pomp of renouncing, quiet, patiently waiting virtue, as if the very weakness of the weak—that is to say, his *essence*, his effecting, his whole unique, unavoidable, undetachable reality—were a voluntary achievement, something willed, something chosen, a *deed*, a *merit*. This kind of human *needs* the belief in a neutral "subject" with free choice, out of an instinct of self-preservation, self-affirmation, in which every lie tends to hallow itself. It is perhaps for this reason that the subject (or, to speak more popularly, the *soul*) has until now been the best article of faith on earth, because it made possible for the majority of mortals, the weak and oppressed of every kind, that sublime self-deception of interpreting weakness itself as freedom, of interpreting their being-such-and-such as a *merit*.

16. Let us conclude. The two *opposed* values—"good and bad," "good and evil"—have fought a terrible millennia-long battle on earth; and as certainly as the second value has had the upper hand for a long time, even so there is still no shortage of places where the battle goes on, undecided. One could even say that it has in the meantime been borne up ever higher and precisely thereby become ever deeper, ever more spiritual: so that today there is perhaps no more decisive mark of the *"higher nature,"* of the more spiritual nature, than to be conflicted in that sense and still a real battle-ground for those opposites.

Note: I take advantage of the opportunity this treatise gives me to express publicly and formally a wish . . . that some philosophical faculty might do a great service for the promotion of *moral-historical* studies through a series of academic essay contests:—perhaps this book will serve to give a forceful impetus in just such a direction.

The question: what is the *value* of this or that value table or "morality"? demands to be raised from the most diverse perspectives; for this "value relative *to what end?*" cannot be analyzed too finely. Something, for example, that clearly had value with regard to the greatest possible longevity of a race (or to a heightening of its powers of adaptation to a specific climate, or to the preservation of the greatest number), would by no means have the same value if it were an issue of developing a stronger type. The welfare of the majority and the welfare of the few are opposing value viewpoints: to hold the former one to be of higher value already *in itself*, this we will leave to the *naïveté* of English biologists.

Beyond Good and Evil[19]

221. It happens, said a moralistic pedant and dealer in trifles, that I honor and esteem a man without self-interest: but not because he is without self-interest, rather because he seems to me to have the right to benefit another person at his own cost. Enough, the question is always who *he* is and who the *other* is. In one, for example, who is called and made to command, self-denial and modest self-deprecation would not be a virtue but the waste of a virtue: so it seems to me. Every unegoistic morality, which takes itself as unconditional and turns to everyone, sins not only against taste: it is an incitement to sins of omission, one seduction *more*—under the mask of philanthropy—and exactly a seduction and injury for the higher, scarcer, privileged. One must force moralities to bow down first of all before the *order of rank*, one must shove their presumption before their consciences—until at last they come to agree that it is *immoral* to say: "what is right for one is fair for another."—Thus my moralistic pedant and *bonhomme*:[20] does he deserve to be well laughed at, that he enjoins moralities to become moral? But one should not be too much in the right if one wants the laugh on one's *own* side, in fact a kernel of wrong belongs to good taste.

259. Forbearing mutually from injury, violence, and exploitation, and setting out one's will as equal to others: this can become in a certain rough sense good manners between individuals, if the proper conditions are present (namely so long as they are actually similar in strength and value standards and belong together in *one* body). But as soon as one would take this principle further and possibly as far as the ground principle of society, so would it show itself as what it is: as will to the *denial* of life, as principle of dissolution and decay. Here one must think things through and beware of all sentimental weakness: life itself is *essentially* appropriation,

---

19. The following selections from *Beyond Good and Evil* have been translated by Clancy W. Martin, who also supplied the notes (unless otherwise indicated).
20. *Bonhomme*, French, "good man."

126

injury, overpowering what is foreign and weaker, oppression, hardness, imposition of one's own forms, incorporation and at the least, at the mildest, exploitation—but why should one always straightaway use those words on which for ages a slanderous intent has been stamped? Within every body within which, as was suggested before, individuals treat one another as equals—it happens in every healthy aristocracy—if it is a living and not a dying body, that body must itself do to other bodies everything that the individuals within it refrain from doing to one another: it will have to be an incarnate will to power, it will want to grow, stretch, seize, achieve dominance—not out of some or another morality or immorality, but because it *lives* and because life just *is* will to power. But there is no place at which the ordinary consciousness of Europeans is more resistant to instruction than here; one rants everywhere now, even in scientific costumes, about coming conditions of society in which "the exploitative character" shall be removed—which rings in my ears like a promise to invent a life that dispensed with all organic functions. "Exploitation" does not belong to a corrupt or unrealized and primitive society: it belongs to the *being* of the living, as basic organic function, it is a consequence of the genuine will to power, which is just the will to life.—Suppose this is, as theory, a novelty—as reality, it is the *primordial fact* of all history: one should be honest with oneself at least that far!—

260. On a journey through the many finer and coarser moralities that have so far ruled or still rule on earth I found that certain properties recurred regularly together and were closely related: until at last I found two fundamental types and one fundamental difference. There are *master morality* and *slave morality*—I add immediately that in all the higher and mixed cultures there also appear attempts at a blending of both moralities, and still more often the interpenetration and mutual misunderstanding of both, indeed at times they are hard against one another—even in the same human being, within a *single* soul. The moral discrimination of values has originated either in a ruling group whose understanding of its difference from the ruled was felt with well-being—or among the ruled, the slaves and dependents of every grade. In the first case, when it is the rulers who determine what is "good," the lofty proud states of soul are experienced as conferring distinction and determining the order of rank. The noble human distances

from himself those in whom the contrary of such lofty proud states finds expression: he despises them. One should immediately note that in this first kind of morality the opposition of "good" and "bad" means about the same as "noble" and "contemptible"—the opposition of "good" and *"evil"* has a different origin. Despised are the cowardly, the anxious, the petty, those who think about narrow utility; even so the suspicious with their constrained glances, those who humble themselves, the dog-kind of humans who allow themselves to be maltreated, the fawning flatterers, above all the liars—it is a fundamental belief of all aristocrats that the common people lie. "We truthful ones"—thus the nobility of ancient Greece named itself. It is obvious that moral designations that were everywhere first applied to *humans* and only derivatively and late to actions: which is why it is a serious error when historians of morality begin with questions like "why was the pitying act praised?" The noble kind of human feels *itself* as establishing values, it has no need for approval, it judges "what is harmful to me is harmful in itself," it knows itself to be that which first grants things their honor, it is *value-creating*. It honors everything that it knows as part of itself: such a morality is self-glorification. In the foreground stands the feeling of fullness, of power that will overflow, the happiness of high tension, the consciousness of riches that would give and grant—the noble human helps the unfortunate too, but not or almost not from pity, rather more from an urge generated by an excess of power. The noble human honors himself as one who is powerful, also as one who has power over himself, who knows how to speak and to keep silent, who takes pleasure in being stern and hard with himself and respects all that is stern and hard. "A hard heart Wotan[21] laid in my breast," says an old Scandinavian saga: thus it is well written from the soul of a proud Viking. Such a kind of human is even proud of it that he is *not* made for pity: therefore as a warning the hero of the saga continues "if the heart is not hard in youth, it will never harden." Noble and courageous humans who think in this way are furthest from that morality which finds the merit of morality precisely in pity or in acting for others or in *desinteressement*; belief in oneself, pride in oneself, a profound enmity and irony against "selflessness"

---

21. Wotan, or Odin, was a Norse god of war, one of the preeminent Norse deities, who was a protector of warriors and of poets. *Ed.*

belong just as certainly to noble morality as does a slight contempt and wariness about compassion and a "warm heart."—It is the powerful who *understand* how to honor, it is their art, their empire of invention. The deep reverence for age and tradition—the whole of law stands on this double reverence—the belief and prejudice in favor of ancestors and disfavor of those who are coming are typical of the morality of the powerful; and when conversely the people of "modern ideas" incline almost instinctively toward "progress" and "the future" and increasingly lack respect for the old, this alone would sufficiently betray the ignoble origin of these "ideas." But the morality of rulers is most foreign and embarrassing to today's taste in the severity of its principle that one has duties only to one's peers; that against beings of an inferior rank, against all that is foreign one may behave as one pleases or "as the heart desires" and in any case "beyond good and evil"—: here pity and the like belong. The capability and the duty of long gratitude and long revenge—both only among one's peers—elegance in repayment, the refined concept of friendship, a certain necessity for having enemies (as if to serve as runnels for the affects of envy, dissidence, exuberance—fundamentally, so that one could be a good *friend*): all these are typical qualities of noble morality which, as suggested, is not the morality of "modern ideas" and therefore is difficult to empathize with today, also difficult to dig up and reveal.—It is different with the second type of morality, *slave morality*. Suppose the raped, oppressed, suffering, bound, unsure of themselves and exhausted moralize: what will their moral valuations have in common? Probably a pessimistic suspicion about the whole human condition will make itself known, perhaps a condemnation of human kind along with its condition. The glance of the slave is adverse to the virtues of the powerful: he has skepticism and mistrust, he has *subtle* mistrust of all the "good" that is honored there—he would like to persuade himself that even their happiness is not real. Conversely those qualities are brought forth and brightly illuminated that serve to lighten existence for the suffering: here pity, the obliging helpful hand, the warm heart, patience, industry, humility, and friendliness come to be honored—for here these are the most useful qualities and nearly the sole means for enduring the stress of existence. Slave morality is essentially a morality of utility. Here is the place for the source of that famous opposition between good and *"evil"*—into evil were projected power and dangerousness, a certain fearfulness, subtlety, and strength, that does not permit contempt to arise. For slave morality the "evil" therefore inspire fear; for master morality it is precisely the "good" that inspire and want to inspire fear, while the "bad" are felt to be contemptible. The opposition comes to a peak when, as a direct consequence of slave morality, a touch of scorn comes along with the "good" of this morality—this may be slight and benevolent—because the good must be *harmless* in the slave's way of thinking: he is good-natured, easy to deceive, a bit dumb perhaps, *un bonhomme*. In general, where slave morality becomes predominant language tends to bring the words "good" and "dumb" closer together.—One last fundamental difference: the longing for *freedom*, the instinct for happiness and the subtleties of the feeling of freedom belong just as necessarily to slave morality and morals as the art and enthusiasm in reverence, in devotion are the regular symptoms of an aristocratic manner in thinking and evaluating.— Herein lies the reason why love *as passion*—it is our European specialty—simply must be of noble origin: we know that its invention belongs to the Provencal knight-poets, those splendid inventive humans of the *"gai saber,"*[22] to whom Europe owes so much and also owes itself.—

261. Vanity belongs among the things that a noble human being perhaps finds most difficult to grasp: he will be tempted to deny it, where another kind of human seizes it with both hands. The problem for him is to imagine a nature that seeks to inspire a good opinion of itself that it itself does not hold—and therefore also does not "deserve"—and that nevertheless winds up *believing* this good opinion of itself. This seems to him half so tasteless and disrespectful to oneself, and half so baroquely irrational, that he would like to consider vanity an exception, and in most cases when it is spoken of he doubts it. He will say for example: "I can be mistaken about my own value and nevertheless demand that my value, precisely as I assess it, also be acknowledged by others—but that is not vanity (rather arrogance or, in the more common case, what is called 'humility' or 'modesty')." Or also: "I can for many reasons take pleasure at the good opinion of others, per-

---

22. *Gai saber,* "gay science" or art of troubadours, i.e., poets and singers of medieval Provence. *Ed.*

haps because I honor and love them and all their pleasures please me, perhaps also because their good opinion underwrites and strengthens my belief in my own good opinion, perhaps because the good opinion of others, even in cases where I do not share it, is still useful to me or promises use—but all that is not vanity." The noble human being compels himself, above all with the help of history, to recognize that, since time out of mind, in all somehow dependent social classes the common man *was* only what he was *considered*—in no way accustomed to establishing values himself, he also affixed no other value to himself than his masters fixed on him (it is the characteristic *right of masters* to create values). It may be understood as the result of an immense atavism that even now the ordinary man still always first *waits* for an opinion about himself and then instinctively submits to it: but by no means only a "good" opinion, rather a bad and unfair one too (one thinks for example of the great majority of self-estimates and self-underestimates that faithful women gather from their father-confessors, and faithful Christians gather quite generally from their church). In fact now, in accordance with the slowly arising democratic order of things (and its cause, the mixing of bloodlines of master and slave), the originally noble and rare urge to ascribe value to oneself on one's own and to "think well" of oneself will be more and more encouraged and distributed: but every time it has an older, broader, and more deeply ingrained inclination against it— and in the phenomenon of "vanity" this older inclination masters the younger. The vain is pleased at *every* good opinion he hears about himself (entirely apart of all considerations of its usefulness, and just as apart from truth or falsity), precisely as every bad opinion of him pains him: for he submits to both, he *feels* subjected to them out of that oldest instinct of submission that breaks out in him.—It is "the slave" in the blood of the vain, a vestige of the slave's impishness—and how much "slave" is for example still residual in woman!—that seeks to *seduce* him to good opinions of himself; it is also the slave who afterward immediately prostrates himself before these opinions as if he had not summoned them forth.—And said again: vanity is an atavism.

265. At the risk of upsetting innocent ears I propose: egoism belongs to the being of the noble soul, I mean that unshakable belief that to a being such as "we are" other beings must be subordinate by nature and have to sacrifice themselves. The noble soul

accepts this fact of its egoism without any question mark, also without any feeling therein of hardness, constraint, or caprice, much more as something that may be established in the primordial law of things:—if it sought a name for this, then it would say "it is justice itself." It admits, in some cases that at first make it hesitate, that there are some with rights on a par with its own; as soon as it is clear on this question of rank, it conducts itself among these equals with their equal rights with the same sureness in modesty and delicate reverence that it shows in dealing with itself—following an inborn heavenly mechanism understood by all stars. It is one *more* piece of its egoism, this refinement and self-restraint in dealing with its equals—every star is such an egoist—: it honors *itself* in them and in the rights it cedes to them, it does not doubt that the exchange of honors and rights is the essence of all relation and likewise belongs to the natural order of things. The noble soul gives as it takes, from the passionate and irascible instinct of repayment that lies at its foundation. The concept "favor" has *inter pares* no sense and fragrance; there may be a sublime manner of, say, letting presents from above happen to one and to drink them up thirstily like drops: but for this art and gesture the noble soul has no talent. Its egoism hinders it here: in general it dislikes to look "up"—rather either *ahead*, horizontally and slowly, or down—*it knows itself at a height.*—

272. Signs of nobility: never to consider lowering our duties to duties for everybody, not to want to hand over, nor to share, one's own responsibility; to reckon our privileges and their exercise among one's *duties.*

284. To live with immense and proud calm; always beyond—. Willingly to have and not have one's for and against, one's affects, to indulge them for a few hours; to *seat* oneself on them as on a horse, often as on an ass—indeed one must know how to use their stupidity as well as their fire. To retain one's three hundred foregrounds; also the dark glasses: for there are cases when no one may look into our eyes, much less in our "grounds." And to choose for company that mischievous and cheerful vice, politeness. And to stay master of one's four virtues, courage, insight, sympathy, solitude. For solitude is a virtue for us, as a sublime inclination and need for cleanliness which guesses how all contact between man and man— "in society"—must tend toward inevitable uncleanliness. All community makes, somehow, somewhere, sometime—"common."

287. —What is noble? What does the word "noble" still mean to us today? What betrays, what allows one to recognize the noble human being, beneath this heavy overcast sky of the beginning of mob rule, through which everything becomes obscure and leaden?— It is not actions that prove him—actions are always ambiguous, always unfathomable—; it is also not "works." Today one finds among artists and scholars enough of those who betray through their works how a deep desire for the noble drives them: but precisely this need *for* the noble is fundamentally different from the needs of the noble soul itself, and in fact is the eloquent and dangerous mark of its absence. It is not the works, it is the *faith*[23] that here decides, that here establishes the order of rank, to take up an old religious formula in a new and deeper sense: some fundamental certainty that a noble soul has about itself, something that cannot be sought, not found and also perhaps not lost.—The noble soul has reverence for itself.

SUGGESTIONS FOR FURTHER READING

A complete critical edition of Nietzsche's collected works, in English translation, is in progress. See Bernd Magnus, ed., *The Complete Works of Friedrich Nietzsche*, twenty volumes (Stanford, CA: Stanford University Press, 1995–).

Myths about Nietzsche's life and views make early secondary literature unreliable. Walter Kaufman's *Nietzsche: Philosopher, Psychologist, Antichrist*, 4th ed. (Princeton, NJ: Princeton University Press, [1950] 1974) was groundbreaking in showing how many of these damaging myths were false. A more recent and very accessible book by Robert C. Solomon and Kathleen M. Higgins, *What Nietzsche Really Said* (New York: Schocken Books, 2000), is a very helpful guide for the general reader with a particular interest in Nietzsche's views on moral character. Ronald Hayman's *Nietzsche: A Critical Life* (New York: Oxford University Press, 1980) is an excellent biography for general readers.

More recent intellectual biographies and studies of note include R. J. Hollingdale, *Nietzsche the Man and His Philosophy*, rev. ed. (Cambridge: Cambridge University Press, [1965] 1999); Alexander

---

23. *Glaube*, "faith" or also "belief."

Nehamas, *Nietzsche: Life as Literature* (Cambridge, MA: Harvard University Press, 1985); Richard Schact, *Nietzsche* (London: Routledge and Kegan Paul, 1983) and *Nietzsche, Genealogy, Morality: Essays on Nietzsche's "On the Genealogy of Morals"* (Berkeley: University of California Press, 1994); Lester H. Hunt, *Nietzsche and the Origin of Virtue* (London: Routledge, 1991); Peter Berkowitz, *Nietzsche: The Ethics of an Immoralist* (Cambridge, MA: Harvard University Press, 1995); Bernd Magnus and Kathleen M. Higgins, *The Cambridge Companion to Nietzsche* (Cambridge: Cambridge University Press, 1996); and Robert C. Solomon's *Living with Nietzsche: What the Great Immoralist Has to Teach Us* (Oxford: Oxford University Press, 2004). For feminist responses, see Kelly Oliver and Marilyn Pearsall, *Feminist Interpretations of Friederich Nietzsche* (University Park: Pennsylvania State University Press, 1998).

Brief introductions to Nietzsche's virtues of note include Christine Swanton, "Nietzschean Virtue Ethics," in Stephen Gardiner, ed., *Virtue Ethics Old and New* (Ithaca, NY: Cornell University Press, 2005); and "Nietzsche's Virtues," in Robert C. Solomon and Kathleen M. Higgins, *What Nietzsche Really Said* (New York: Schocken Books, 2000). For a lighthearted discussion, see Mark T. Conrad, "Thus Spake Bart: On Nietzsche and the Virtues of Being Bad," in *The Simpsons and Philosophy*, William Irwin, Mark T. Conrad, and Aeon J. Skoble, eds. (Chicago: Open Court, 2001).

PART II
CONTEMPORARY READINGS IN VIRTUE THEORY

Rosalind Hursthouse

Applying Virtue Ethics
to Our Treatment of the Other Animals

Applying virtue ethics to moral issues should be straightforward. After all, it basically just amounts to thinking about what to do using the virtue and vice terms. "I mustn't pull the cat's tail because it's cruel," I might say to myself, and surely that is simple enough. But somehow, when one turns, as a virtue ethicist, to engaging in current moral debates, applying virtue ethics becomes very difficult. Of course, applying the virtue and vice terms correctly may be difficult; one may need much practical wisdom to determine whether, in a particular case, telling a hurtful truth is cruel or not, for example, but that does not seem to be the main problem. In my experience, the main problem is just getting started. Why is this? Well, the thing I found most difficult when I was first trying to work out the virtue ethics approach to abortion was shedding the structure of thought about the issue imposed by the other two approaches, and I had the same difficulty trying to think about applying virtue ethics to our treatment of the other animals. We can't get started until we have cleared enough space to think in our own way and have found the right questions to ask.

AGAINST MORAL STATUS

In the abortion debate, the question that almost everyone began with was "What is the moral status of the fetus?" and I wasted a lot of time asking myself "What is the virtue ethicist's answer to that question?" (and, indeed, "What does virtue ethics say about that question?" and "What would the virtuous agent's answer to that question be?" and even "What would the virtuous answer

136

to that question be?"). Eventually it occurred to me to wonder *why* we were all trying to determine the moral status of the fetus and, once I saw why everyone else was, it became clear that virtue ethicists needn't bother. For everyone else was assuming the correctness of some moral rule or principle about respecting the rights of, or giving equal consideration to the interests of, or the wrongness of killing, Xs, and so they really needed to know, Are fetuses Xs or not? But we virtue ethicists had roundly declared that normative ethics did not have to consist of a system of such moral principles and that practical ethical thought was better conducted in terms of the v-rules.

The consequentialist and deontological approaches to the rights and wrongs of the ways we treat the other animals (and also the environment) are structured in exactly the same way. Here too, the question that must be answered first is "What is the moral status of the other animals (or other living things, such as trees, or indeed other natural things such as rocks and mountains)?" Here too, it is supposed that to establish that the other animals (or some subset of them) are Xs would be to establish that they have rights, or that their interests should be given the same moral weight as those of other Xs, or that prohibitions that apply to other Xs apply to them. And here too, virtue ethicists have no need to answer the question.

Moreover, we have reason to reject it. Kant's infelicitous distinction between *persons* and *things* highlights a problem inherent in this structure which virtue ethics, with its case-by-case approach, should be well fitted to avoid. Suppose that the distinction has been drawn in such a way that Xs are, in practice, mostly very similar. Xs are, let's say, rational, or self-consciousness, or human. Then the problem is that the non-Xs are bound to be a very heterogeneous class. Let us grant, for the sake of the argument, that if I am faced with an X then there are certain things I must or must not do to it. But what if I am faced with a non-X? Where is my action guidance? May I do anything to it I please, however wicked my desires? Well, if it is indeed a thing such as a bit of wastepaper or mud it is hard to imagine any wicked desires engaging with it, and perhaps the answer is, indeed, "Yes, do as you please." However, precisely because the class of non-Xs is so heterogeneous, that clearly can't be the right answer every time. Not every non-X is "just a thing" in a colloquial sense, and much of what I may or may not or ought to do to a particular non-X is going to depend in part on what features it has, other than failing to be an X.

While debates about the status of the fetus were so exclusively concerned with the issue of abortion, this problem was not glaringly obvious. What, after all, did anyone want to do with a human fetus, or embryo, but preserve it or kill it? If it was a non-X, it was something you could kill, and that was all anyone wanted to know. But then it turned out that there were other things people wanted to do with the fetuses or embryos, such as use them for experimental purposes, and the question "What may I do to this rather special sort of non-X, beyond killing it?" became pressing.

What happens when we turn to debates about the status of the other animals? Most philosophers writing on this come down on the animals' side, classifying them as Xs and thereby generate the complementary version of the problem. Now it is the Xs that form a heterogeneous class, not, it is true, as heterogeneous as Kant's "things," but still encompassing, arguably, fish and birds, mice, rats, and cockroaches, as well as the familiar domestic animals and mammals quite generally, including us. This heterogeneity makes it extremely difficult to maintain the "All Xs are equal" stance which, in the name of antispeciesism, had motivated awarding the other animals moral status in the first place.

As is well known, the chick's interest in a few years of simple henny pleasures, or its right to life as something of inherent value, turn out, in Singer and Regan,[1] to guarantee very little when they come up against my consciously contemplated future sophisticated pleasures or my right to life. The quasi-Kantian person/nonperson distinction is now drawn within the class of items accorded moral status and, although Singer and Regan can both plausibly claim that they still avoid speciesism (because of their stances on mentally incompetent humans), they do not avoid (what we might call) animal elitism. In their systems, some animals are more equal—

---

1. See Peter Singer, ed., *In Defense of Animals* (Oxford: Basil Blackwell, 1985) or for full statements of Regan's and Singer's positions, see Tom Regan, *The Case for Animal Rights* (Berkeley: University of California Press, 1985) and Peter Singer, *Animal Liberation*, rev. ed. (New York: Avon, 1990).

have a higher moral status—than others. Some moral philosophers, working within the same structure, have made this explicit.[2]

Well, one might say, what's wrong with saying that differing animals—and even human beings at differing stages of their development—have differing moral status? Isn't this just to recognize a whole variety of morally relevant features that should be taken into account when deciding what to do, instead of lumping everything together under a single principle, and isn't this what virtue ethics recommends?

I would say there are two things wrong with it.

One is that the "variety" of features recognized is so paltry, a few psychological capacities selected ad hoc to capture a few crude intuitions about which animal should win in cases where interests conflict. In this context we should note in passing the standard objection environmentalists make to the animal liberationists. It is that the latter draw no distinction between domestic and wild animals, and that what their positions on "animals" entail might be all right with respect to the former but are absurd with respect to the latter.[3]

The second is that the assigning of differing moral status is not merely recognizing a few features often relevant to good practical decision-making. It is recognizing them *and ranking* the possessors of those features accordingly. That, after all, is what the concept of status does. In welcoming recognition of (some of) the obvious differences between cats and men as an improvement on always lumping them together as sentient, or experiencing subjects of a life, virtue ethicists are not going to commit themselves in advance to saying that the cited differences will always guarantee that, in cases of conflict, it is the cats that will go to the wall because of their inferior status. After all, we can recognize differences between women and men as features that should often be taken into account when deciding what to do, without for a moment thinking that we thereby commit ourselves to any kind of ranking.

---

2. For example, Donald VanDeVeer, "Interspecific Justice," *Inquiry* 22 (1979): 55–70; and Mary Anne Warren, "Difficulties with the Strong Animal Rights Position," *Between the Species* 2 (1987): 163–173.

3. See J. Baird Callicott, "Animal Liberation: A Triangular Affair," *Environmental Ethics* 2 (1980): 311–338.

To illustrate the wrongness of both, we might briefly consider me and my cat. On any prevailing assignment of differing moral status, my psychological capacities easily outrank my cat's. If you can only rescue one of us from the burning building without danger to yourself, you should rescue me, preserving the animal that has the higher status. What if I have escaped by myself, should you then rescue the cat? Most people say no, unless you really can do it with no danger to yourself at all, because you outrank the cat too and should preserve the animal with the higher status. Is the same obviously true of me?

I would say that this is, at least, not obvious. For a further feature of the cat relevant to my decision-making is that he is *my* cat, a cat for whom I have assumed responsibility. Although it would, I take it, be sentimental idiocy of me to run a high risk of dying to rescue him, and highly irresponsible if I have family and friends, I am inclined to say that, if the risk, though real, is fairly low, and no one will be devastated by my death, going to rescue him might well be a good decision. After all, despite my superior moral status, my life mightn't be worth much, and although I can't risk your life on the grounds that it isn't worth much, I can surely risk my own.

Moreover, it is not obviously the case that, just because you outrank my cat, you are not in any way called upon to rescue him. I am reliably informed that people with the further feature of being firemen regard rescuing animals from burning buildings (when the risk is not extreme) as part of their normal duties.

Given these problems, virtue ethics can dismiss the question of the moral status of animals without a qualm. As a tool in the abortion debate, the concept of moral status had its uses. In my view, assigning the embryo or fetus a certain moral status was a clumsy (and often wildly inaccurate) attempt to capture what I called "the right attitude to the familiar biological facts" of how we come to be, and that's worth doing. However, in the context of the ethics of our treatment of the other animals it is simply useless. There isn't one familiar set of facts concerning *the* other animals, but a whole host of sets of (largely unfamiliar) facts about different species, and another host of sets about individual animals, and another host about groups—pets, zoo animals, the animals we eat, the animals we experiment on. . . . Questions about right and wrong actions in relation to animals arise in a wide variety of contexts, far too many to be settled by a blanket assignment of status.

Since there are so many different questions about right and wrong, I'll just jump into one of the most familiar areas, *viz.*—

VEGETARIANISM

The first thing for a virtue ethicist to say about vegetarianism, to correct a surprisingly common mistake, is that it cannot be a virtue. This is a grammatical, not an ethical, claim. Vegetarianism can't be a virtue because it is not a character trait but a practice, and virtues have to be character traits. Well, is it a virtuous practice? If we take that as asking "Is it a practice which, as such, manifests or expresses virtue?" the answer is "Obviously not" because people can become vegetarians for such a range of different reasons. If I become vegetarian on health grounds it might well manifest temperance, but if I go in for it simply because it is fashionable it would be a mark of folly.

However, if we take "Is it a virtuous practice?" as asking "Is it a practice that the virtuous, as such, go in for (or ideally, would go in for); i.e., a practice it is right to go in for?" we get to the question that someone employing a normative virtue ethics is supposed to address.

One way I begin to approach it is by taking several leaves out of Singer's first book, *Animal Liberation*. As some reviewers on the Amazon.com Web site note, you can skip over Singer's philosophy in this book without missing anything important. What is doing the work are the detailed descriptions of factory farming (and animal experimentation). Thirty years ago,[4] they showed his readers that what we are being party to in eating meat is a huge amount of animal suffering that could be substantially reduced if we changed our habits. So I take the leaves on which he does that and think about them in terms of, for example, compassion, temperance, callousness, cruelty, greed, self-indulgence—and honesty.

Can I, in all honesty, deny the ongoing existence of this suffering? No, I can't. I know perfectly well that although there have been some improvements in the regulation of factory farming, what is going on is still terrible. Can I think it is anything but callous to shrug this off and say it doesn't matter? No, I can't. Can I deny that

---

4. The first edition of Singer's *Animal Liberation* appeared in 1975.

the practices are cruel? No, I can't. Then what am I doing being party to them? It won't do for me to say that I am not actually engaging in the cruelty myself. There is a large gap between not being cruel and being truly compassionate, and the virtue of compassion is what I am supposed to be acquiring and exercising. I can no more think of myself as compassionate while I am party to such cruelty than I could think of myself as just if, scrupulously avoiding owning slaves, I still enjoyed the fruits of slave labor.

What if I needed to eat meat to survive? That would, of course, be a very different situation. No one would think of many Africans, situated as they are, as being short of compassion solely on the grounds that they ate whatever the aid agencies provided. But that is not how it is with me, nor with anyone in a sufficiently privileged position to be reading this book. Once again, honesty compels me to admit that I do not *need* meat, I just *like* it. A lot. It gives me an enormous amount of pleasure. However, precisely what temperance requires is that I do not pursue such pleasure while ignoring the claims of the other virtues. Pursuing the pleasures of consuming meat, in the teeth of the claims of compassion, is just plain greedy and self-indulgent.

Suppose that, on occasion, I eat meat not in the pursuit of pleasure, but for some other reason? I have many hospitable meat-eating friends. Before they all know that I am vegetarian, am I to be Banquo at their feasts, refusing not only the meat, but the anchovy-corrupted salad and the stock-made soup, inflicting on my hosts the embarrassment of having nothing to offer me but bread, potatoes, and a couple of bananas? Politeness and consideration would give me good reason to eat what was put in front of me and that would not count as greedy or self-indulgent. Should I not have telephoned them well beforehand to tell them that I have become a vegetarian? Well, sometimes yes; there would be circumstances in which it was either thoughtless or (supposing I had thought about it) cowardly, in a way, not to do so. I don't telephone, and I eat what is put in front of me, because I want to avoid the confrontation and the cries of "Oh no, not you too! I thought you had more sense." But, after all, I think I have sense on my side; in ducking the issue I merely manifest the fact that I lack the courage of my conviction.

Of course all my friends will have to know one day that I have become vegetarian, and most will change their menus accordingly, at least somewhat, when they have me to dinner. Some may choose to ignore it (this is less common than it used to be) and what then? Their doing so is hardly a mark of the quasi-virtue of friendship, but neither is my continuing to attend their dinner parties, bringing embarrassment and censure to the table every time I do. (Other guests will notice how little I am eating and ask why, or whether I am vegetarian; on learning that I am they will naturally ask, Did our hosts not know? I can't lie about it so I will say yes, they know, or imply by my smile or shrug that that is so.) So I could give up the friendship, or I could excuse myself from their invitations but continue to have them to my (vegetarian) dinner parties in the hope they will come round. Or I could initiate our talking about it—not about their becoming vegetarian, but about their being more conciliatory about my having done so.

So, with respect to vegetarianism, a virtue ethicist may reach roughly the same practical conclusions as Singer and, albeit to a lesser extent, Regan, though on different grounds. The practices that bring cheap meat to our tables are cruel, so we shouldn't be party to them.

EXPERIMENTS ON THE OTHER ANIMALS

Does virtue ethics run the same line of thought about using sentient animals in scientific experiments? To a limited extent, yes. In other ways, no—not, or at least not immediately, because of virtue ethics' "human centeredness" (of which more later) but, surprisingly, because of virtue ethics' extreme practicality.

Let me deal very briefly with the first, in part because it will allow me to clear up a common misconception of cruelty. Consider the use of the other animals to test cosmetics. A virtue ethicist should agree with Singer and Regan that this is wrong, for it is, in my view, quite certain that such experiments are cruel. However, this is not beyond question, since some philosophers, such as Regan, maintain that cruel actions are limited to the intentional causing (or allowing) another to suffer by an agent who either enjoys or is indifferent to it.

This claim enables Regan and those who follow him to reject the idea that the prohibition against cruelty will suffice to ground any robust negative duties to animals. For, they point out, it allows people to subject animals to suffering as long as they regret the necessity. However, the claim is quite false, as a quick look at a dictionary should remind us. The causing of pain or suffering can count as cruel even when it is unintentional; people can be found guilty of cruelty to children and animals without the prosecution having to establish intent. More commonly, a cruel action is intentional, but the agent's professed or manifest purpose is quite enough, and neither his pleasure, his indifference, nor his regret is required for the assessment of his action as cruel or not. All that is needed is that the action is the infliction of pain for a purpose that does not justify it. Some experimenters on animals have inflicted horrifying suffering on cats; their purpose was to discover how much pain cats can stand before it kills them. Such experiments can be rightly condemned as cruel simply on the grounds that the knowledge gained was far too insignificant to justify the experiments, without any consideration of the experimenters' feelings.

The same is true of experiments to test new cosmetics, for, as Singer so rightly remarks, we don't *need* any new cosmetics, and, as virtue ethicists mindful of the vices of vanity and self-indulgence could add, we don't actually need any cosmetics at all. Their use could be a harmless pleasure, but only if limited to the use of those produced by companies that do not test their products on the other animals.

So, as before, the three different approaches may reach the same practical conclusion regarding the use of animals to test cosmetics—that we should refrain from being party to these practices. A utilitarian shouldn't be party to the infliction of unnecessary suffering, a deontologist to the violation of rights, and a virtue ethicist to cruel practices.

However—moving on now to the ways in which a virtue ethicist cannot continue to pursue this line—this is action guidance only if "refraining from being party to such practices" can amount to something that I can *do*, something that people who are being party to them don't do. It is ironic that the critics of virtue ethics, claiming that it couldn't give an account of right or wrong action and *hence* couldn't provide action guidance, failed to notice that, in many cases, for most of us, their establishing that an action type is wrong provided no action guidance whatsoever. This is true for many people regarding experiments on animals to test cosmetics, and becomes striking when we turn to the field of medical experimentation.

It is here that the issue of moral standing is assumed to be crucial. Medical experimentation on the other animals is directed toward saving, and improving, the lives of human beings. If many of the other animals used have the same moral status as human beings, then either we should be using brain-damaged orphans instead, or we shouldn't be doing it at all; it is wrong. What could be more important than establishing whether or not this is so?

But why is it so important, practically speaking? Suppose I had accepted that Singer and Regan have, in their different ways, shown that most/all experiments on the other animals are wrong. How does that provide action guidance? What does it tell me to do? Obviously, to refrain from performing such experiments. For most of us, that's not an issue. I'm not an experimental biologist or technician, I'm a philosopher. So is just continuing to be a philosopher all their arguments tell me to do? That's also what I would do if I had rejected their conclusions.

As we have just seen, for some people, for some of the experimental practices, what one should do is obvious enough. Women who regularly buy cosmetics, and the few men who buy them for themselves or their partners, should refrain from buying them from companies that test their products on animals because we shouldn't be party to that practice. This leaves those who have no reason to buy cosmetics unaddressed, and, more importantly, leaves us without any action guidance with respect to the vast field of medical experimentation. What *is* it to refrain from being party to medical experimentation on animals? One might, if the choice were offered, refuse to save or prolong one's life by accepting a transplant of a vital organ from a nonhuman animal, but that is an issue for very few of us. And, short of refraining from *any* of the benefits modern medicine has to offer, there doesn't seem to be anything that most of us could do that would count as "refraining from being party to the practice."

If normative ethics is to be truly about action, finding things to do with respect to medical experimentation on animals is far, far more important for philosophers concerned about our treatment of the other animals than trying to work out whether or not human lives and suffering count in some way more than the lives and suffering of the animals used, or whether the rights of human beings outrank theirs. Whichever way the arguments fall out, for or against, the conclusions on their own won't say anything practical to most of us.

They are philosophical exercises we engage in, but not to discover what each of us, individually, should do about medical experimentation on animals. Suppose I do reach the conclusion that experimenting on a nonhuman animal is every bit as wrong as experimenting on a brain-damaged orphan. "So," I say to myself, "I must . . ." Must what? Practically speaking, I am no better off than I would have been if I had concluded that it isn't as wrong, but still, in many cases, it may be very wrong, or quite wrong. Now, why is this?

Here we come to another piece of the structure imposed by the other two approaches that needs to be unpicked. I should note that I do not think the following mistake is intrinsic to the other two approaches, only that, in practice, their overly theoretic stance has resulted in its prevalence.

Suppose one begins doing normative theory by thinking in terms of providing a systematic account of why "act X" or "such and such an action" is right or wrong. The intentionally abstract phrases leave it unsettled whether one is talking about action types or action tokens, and, moreover, whether the action—type or token—is, or forms, part of a practice. Sometimes this doesn't matter. Given an act description such as "lying," direct utilitarianism will tell you when a token is right and when it is wrong, and deontology will tell you that the action type is wrong and hence each token is (or that the action type lying-in-such-and-such-circumstances is wrong though the action type lying-in-so-and-so-circumstances is justifiable), and with the ascription of wrongness to a token, that is, an individual action, we have our general action guidance.

The prevalent mistake lies in assuming that what goes for something like "lying" goes for any other act description; that is, that getting "is wrong" attached to it is going to provide general action guidance by somehow hooking up with an action token. Lying is not a practice, but a type of individual action that any one of us might do on almost any occasion. When practices are what is at issue, it is much harder to get to individual actions that any one of us might do or refrain from doing.

Singer overlooked this problem in the first edition of *Practical Ethics*,[5] failing to notice that while the direct utilitarianism he had committed himself to might support the conclusion that farmers

---

5. Peter Singer, *Practice Ethics* (Cambridge: Cambridge University Press, 1979). A second, expanded edition appeared in 1993.

should stop meat production; it did not license his conclusion that I should not buy meat in supermarkets. He had argued that the *practices* of producing meat were wrong, that those who engaged in it were failing to give equal consideration to the interests of the animals involved. Yet when I turn up at the supermarket and follow his instruction "to take account of the interests of all those sentient beings affected by my decision," I know that my individual action of buying meat is not going to affect the interests of any nonhuman animal, except, perhaps, my dog. His claim that I should not be party to these wrong practices needed the support of the indirect utilitarianism he introduced in the second edition.

Here again, it is a mistake to assume that what goes for one description of a practice goes for any other description; that is, that attaching "is wrong" to it is always going to provide corresponding guidance to be derived from "being party to the practice is wrong." You have to look at the practice at issue and see what it is like.

Medical experimentation is, unlike lying, a practice. But, unlike meat production, it is not a practice that any one of us can readily, in our individual actions, refrain from being party to. What is it like?

It is a practice that is deeply entrenched in a powerful, and also well entrenched, set of institutions—not only medical schools training doctors, medical research centers, and corporate research centers and laboratories seeking drugs or treatments that will make money, but also universities training students who can then work in such places, some of whom will remain in the universities doing research that may feed back into the training of the doctors and medical and corporate research centers. This set of interlocked institutions is something that most of us, individually, are utterly powerless to change.

That is why the debate over whether "*it*," or only *many*, or *some*, aspects of it, are wrong is not important, practically speaking. Settling that issue one way or the other will not make most of us one whit less powerless.

Conversely, making no more than the modest assumption, consistent with any outcome of the debate a philosopher might reach, that at least *some* of it is wrong, is enough to get us going, once we have it under that description—a practice entrenched in an interlocked and also entrenched set of institutions. We have to begin by thinking about what changes that sort of setup. Racism was like that, and although it still is to some extent, things have improved enough in the last forty years for us to be able to look back and learn something from the changes. What brought them about?

In part, as we know, the leadership of some great figures such as Martin Luther King and Nelson Mandela. In part, as we know, the courage and determination of a great number of black people. However, as we also know, in part the individually insignificant but collectively influential actions and reactions of a great number of white people. Some people were in a position to do more than others; for example, lawyers, journalists, writers, and teachers— and academics, being both writers and teachers. Some of them joined in the collective action and some of them didn't. A lot of what was done was, individually, very insignificant indeed. People signed petitions, joined pressure groups, went on perfectly safe marches, voted for politicians who spoke against racism. And, I suppose, argued and often broke off relations with their parents and some of their friends. These are not the sorts of things one can recount with justifiable pride when asked "What did you do about racism in the sixties, Mummy?" but they were things that almost anybody white could do, they were worth doing, and again, not everybody did them.

We are, perhaps, inclined to think that "What would a virtuous agent do in the circumstances?" has to be answered by the description of an action that merits praise. That certainly is not always true; it depends on the circumstances. When I do something as ordinary as tell the truth in response to the stranger's question "How do I get to the station from here?" I do what is honest. When I leave a standard tip for the waiter who brought me my coffee I do what is just. Such actions are too minimally decent to call for praise, and since "virtuous" is a term of praise, it is contrary to common usage to call them "virtuous." However, they are no less "what a virtuous agent would do in the circumstances" just because they hardly call for virtue and are regularly done by a lot of people who doubtless fall far short of possessing it. In the circumstances imagined here, there isn't anything else for the virtuous agent to do, the doing of which would distinguish her from the nonvirtuous, either the merely conventional or the dishonest and unjust.

Now the white antiracists who signed petitions and so on did a bit better than that. Protesting against the prevailing convention, they did distinguish themselves from the merely conventional, and from the unjust racist and also from the cynics and those who despaired of bringing about change and were paralyzed by their individual powerlessness. If they hadn't, things would still be just as bad as they once were.

Much of this is directly transferable to the issue of medical experimentation. Any of us can sign petitions, support animal-rights pressure groups, and vote for politicians who speak up on behalf of the other animals. In this context, the role that lawyers play in combating the racism entrenched in the legal systems will mostly have to be played by scientists within the set of institutions that enshrine the practice, but it is up to the rest of us, collectively, to make enough noise to get more of them concerned about bringing about changes.

Some people are in a position to do more than others. A growing number of science undergraduates now refuse to do animal dissections. I gather (without being quite sure) that some have just been kicked out of their classes and thereby forced to fail them, but I have also been told on good authority that, in some universities at least, the system has been changed to accommodate them. Some people can get onto the ethics committees that, in some institutions, now regulate, to some extent, the use of the other animals, and some can campaign to get such committees established.

Suppose one does get on such a committee, what should one do? Isn't this a situation in which one would have to make up one's mind one way or the other whether at least some of the other animals had the same moral status as human beings? In my view, no, because if you decide that they do, and argue and vote against every experiment that comes under scrutiny, you will just be thrown off the committee. Your only chance of staying on and achieving anything at all is to join forces with those who are arguing and voting against the experiments whose benefits to humans are (in Singer's words) "either non-existent or very uncertain." But suppose you really, truly believe it? Is it not a failure of integrity, or shameful hypocrisy, to allow any of the experiments to pass without protest, however fruitless? How could a virtuous agent do that?

Well, if you really believed in the equal moral status, for you the set of institutions in which medical experimentation is entrenched would, I think, be comparable to the set of institutions imposed by the Nazis. Yet most of the people we admire from that dreadful time concentrated on doing the very little that they could, "allowing" many Jews to go to the death camps "without protest," and we do not condemn them for hypocrisy or lack of integrity. Think of Schindler, jovially entertaining powerful members of the SS while he schemed to get more Jews into the protection of his factory.[6] How, situated as he was, could he have shown more virtue?

True, everyone who did anything to help the Jews in Germany or the occupied countries risked their lives, and so we admire them for their courage as well as their compassion, justice, and practical wisdom. Their virtue was, in Philippa Foot's words, "severely tested" and passed the test.[7] It may be that some of those who are strongly committed to the cause of animal liberation yearn for some appropriately heroic expression of this strong commitment, something that would severely test their virtue, finding it intolerable that all they can find to do are such trifling things as sign petitions and join pressure groups.

There is no reason to suppose that, for many of us, there is any such expression. Think of racism again. There was very little most people living outside South Africa could do to express their commitment to ending apartheid beyond boycotting South African goods and the usual trifling things one hopes will, eventually, influence one's government to bring more pressure to bear. Aristotle does not give enough attention to the nameless virtue, which we might now call proper modesty, that consists in correctly assessing one's limited capacities to achieve great things, being more interested in its grand form, *megalopsuchia*. No doubt in such a tiny democracy as his Athens, the idea that change could be brought about only through years of collective endeavor made up of individually insignificant actions was unlikely to occur to him. However, that is how things are with us now. It is not heroic courage but unexciting virtues that call us to such actions—amongst them, hope, patience, and modesty.

You may complain that none of what I have said about our actions in relation to the other animals is exciting but all pretty obvious. I think myself that this is how it should be. Most of the results of applying virtue ethics *should* be pretty obvious, because,

---

6. Thomas Keneally, *Schindler's Ark* (London: Hodder and Stoughton, 1982).

7. Philippa Foot, *Virtues and Vices* (Oxford: Oxford University Press, 2002).

rather than constructing theoretical principles, virtue ethics just applies the everyday virtue and vice terms to our actions in the world as we find it. But what is there to be found, even right under our noses, is often not obvious until it is pointed out. We have to make sure we really are looking at the ways human beings are affecting the world and, if they are bad, that we ask ourselves "What can I do?" instead of getting tied up in abstruse questions about moral status.

HUMAN-CENTEREDNESS

It will not have escaped the observant reader that much of the preceding discussion smacks more of consequentialism than of an absolutist rights-based position. Of course, virtue ethicists have always shared a form of antiabsolutism with consequentialists, agreeing with them that many act types—lying, killing, meateating—are right in some circumstances, wrong in others, adding "depending on the circumstances" rather than "on the consequences." This might lead a committed animal-rights advocate to protest—as Regan protests against Singer—that someone approaching the matter via the virtue ethical term "cruel" has really missed the point. "[W]hat is fundamentally wrong," Regan says, "isn't the pain, isn't the suffering . . . [though] [t]hese compound what's wrong. The fundamental wrong" is viewing animals "as *our resources.*"[8] Hence his insistence that the other animals have inherent, rather than merely instrumental, value. Can virtue ethicists take some leaves from Regan's book too?

Well, we had better not do so by taking on the blanket ascription of inherent or intrinsic value, because that will take us straight back into moral status territory and the usual problems of whether Xs have the same value as, or less value than, non-Xs. We can recast talk about things having intrinsic value as talk about their being worth our pursuing or having or preserving (or bringing into being, protecting, maintaining, restoring, desiring, loving . . .) for their own sake, and there is no reason why virtue ethicists shouldn't

---

8. Tom Regan, "The Case for Animal Rights," in Peter Singer, ed., *In Defense of Animals* (Oxford: Basil Blackwell, 1985), p. 13.

agree with Regan that the good of the other animals is such a thing and thereby has intrinsic value in that sense.

Unconstrained by the need to assign moral status, and thereby to find a feature (such as being the experiencing subject of a life) that grounds it, there is no reason for us to stop there. The environmental ethics literature has compellingly reminded us that species, and the good of plants and ecosystems, also have "intrinsic value"—that is, in our terms, they are also worth our pursuing or preserving, protecting, desiring, and so on for their own sake, not merely for our own.[9]

However, it is often supposed that virtue ethics (or at least, Aristotelian or eudaimonistic virtue ethics) has a peculiar problem in ascribing intrinsic value in *any* robust sense to the other animals, let alone to plants or ecosystems, because, it is thought, it counts *human* flourishing or the good *human* life (*eudaimonia*) or *human* virtue as "the fundamental" or "top" value. Thereby, it is thought, virtue ethics is objectionably "human-centered," regarding the rest of nature as no better than a resource for *us*.[10]

This is a mistake (or set of mistakes) but it is hard to pin down how it arises. Let's begin by considering *eudaimonia*—i.e., human flourishing or the good human life—separately from virtue. At least part of the trouble arises from misunderstanding the role this plays in eudaimonistic virtue ethics and trying to identify that role in terms of its "counting as the top value."

According to ancient Greek ethics, my final, architectonic end—and everyone else's—is indeed *human* flourishing, living a good human life. But, as Julia Annas has frequently pointed out,[11] this is not, in itself, a form of egoism, nor, we may now add, does it in any way privilege the value of *human* flourishing or *human* life. It

---

9. It is, I think, in the area of "environmental," rather than "animal" ethics—assuming that to be a currently comprehensible division of the academic literature—that discussion of wild animals belongs, though space does not permit it here.

10. See, for example, Holmes Rolston III, "Environmental Virtue Ethics: Half the Truth but Dangerous as a Whole," in Philip Cafaro and Ronald Sandler, eds., *Environmental Virtue Ethics* (New York: Rowman and Littlefield, 2005), pp. 61–74.

11. In many places, but see *The Morality of Happiness* (Oxford: Oxford University Press, 1993), especially pp. 127–128, 223, 322–325.

is not egoistic in virtue of its directing me to think about *my* flourishing, *my* good life. I am to think about how I should live *my* life, how to give it a shape, simply because it is only *my* life that I can live, not because I am to take it to be necessarily more worth preserving than yours. It is not chauvinistic in virtue of its saying that my end—and everyone else's—is human flourishing, living a good human life. This doesn't rank human life over other animals' lives and direct me to choose to live a human one because it is more valuable. I have no choice. Since I am a human being, there is no other kind of life I could live.

So far, the content of human eudaimonia has been left unspecified. Let us move on to (human) virtue. As Annas has also stressed,[12] ancient eudaimonism could, and did, take an egoistic form—when, that is, *eudaimonia* is taken to be the life of pleasure. No doubt someone who lived only for pleasure (of the egoistical sort) would indeed regard the rest of nature, as well as other human beings, as no better than resources, but things are very different when we take *eudaimonia* to be the life of virtue. Just as the exercise of virtues such as charity, generosity, justice, and the quasi virtue of friendship, necessarily involves *not* focusing on oneself and one's virtue but on the rights, interests, and good of other human beings, so the exercise of compassion and the avoidance of a number of vices, involves focusing on the good of the other animals as something worth pursuing, preserving, protecting, and so on.

It is a commonplace of our thoughts about virtue—not only philosophical virtue ethicists' thoughts, but everyday thoughts, reflected in common usage—that the exercise of virtues such as charity, friendship, courage, honesty, and justice may, if one is unlucky, turn out to involve laying down one's life. This not only makes it clear that one's individual virtuous actions are not aimed directly at either one's *eudaimonia* or one's personal virtue, but also that it is not virtue ethics, *per se*, which says that such self-sacrifice could not be required by virtue if what was at stake was "only" another animal, or the survival of a species or an ecosystem. It is not virtue ethics that says such things are not worth dying for; it is our everyday use of "worthwhile" and the virtue and vice terms.

---

12. Ibid.

Everyday usage of the virtue and vice vocabulary is indeed human-centered by and large (compassion and cruelty are the obvious exceptions) and we know why; namely, that centuries of Western ethical thought have been human-centered. Thereby, the same is true of our everyday use of such terms as "duty," "obligation," "rights" and "right" and "wrong" applied to actions. The problem of traditional human-centeredness is one that every philosopher who wants to change our attitudes toward the other animals and the rest of nature has to face, not one peculiar to virtue ethics.

Singer and Regan have become rightly famous for making it obvious to many of us that a great deal of gratuitous suffering is involved in our use of some of the other animals for food and experimental purposes. Once we have brought ourselves to recognize this fact, the ordinary usage of "cruel" and "compassionate" latches on to it quite unproblematically. However, as environmentalists constantly urge, we need a substantial change in our outlook to get any further—in virtue ethics' terms, a clearly seen and affective recognition of the fact that human beings, and thereby human lives, are not only interwoven with each other but with the rest of nature. Then, and only then, will we apply virtue ethics correctly to what we are doing.

SUGGESTIONS FOR FURTHER READING

Much of the literature analyzing contemporary issues from a virtue ethics perspective makes use of Aristotelian conceptions of virtue, even when the source of these conceptions is not named. Simply by combining the search term "virtue" with any topic of interest in databases of philosophical, ethical, and/or social criticism, one can find a wealth of material (although care must be taken to determine that the conceptions employed really are Aristotelian and not drawn from some other source).

Edmund D. Pellegrino has argued for a virtue ethics approach to medicine grounded in both Aristotle and Aquinas in a number of essays, including "The Virtuous Physician and the Ethics of Medicine," in *Virtue and Medicine*, Earl E. Shelp, ed. (Dordrect: Reidel, 1985). Justin Oakley and Dean Cocking have argued for a more strictly Aristotelian virtue ethics of medicine and other traditional professions in "A Virtue Ethics Approach to Professional Roles,"

Chapter 3 of their book, *Virtue Ethics and Professional Roles* (Cambridge: Cambridge University Press, 2001), pp. 74–94. Rosalind Hursthouse discusses such an approach to the morality of abortion in "Virtue Theory and Abortion," *Philosophy and Public Affairs* 20 (1991): 223–246. Susan S. Stocker discusses the views of Aristotle and Nietzsche in "Facing Disability with Resources from Aristotle and Nietzsche," *Medicine, Health Care and Philosophy: A European Journal* 5 (2002): 137–146. On the ethics of extending life and age-based rationing of health care, see Susan M. Purviance, "Age Rationing, the Virtues, and Wanting More Life," *Journal of Medical Humanities* 14 (1993): 149–165; and Juliet Cassuto Rothman, *Aristotle's Eudaimonia, Terminal Illness, and the Question of Life Support* (New York: Lang, 1993).

Aristotelian approaches to the ethics of other professions are not lacking; see, e.g., Michael Milde, "Legal Ethics: Why Aristotle Might be Helpful," *Journal of Social Philosophy* 33 (2002): 45–66; Louis G. Lombardi, "Character Versus Codes: Models for Research Ethics," *International Journal of Applied Philosophy* 5 (1990): 21–28; and Douglas J. Crawford-Brown, "Virtue as the Basis of Engineering Ethics," *Science and Engineering Ethics* 3 (1997): 481–489. There is also increasing interest in Aristotle's work in business ethics; see, e.g., Robert C. Solomon, "Corporate Roles, Personal Virtues: An Aristotelian Approach to Business Ethics," *Business Ethics Quarterly* 2 (1992): 317–339; Howard Harris, "Courage as a Management Virtue," *Business and Professional Ethics Journal* 18 (1999): 27–46; and Peter Hadreas, "Aristotle on the Vices and Virtue of Wealth," *Journal of Business Ethics* 39 (2002): 361–376. On environmental issues, see Susanne E. Foster, "Aristotle and the Environment," *Environmental Ethics* 24 (2002): 409–428.

Julia Annas

Seneca:
Stoic Philosophy as a Guide to Living

Seneca is a philosopher who appeals to people who are not philosophers. He writes in a way that is accessible to a variety of readers, and draws us in with his forceful and intense style. Moreover, he writes, in the main, about topics that concern all of us: what happiness really is, what we truly want out of life. And he writes in an engaged way: he wants his writing to make a difference, both to himself and to the reader, to make both parties better people. At some periods he has been a popular writer, one whose works trickle down, often in simplified form, to a broad, diverse audience looking for advice. Interestingly, this is increasingly happening today, as popular forms of stoicism appear among, and are sometimes influential in, self-help books and popular manuals about living your life better. I have seen an Italian popular book called *Seneca for Managers*, and Seneca recently figured as one of the "Five Greatest Advice Books of All Time" in the syndicated column of the business advice writer Dale Dauten.[1]

This may at first appear rather surprising, for two reasons. One is that when we actually read Seneca we find claims that run quite counter to common sense. Virtue is sufficient for happiness, Seneca tells us; reason is what is natural for humans and so virtue is the perfection of reason. Moreover, virtue is the only good; everything else (and he does mean *everything* else: riches, health, status) is not good, and is "external" to happiness. Whatever we think of these claims, how can they be the basis of good advice as to how we are

---

1. "Stoic advises focus on virtue, wisdom en route to success," Dale Dauten, *The Corporate Curmudgeon*, published in the *Arizona Daily Star*, Business Section, January 10, 2003.

to live? If we take these claims seriously, aren't they likely to turn us away from everyday life, if anything? How can anything so high-minded help managers and businesspeople?

Second, if we read Seneca looking for advice, we may at first find ourselves persistently frustrated by the highly general level at which he speaks. We tend to think of advice as being what we need when we have a particular problem to solve. Should I persist in a relationship in which my partner is acting selfishly? What difference does it make whether children are involved? Should I give an employee a deserved promotion when this will create resentment and office disharmony? What we want from advice, we may think, is a directive, to be told "Yes" or "No" to such questions. Advice, we think, should surely tell us what to do. Seneca tells us to strive to become virtuous, even where this is very difficult, to try to rise above being concerned with money, health, and everyday matters that tend to claim our attention. This isn't telling us what to do in the sense of directing us to specific actions. It may seem that it is uselessly general for answering our problems, and thus for giving us advice.

Yet Seneca remains among the popular self-help and guidance books, so there must be something he is getting right. People clearly do not reject ethical guidance just because it is pitched at a demanding level and they clearly do get practical help in living their lives from being told to care more about wisdom and virtue than money.

Seneca is grounded in stoic philosophy; that is, in logic and metaphysics as well as ethics, and his grounding is thorough— there is no doubt that he has worked through all areas of stoic philosophy rigorously. He is not, however, writing for other experts in stoic philosophy; he writes for people who are aspiring beginners in living a stoic life, and he regards himself as being one of them, able to help others but still direly in need of help himself. He is not writing an easy introduction to stoic philosophy for people who merely have a detached interest in knowing about it; he is writing to make a difference, to himself and others, in living in a stoic way.

This committed feature of Seneca's writings has continued to attract readers, but it also means that Seneca is doing something very difficult, which is being constantly in danger of falling between two stools. He thinks that we will not live better lives until we become stoics; that is, come to accept a particular theory of what is valuable and how to live our lives in a way that reflects this. We need to accept this theory, moreover, as a result of reasoning and thinking deeply about it for ourselves, not just as a result of parroting a teacher or being influenced by a book. Seneca realizes that it would be counterproductive just to face people with the full stoic theory; few, other than professional philosophers, will be motivated to work through all the technicalities and the full range of issues, which to a beginner may well appear daunting and irrelevant to everyday concerns. He needs, therefore, to give us the basic ideas that are central to concerns we already have, especially the pressing concern of how to live our lives better, and to engage us in a way which will encourage us to think about these issues for ourselves, rather than think that the job is done once we can recite a few formulas. We won't understand these ideas properly, and hence will not use them properly to guide our lives, unless we ourselves ask for the reasons supporting them, and thus broaden our own understanding of the stoic account of ethics (and ultimately of the wider background to ethics). We won't get going on this at all unless we engage, from where we are, with the right ideas in a way that will get us involved. What Seneca is doing here is recognizably similar to the aims of many contemporary self-help books; they aim to convey a specific set of ideas which the reader has to accept, not just passively but as something to internalize and put to work in his or her own life. In Seneca's case his aim is to get us to care, in a deeper way than we do, about virtue.

What are the specifically stoic ideas we must accept in order to live better? How can accepting these ideas do anything for us by way of practical advice?

Stoic ethics is in the mainstream of ancient ethics in being eudaimonist: it takes it to be a shared assumption that we all seek happiness. Happiness here is not to be understood, as it often is nowadays, as feeling good, or any kind of enjoyable feeling. Happiness here applies to your life as a whole, not to feelings or episodes. In aiming to be happy we are aiming to live flourishing lives, live well, and this is an achievement that we have to work at rather than a feeling that just comes to us. Questions that for us tend to be posed in terms of how best to live our lives are structured in ancient theories in terms of happiness. This is something we need to bear in mind, as otherwise stoics may appear to be making implausible claims about getting what we want, or getting what makes us feel good.

What actually renders us happy in this sense, gets us to think that we have achieved a flourishing life? Common sense gives us answers like these: having money; having a certain standard of living, or, perhaps more importantly, having a certain status involving respect for what we do; having good health and the opportunities for varied activity.

Eudaimonist ethical theories, including many that are currently called types of "virtue ethics," check us right at the start by telling us that this is the wrong *kind* of answer. Happiness is not a matter of the stuff you have—things like cars and houses, money, even factors like health and status. As you start thinking reflectively about living your life in one way rather than another, in a way that reflects and expresses a particular view about what is valuable, you are taking control of living your life and trying to *do* something with it. From this point of view, things like cars, houses, and money, as well as factors like health and status, are all just material you have to work on, what we could regard as the circumstances of our life that we have to do something with before we can regard our life as something that we are *living*, rather than just going along with.

It is not the stuff, the material of your life, that makes you happy. *You* make yourself happy (or not) in the way you live your life. Like a craftsperson making something from raw materials, you make something of your life by using your reason, particularly by reasoning about how to live your life in a way in which money, health, and other things play one kind of role rather than another. Someone who has just picked up from the culture the idea that wealth is a good thing, and devotes their life to accumulating ever more money, is making the mistake of thinking that stuff makes you happy. At some point he or she has to realize that just accumulating money leaves the person unsure what to do with it and how to spend it. She may well find it hard to use it meaningfully rather than in ways ever more pointlessly devoted to the accumulation of more. It is because common sense does not tell us what to do in our lives with health, money, and status once we have got these that people who are successful in all these ways are still often left with confused and unsatisfactory lives, and seek help from people who offer to help them live better—whether contemporary self-help manuals or writers like Seneca.

How should we live our lives, then? This is where virtue enters in. Most of us accept that virtue is some part of a life that can be called flourishing. We recognize that greedy, competitive, and devious people are disabling themselves from developing deep relationships of mutual trust with others, and that cowardice prevents a person from standing up for what she believes in, and thus lets her life be organized in terms of other people's priorities. We think, at the level of common sense, that if we bring our children up to be fair, brave, and generous they will have better lives than if we bring them up to be dishonest, cowardly, and mean. While we recognize that the fair and generous may encounter bad luck, and end up failures in worldly terms, we don't take this to be reason to bring children up to be grudging and devious.

Ethical theories whose basis is virtue claim more than this. Being virtuous is, they claim, necessary for flourishing; that is, people who aren't virtuous are not happy, however rich, famous, and otherwise enviable they may appear. The stoics go even further: virtue is, they think, both necessary and sufficient for being happy. Not only are rich and famous but wicked people not happy, *nothing* else matters for happiness except being virtuous. Other things, such as health and wealth, are what they call "indifferent."

When these ideas are presented in a technical way, as in some of our stoic texts, with reasons for the claims and arguments linking them, they can seem arid and hard to understand. However, as we can see from Seneca's letters and essays, they can also be presented in a way that makes them attractive to someone who has not studied philosophy but is at least sympathetic to the idea of living her life in a way that systematically reflects a theory about what is valuable, rather than mindlessly going along with what people in her society happen to value.

To hold that virtue is sufficient for happiness is to hold, for a start, that there are two radically different kinds of value that we recognize in our lives. We think it better to be healthy than ill, better to have money than none, better to be respected rather than to be despised, and so on. We can also come to see that none of these things has the same kind of value as the value of acting bravely, generously, or fairly, as we do when we exercise a virtue. The stoics make this point by saying that strictly speaking only virtue is good (and vice bad), while everything else is "indifferent." They do not mean that these things are indifferent in the ordinary sense—that we either don't or shouldn't care about whether we have them or not. Someone who didn't care whether she was healthy or ill would be making a huge mistake about what humans do and should care about. It is part of being a normal human to strive for health and avoid disease. We also recognize that these things are indifferent to our *happiness* when we realize that being happy is an achievement that comes from the way we live our lives, and that health, along with money and status, is just part of the material we have to work on as we do that. Virtue is the only good, the only thing that benefits us and leads to happiness, because being virtuous is living our lives rightly, and it is *living* rightly that achieves happiness, not the stuff or materials we have to work on in doing this.

We can see from Seneca what a huge difference is made to the way we think of our lives by recognizing this fundamental difference. Once we realize that all that matters for happiness is acting honestly, and not whether profit or loss follows from this, we shall feel ourselves becoming detached from the conventional fixation on making profit and avoiding loss as being the most important thing in life. This is not the same as ceasing to care about making a profit and avoiding loss; rather, it is to assign to that its appropriate place in your life. The stoic distinction between the value of virtue and the value of things conventionally considered good, like health and wealth, prevents us, for example, from making trade-offs between doing what is honest and making a profit; making a lot of money will never justify any dishonesty. This huge difference to the way we think of our lives is not, demanding though it is, difficult to grasp in principle. We are just focusing on living our lives rightly, exercising virtues, and realizing that this is what matters for happiness rather than things like health and wealth, which are conventionally prized. It is not hard for us to grasp that it is how we live, rather than stuff, that matters for our lives to flourish; the stoics tell us that finally to get this right is extremely demanding, and turns out to involve revising many of our conventional evaluations and attachments.

Living virtuously is, for the stoics, natural for us, for it is natural for humans to exercise their reason, and virtue is the perfection of reason. These are theses, fully to understand which we do need to enter further into technical stoic arguments, but again the general idea can be displayed in a way that is reasonably plausible and attractive. It is characteristic of humans to have and act on reasons, to ask why they are acting and to seek to explain and justify their actions in terms of reason. This does not mean that statistically most humans do this—clearly they don't; those who reason effectively, whether about their actions or further matters, are relatively few. Still, we recognize that reflection, rather than mindlessly going with the flow, is something we expect of ourselves as human beings, and recognize as irrelevant in the case of the other animals.

Why is the perfection of reason virtue, rather than, for example, unprincipled cleverness? Once again, this is a claim that cannot be properly understood until we have gone further into stoic value theory and moral psychology, and ultimately into further areas, but again we can see the general idea in attractive form. A right action is not one that happens to produce a good outcome; it is one done for the right reason. Acting for the right reasons, however, turns out to involve much more by way of commitment to good reasoning. Someone who acts for the right reasons is someone who has gone further than reflecting on particular reasons; she has a character in which the virtues have been developed, so that she has overall commitment to acting in ways that are honest, fair, and so on, and thus to acting on certain reasons. This commitment shapes her life and thus her attitudes, and in turn her actions. The virtues develop as she comes not only to grasp the importance of certain reasons but to respond in corresponding ways. As she comes to be honest, she not only acts honestly but becomes repelled by dishonesty, and the grip of conventional fixation on money, health, and beauty is thereby weakened. Everything in her life thus expresses her deep commitment to, and understanding of, the profound difference between the value of virtue and the value of everything conventionally prized. Reasoning, if carried through rigorously and consistently, leads us away from trying to justify what we happen to want, and toward living a life guided by a systematic and reasoned account of what is valuable. Unprincipled cleverness, by contrast, is valuable to us only for getting us whatever it is that we happen to want at the time. It is not something that can direct and give shape to a life.

Seneca sketches for us some aspects of what it would be like to have such an ethical outlook, grounded on systematically understanding what is truly valuable, and how this would ensure the attainment of happiness. This happy person is not worried by the raw material of life, neither obsessed with status or power nor terrified of being one of society's losers. She is not exhilarated or lowered by events that concern only things external to her happiness, and so is calm and reliable, confident in herself and with sources of joy within herself, not dependent on the way other people and events happen to turn out. She is not dependent on getting whatever she happens to want, in order to have successfully achieved what she aims for in life. Her life is harmonious, containing no internal conflict, since it is based on what has been reasoned out in a thorough and consistent way, and someone who has achieved this is not made wretched by things like illness or lack of money, which wreck others' lives because they have no systematic grounding from which to assess the importance of these things in their lives.

This is a life based on a notable realignment of values from what we conventionally accept, and the happy person will be one whose priorities and evaluations will differ from those of unreflective people. Still, we can recognize this as an exacting, but attractive ideal. We recognize the appeal of being in charge of our lives, of leading a life in which achievement depends on ourselves and not on the way others chance to be. And, although revisionary, this ideal is not completely out of touch with what we cared about before reflecting on our values. Health, money, and power are on this account indifferent as regards happiness, but very far from indifferent in the ordinary sense. We can still draw distinctions between matters that are trivial and those that are important, in a positive or negative way, among the circumstances and matter of our lives. Moreover, even the virtuous can draw distinctions between virtuous actions performed in preferable circumstances and those performed under conditions that we would prefer not to hold. The wise and virtuous person, as Seneca says, will prefer to be tall and have money, though he will not despise himself if he is short and poor. The rightness of an action does not depend on its outcome, but it is still reasonable for us to prefer a right action with a good outcome (for example, an act of generosity that helps many) to one that, though equally right, has a less preferable outcome (helping only one person). Hence the wise and virtuous person, far from ignoring or trying to rise above such matters as money, will prefer to have money than not to have it—not for the reasons that most people have, namely the belief that money is a good thing, still less that life is not worth living without it, but because she prefers virtue to have a broader impact, more people to be helped rather than fewer.

We can see, then, from a writer like Seneca what it is like, in a general way, to be someone who finds living virtuously to be sufficient for happiness, as opposed to those of us who think that to live a happy life we need another car, a bigger house, or a promotion. He has given us the sketch of an ideal at which to aim, and pointed us on the right road to progress toward it—trying, as he is trying, to become a stoic, by reasoning ever more profoundly about everyday values and their place in our lives and by learning more about stoic ethics and integrating what we learn ever more deeply into the way we live. If we read Seneca in the right way, we will recognize his ideal as one we can have too, but we will also come to see that we cannot rely on Seneca to get us to the goal; we have to learn more for ourselves about what virtue really is and how to achieve it. In principle, Seneca's writing plays the same role for himself; it is in articulating for others what virtue is like that Seneca discovers the limits of his own understanding and the ways in which he can himself improve and approach nearer to the stoic ideal.

Demanding as this ideal is, it is available to us as an ideal that we can find attractive. It has attracted people from Seneca's own times up to the present day. While humans have behaved badly in all ages, they have also proved capable of responding to demanding ethical ideals.

Still, we may say, how does all this help managers to be good managers? How does it help businesspeople to get through the day at the office? Where is the concrete advice?

This raises the issue of what we expect an ethical theory actually to do for us. Sometimes philosophers write as though we could reasonably expect an ethical theory to tell us what to do, where this means that the theory will generate for us a list of directives to do, or not do, specific things. If we do, then we have problems, for the idea that an ethical theory should tell us what to do in this way runs into problems familiar to philosophers. A theory is supposed to tell us what to do and not to do in a determinate way, as when we are told not to kill, not to steal, and so on. But these injunctions are not determinate enough to settle difficult cases, where I might wonder whether, in the circumstances, this case could be justified, or should not really count as killing, or stealing. This kind of problem might get us to demand that a theory give us rules that specify not just that we shouldn't kill or steal, but that we should not kill (or steal) unless . . . , where we think that we could produce a list of circumstances that nullify or modify the rule. However, any attempt to produce a realistic list of circumstances of this kind soon runs into the problem that, while the rule becomes unwieldy and cluttered with complications, it still is not determinate enough to give clear guidance in the cases where this is most needed; that is, cases in which the application of the rule is difficult and disputed.

There is another problem with the idea that an ethical theory should produce a list of determinate rules or directives for us, one that a theory based on virtue is well placed to meet. Suppose that we could in some way meet the problem that the rules an ethical theory produced for us have to be determinate enough to tell us what to do even in difficult cases in which it is not clear how existing rules apply. We would then have an ethical theory that successfully told us what to do, that is, told us "Yes" or "No" to all our questions and directed us to perform a particular action, or not. It would have provided us with what is called a decision procedure for action—a list of rules or a determinate way of producing such a list.

Is this really what we want from an ethical theory? Here is an analogy. Suppose we know someone who always does what his mother tells him to do. In daily life, he follows the rules he was given by his mother; when faced by a difficult case, he either asks his mother what to do, or, if she is not around, works out what she would tell him to do about this particular case, and then does it. This strikes us as disturbing. Why? Suppose his mother to be an excellent ethical reasoner; her directions are always right. We are still left thinking that there is something importantly lacking in the son. What is it? He is not, as we put it, making his own decisions. He is being told what to do, and doing it, but we feel that something is lacking; we have a case of arrested development. What is lacking is the thought that the decisions are his own, arrived at through his own reasonings.

The kind of theory we find in Seneca has different expectations of what ethical theory can do for us. This is true not just of stoicism, but of the kind of ethical theory which is now called virtue ethics, at least the kinds which are eudaimonist, seeing virtue as a way of achieving happiness or a flourishing life. As we have seen, acting rightly requires acting for the right reasons, and this in turn demands that you have the right ethical outlook in general, that your character has developed in a way reflecting your understanding of the right account of value. Every one of your actions will express this understanding, and will in turn strengthen or weaken the outlook that expresses it. It would thus be the merest start for an ethical theory to give you a list of rules or directives to follow, as children follow their mother's directives. It would even be misleading if this encouraged the idea that nothing more was needed.

Rather, an ethical theory leads you to an account of what is valuable, which will inform your whole outlook; if you become a stoic, for example, this will give you an outlook that is systematically different from that of nonstoics. But your deliberations and decisions will be yours; each will be made as you respond to a particular situation and reason about it, and will not just be read off a list provided by a theory, or generated by applying the theory in a mechanical way. The theory guides the way you deliberate and act, since the way you think, act, and feel will express your grasp of the theory's account of what is truly valuable and what is not. Such guidance cannot be reduced to a list of directives, as though the theory were a handbook that you consult.

Seneca is trying to get us, and himself, to progress along the path toward becoming a stoic. We, his readers, get from him the idea of what it would be like to be a stoic, to hold that all that matters for happiness is becoming virtuous. Just as Seneca does, we try to apply this in our own life. Just as he does, we try to deepen our understanding of the various stoic ideas about virtue and happiness, and at some point we will leave the teacher behind and make progress on our own, seeking understanding of virtue and happiness through our own reasoning and applying it to our own situations. Thus we don't try first to understand the theory fully and then start to apply it; increased grasp of the theory is part of a progress integrated with increased ability to apply it in our own case.

Seneca's advice, as I said at the start, can seem overgeneral, too indeterminate to help any actual manager, parent, teacher. We should remember that we do not have two jobs: first learn the theory ("virtue is sufficient for happiness") and then apply it to our own lives ("virtue is sufficient for happiness, but how does that help me decide whether to leave my partner, give the promotion, and so on?"). We start to learn the theory from within our own situations, each of us being profoundly embedded in social and cultural contexts. Our progress toward understanding how virtue could make us happy comes through realizing what it would be to care more about doing the right thing than making a profit, or to be detached from consumerist obsessions rather than feeling the need to buy the latest gadget. We make sense of virtue from here, from within our own lives. Our lives are already full of determinate rules, demands, and expectations; we don't need ethical theory to give us more of these. Ethical theory gives us an altered outlook on our already determinate demands.

Moreover, thinking in terms of the virtues gives us a distinctive approach to practical problems. When we have to make a difficult decision, like the ones mentioned at the start, thinking in terms of the virtues gives us a focus that excludes certain types of consideration and foregrounds others. If I am thinking of leaving a selfish partner, for example, it excludes some approaches, such as focusing on the loss of time and resources the selfish person is inflicting, and the annoyance this causes. A virtues approach asks what a response would be which is loving but fair, concerned for the good lives of all the people concerned. Similarly, in the case of the deserved promotion: a virtues approach will be one which focuses on what people deserve, rather than automatically giving weight to feelings even when these are spiteful. It will also not give weight to any desire to avoid the effort required to encourage the rest of the office staff to accept the promotion and to take a more fair-minded attitude to it. Applied to a particular context, then, this virtues approach will give determinate guidance. The person who applies this approach will come up with answers that are different from those she would have got had she focused only on her own loss of time and resources. This is, to repeat, not to take the unrealistically high-minded view that these don't matter, or that we should try to rise above them. They do matter, but they matter as the material of a well or badly lived life; on their own they cannot make a life be lived well or badly.

A virtue approach is, then, highly general when we talk about it, but gives us determinate guidance when we apply it in a particular context. This shows us how Seneca can have appealed to ancient Romans, eighteenth-century gentlemen, and modern business-advice columnists. From within these very different societies and cultures people have read and been attracted by the account of virtue and happiness that Seneca has given us from within his own. Seneca's actual practical problems were very different from our own. Any actual concrete advice he gives or could give would almost certainly lack application in very different societies and cultures. That he is still read, with profit, in these very different societies indicates that concrete advice is not what we want from him. What he can convey, to us and to other people in very different societies, is the way to begin our own path to understanding what in life is truly valuable, and thus to revising our own priorities and acquiring a new outlook on our lives.

We may of course find Seneca's own stoicism too exacting, or unrealistic in what it expects from human nature, but it is interesting that, whatever the fortunes in academic philosophy of the more technical and professional accounts of stoic ethics that we have, there has been considerable appeal across the centuries in what Seneca says. We can respond to the idea that what matters in life is not your circumstances but the way you live your life whatever your circumstances; that the well-lived life is one lived in a way that expresses virtue; that virtue is achieved by aiming at wisdom, seeking, in an ever-deepening way, the reasons for what we do. Such ideas pull us away from the flow of life in our societies. For they pull us away from the assumption that what matters is success, status, having the latest fashionable things. The thought that it is better to be independent of such things, rather than living a life shaped by their pursuit, seems to be surprisingly constant in different cultures. Modern businesspeople are, it appears, ready to be told to "focus on wisdom and virtue rather than the material."[2] We seem to be as ready as people in other cultures and other times to aspire to virtue and to wisdom, and to think that there is a deep connection between the two.

SUGGESTIONS FOR FURTHER READING

An excellent place to start one's study of the application of stoic virtues to practical life is with the stoics themselves. The short collection of sayings of Epictetus, known as *The Enchirideon*, or *Handbook*, gives advice on how to cope with a variety of chal-

---

2. From the Dale Dauten column mentioned in note 1.

lenges from daily life (see *The Handbook of Epictetus*, trans. by Nicholas White (Indianapolis: Hackett Publishing Company, 1983). Seneca discusses an even wider range of topics in his *Letters*. The *Meditations*, a journal of stoic precepts collected by the Roman emperor and stoic, Marcus Aurelius, for his own reflection, is another rich resource (see *The Meditations of Marcus Aurelius*, trans. by G. M. A. Grube (Indianapolis: Hackett Publishing Company, 1983).

Nancy Sherman explores the power and appeal of the stoic outlook for the development of martial character and virtues in her recent study, *Stoic Warriors: The Ancient Philosophy behind the Military Mind* (New York: Oxford, 2005). Admiral James B. Stockdale has written frequently of how stoic philosophy helped him to endure prolonged captivity in a prisoner-of-war camp, most recently in his *Courage Under Fire: Testing Epictetus's Doctrines in a Laboratory of Human Behavior* (Stanford, CA: Hoover Institution on War, Revolution and Peace, Stanford University, 1993). Lawrence C. Becker discusses the value of stoic ideas for bioethics in "Human Health and Stoic Moral Norms," *Journal of Medicine and Philosophy* 28 (2003): 221–238 and argues for a neostoic outlook on human happiness and virtue in his book *A New Stoicism* (Princeton: Princeton University Press, 1998).

Stoicism's value for contemporary environmental ethics has been a subject of much controversy. Carmen V. Castelo reviews the debate and offers a defense of stoic approaches in "Reflections on Stoic Logocentrism," *Environmental Ethics* 18 (1996): 291–296. Ronald Sandler offers a virtue-based defense of certain kinds of genetic engineering, consistent with stoicism, in "A Virtue Ethics Perspective on Genetically Modified Crops," in *Environmental Virtue Ethics*, Ronald Sandler and Philip Cafaro, eds. (Lanham, MD: Rowman and Littlefield, 2005). Recently it has been suggested that Aldo Leopold's famous essay, "The Land Ethic," may be best interpreted as offering precepts for developing an environmentally sensitive *character*. If so, Leopold's conception of the relation of humans to nature could well be viewed as an extension of stoic thought. See Aldo Leopold, *A Sand County Almanac* (New York: Oxford University Press, 1987).

Mark H. Waymack

Francis Hutcheson:
Virtue Ethics and Public Policy

Francis Hutcheson's active years of teaching and writing were in the first half of the eighteenth century in Scotland. The period was the beginning of a great economic and cultural blossoming in Scotland, known now as the Scottish Enlightenment. It was a time that saw, in addition to memorable contributions to arts and letters, great advances in public infrastructure, economic productivity, and urban development. It would seem quite appropriate, therefore, to cast some reflection upon Hutcheson's moral theory in terms of ethics and public policy.

As grist for the mill, so to speak, I will offer a contemporary public-policy controversy. At present, a first-world government is considering whether to subsidize its cotton farmers. These subsidies would not be small, running to a sum in the neighborhood of $10 billion. The subsidies would make it possible for those cotton farmers to sell their cotton at a price below its true cost, and thus give these growers a competitive advantage in the global market. How would Hutcheson's moral philosophy help us think about this issue?

Let us approach the problem from two different angles. First, Hutcheson does offer a kind of account of good versus bad actions. Second, though he does offer an analysis of good and bad in reference to actions, at the core his is a moral philosophy of virtue. Hence, in the final analysis moral judgment, in its strictest, truest sense, is reserved not for actions but for characters, for persons. So we must consider how Hutcheson's virtue theory, as a virtue theory, would address this issue. In order to perform these analyses, though, let us first briefly review Hutcheson's moral philosophy.

HUTCHESON'S THEORY

It may be helpful to begin by considering whom or what Hutcheson is arguing against. He has two chief targets: the egoists and the rationalists.

Certain moral philosophers, now known as ethical rationalists, had argued that morality was a matter of reason, of rationality. Using arguments that David Hume would repeat, Hutcheson insisted that pure reason is not a motivator; it is passion that motivates us to act and because morality is about behavior, it must therefore be based upon passion and sentiment, not reason. (At best, moral approval and disapproval are feelings informed by reason.)

We are each, according to Hutcheson, endowed by our human nature with a moral sense. Some observations give rise in us through this moral sense to a pleasant feeling, which we call approval. Other observations give rise to an unpleasant feeling, which we call disapproval.

According to Hutcheson, the simple fact is that our moral sense reacts favorably when we observe actions that we attribute to benevolence, and it reacts with disapproval when we observe behavior that we believe arises from motives that are contrary to benevolence.

We are also endowed psychologically with a strong streak of self-interest, but self-interest, in and of itself, is morally neutral. In other words, there is nothing morally wrong with pursuing self-interest as long as it does not violate benevolence. Benevolence, love for others, is then the core of morality for Hutcheson.

Of course, if egoists, such as Thomas Hobbes, are correct, then this would create quite a mess. For the egoists' contention is that human beings are motivated solely by self-interest, never by true benevolence. The egoists had taken two approaches to this, both of which Hutcheson rejects. First, some, like Hobbes, accept humans as solely self-interested and then proceed to redefine ethics into terms of self-interest. Others, such as the theologians John Calvin and John Knox, accept that humans are thoroughly egoistic, but retain benevolent love as the measure of morality. From this point of view, virtue becomes impossible for humans. The measure is love of others: we are simply quite unable to meet that measure. Hence, the strict Calvinist theology holds that we are all thoroughly corrupted and we all deserve to go to hell. Those few who are selected to go to heaven, selected so that God might display his virtue of mercy, are not chosen because they in any way deserve it. None of us can possibly deserve salvation. Rather, those who are lucky enough to be given it receive it purely as an unearned gift.

Hutcheson's response is to argue that a candid observation of human nature reveals that in fact we are psychologically geared to act upon benevolence. We are psychologically a complex mixture of self-interest and benevolence. In ordinary life, we exhibit both of these motivations. Neither one "wins" all the time.

So, for Hutcheson, virtue consists in benevolence, and benevolence is at least one of our naturally endowed psychological motivations. Virtue is therefore not only theoretically possible for humans, it is a rather common, everyday experience.

We have, so far, stated that for Hutcheson the moral sense approves of benevolence. This requires a bit of qualification. Yes, the moral sense approves of benevolence, but it also approves more of "wider" benevolence. So the person who does something to benefit her friends, but ignores many other persons, would stimulate less moral approval in us than someone who was motivated by concern for the larger population, including people that she might not know personally. Indeed, for Hutcheson, the highest virtue is what he calls "universal benevolence" and, yes, Hutcheson does even speak of doing the "greatest good for the greatest number."

GOOD AND BAD ACTIONS

The best action, for Hutcheson, will thus be that action that promotes the greatest benefit for the greatest number of people. In terms of identifying right or good actions, Hutcheson sounds very much like a utilitarian. Indeed, with "universal benevolence" as the highest moral virtue, it is not surprising that Hutcheson's notions of what constitute good and bad action sound very utilitarian. The crucial difference that we must keep in mind, however, is that for Hutcheson the moral sense is designed to react not to consequences but to motives. Thus, at least one contemporary scholar, Mark Strasser, has characterized Hutcheson as a "motivational

Utilitarian."[1] A farm tractor might be highly useful, but we do not morally esteem it. An air conditioner may be the source of great pleasure during a hot summer; but we do not give it moral praise. However much such things might contribute to human happiness, we do not feel moral approval or disapproval toward them. This is, according to Hutcheson, because they themselves have no motives. They are not moral agents. Thus, it is conceptually inappropriate to morally praise a machine, because moral approval and disapproval are ultimately reserved strictly for motives.

Hutcheson is aware that on occasion a few individuals may lose out so that the greater good may be attained, and he accepts this unfortunate situation, as long as no established, recognized rights are violated. For to violate established rules of rights threatens the social order and social trust that are so crucial to a flourishing, happy society.

RIGHTS

We should therefore say something about Hutcheson's view of rights. Whereas John Locke, for example, had based property rights upon a law of nature, making property a right that precedes social construction, for Hutcheson rights are, properly speaking, created by society for the benefit of persons. The happiness of a society can be greatly enhanced by the creation of certain sets of moral and legal rights. Once again, Hutcheson's utilitarian-like streak is revealed: we create rights because doing so will promote human happiness.

Hutcheson specifies three different kinds of rights: perfect rights, imperfect rights, and external rights. Perfect rights are those rights on the grounds of which society may compel certain kinds of behavior. If I owe you money, you have a right to appeal to society to compel me to pay my debt. If I try to murder you, you have a right to demand that society compel me, by force if necessary, not to do so. Perfect rights, because they are enforceable, must be clear and easily applied to particular circumstances.

---

1. Mark Strasser, *Francis Hutcheson's Moral Theory* (Wakefield, NH: Longwood Academic, 1990).

A right to charity, however, is an imperfect right, as it cannot oblige any particular individual to give money. Though an unfortunately impoverished family may have some right to charity, their claim cannot be against me in particular (unless I have individually harmed them in some way, in which case what I owe is no longer charity but would be reparations instead). I ought to be courteous to my neighbors, but society will not put me in jail if I simply ignore them. So, perfect rights are socially enforceable, whereas the satisfaction of imperfect rights may be encouraged, but cannot legitimately be compelled.

External rights, as described by Hutcheson, bring up a different concern. What Hutcheson means by external rights are particular rights that we in fact possess, and which society has agreed to observe and should therefore protect, even though their exercise on some particular occasions may be harmful. Thus, the very rich miser has a right to collect rent from a poor family, even though the general happiness might be advanced if in this particular instance he forgave their rent for a month, or reduced the amount. Though the overall sum of happiness might have been greater if the miser voluntarily agreed to do so, society cannot and should not compel him to do so. This is because, according to Hutcheson, compelling such behavior would undermine our established conventions concerning private property, would erode our trust in retaining possession in the future of what we work hard for now. Thus, incentives to work diligently would be dampened, less wealth would be created, and society as a whole would be less happy in the long run. It is our trust in the security of our private property that provides a strong motivation to work hard and produce and acquire more for ourselves and our loved ones. Similarly, suppose I have great potential as a medical researcher to find better treatments for human cancers. Humanity, as a whole, may well be much happier were I to pursue that profession. Yes perhaps my heart is set on being a performance poet. Even further, perhaps I am a very mediocre poet at that. Society, according to Hutcheson, should not have the power and does not have the authority to force me to be a medical researcher, even though society may deem my choice of being a poet a morally much inferior choice. Hutcheson's reasoning, once again, is that to have a social policy whereby individuals are forced by a central authority into career choices that it deemed would most contribute to the general happiness, would cause such a loss of happiness that any positive contribution to overall happiness would be entirely washed away. Furthermore, Hutcheson is insisting, such a system of rights only works when rights are observed generally. To allow exceptions threatens to undermine the whole institution of rights. Hence, human happiness is most advanced when we continue to respect individuals' rights, even when particular individual choices might be contrary to overall human happiness. In this regard, Hutcheson sounds very much like a rule-utilitarian.

SUBJECTIVISM

One might worry here that Hutcheson is putting forward a very subjectivist, perhaps even an emotivist, account of moral judgment. After all, moral approval seems to be nothing more than my emotive reaction to how I perceive the behavior of other persons.

In one sense, of course, Hutcheson is quite obviously a subjectivist. Moral approval and disapproval are feelings, perceptions in an observer. They are our reactions as subjects to what we perceive. Should this worry us?

The threat that we typically associate with subjectivism and emotivism is that I might somehow feel moral approval for something that the rest of the world perceives as morally very odious. Could there be any real moral disagreement, since my perceptions are what they are and your perceptions are what they are?

Hutcheson's answer here would be to argue that there is a given human nature, in particular a given human psychology. Though there may be minor variations between humans, there is a general uniformity to human nature. Psychology, as a natural or social science, depends upon such general uniformity. Medicine would be an incoherent practice if there were not strong similarities between us as humans. Indeed, the very idea of deviant psychology or of disease depends upon a general norm of psychological and physiological health. Likewise, Hutcheson would argue, the moral sense given to us by nature is universal enough that it establishes a norm. That some individuals are color-blind does not destroy our commonly accepted notion of colors. We still post red lights at busy intersections to command drivers to stop, and green lights for them to go. The psychopath is deviant from the norm. And the existence of a few morally corrupt, morally diseased individuals does not destroy the recognition of a norm.

Hutcheson does seem aware that, whether because of individual variation or differences in environment and social upbringing, there will be some variation in our inclinations to benevolence. Some of us will feel it more strongly and more universally than others. Some of us will have greater sympathies and moral imaginations than others. Indeed, it is one of the practical purposes of moral philosophy to enlarge and bolster our moral imagination and passions of benevolence. And this variation in our experience of the passion of benevolence may also help explain why Hutcheson feels that the institutions of rights are so necessary to a flourishing, happy society. Where our benevolence may be only limited or weak, the social institutions of rights may bolster our passion up enough to protect the social fabric that enhances human happiness.

To summarize, however, Hutcheson avoids the alleged threat of subjectivism by relying upon a certain universality to our human nature, especially to our moral sense. Perhaps we are too distracted by our differences sometimes to see just how much we really are alike.

CASE ANALYSIS

As we are trying to understand Hutcheson's virtue at work, let us consider a fairly simple public-policy controversy: governmental agricultural supports. How should we think, in moral terms, of a government paying economic subsidies to its farmers to raise their income far higher than it would have been if they relied entirely upon income from sales at the prevailing marketplace price? In particular, let us discuss the question of a first-world nation providing generous economic subsidies to its cotton farmers.

The emergence of a global market for cotton, occurring simultaneously with substantial rises in production costs in this first-world nation, has created a situation where without the support of government subsidies these farmers would no longer be able to grow and sell cotton without going bankrupt. Without these government subsidies, cotton farmers in this wealthy nation will lose their jobs, lose their incomes, and go out of business. Needless to say, this would harm these particular cotton farmers—the farm owners, the managers, the laborers, and even the communities within which they are located.

Sensitive to this potential harm, politicians consider passing a bill that would create a subsidy program to protect the cotton-growing industry. Now the cotton growers will surely benefit greatly from this subsidy program. They will not only be able to stay in business, they will earn quite respectable profits. As for the taxpayers in general, it is harder to say. Yes, the taxpayers will have to send money to the federal government to pay for this subsidy; yet they are also then the beneficiaries of cheaper cotton prices in the market. I suspect that there is some net loss to taxpayers, but it is arguable that such a loss is fairly negligible.

Nevertheless, there will be losers as a consequence of this subsidy policy. Those losers will be cotton farmers in other parts of the globe. Large parts of Africa, with a relatively hot and relatively dry climate, have been significant producers of cotton. While African farmers tended not to have the highly efficient farm machinery used in first-world agriculture, African labor costs have been consistently and significantly lower than in the first world. Indeed, if one were to remove the subsidies, then African cotton could compete well economically in the global market. With the subsidies, these first-world cotton growers can sell their cotton for roughly one-third of its growing cost and still make a tidy profit. At this greatly reduced price, however, African farmers cannot compete economically. The African cotton industry, therefore, is likely to be devastated by these cotton subsidies.

If we are guided by Hutcheson's standard of universal benevolence, then I, at least, think it is clear that these subsidies to American cotton growers fail to meet that moral standard. Those subsidies will benefit a relatively few farmers, but at the cost of great human suffering to vast numbers of persons in Africa alone. Furthermore, these first-world farmers are almost certainly more adaptable, in terms of shifting to alternative crops, than the African farmers, and even if some of those first-world cotton farmers are eventually forced out of business, it is likely that the massive economy of their nation could absorb them in some kind of gainful employment, whereas many of these African communities have no such economic resilience. Our subsidies are thus liable to contribute to poverty, starvation, and environmental degradation affecting large numbers of persons in Africa.

Thus, the cotton subsidies may represent local benevolence, but they fail the test of universal benevolence.

Do these cotton farmers have a right to the subsidy? This is a more difficult question. It is hard to imagine what kind of claim could exist to classify this as a perfect right. These farmers did not grow the subsidy on their land. Rather, it comes from the generosity of the nation's legislators and taxpayers.

Is there an imperfect right? Sometimes such subsidies are used to relieve the suffering of such individuals when they have been subjected to unexpected, devastating misfortune, and they need some limited time of support in order to either become economically competitive once again or else to shift to other, more financially sound crops. Benevolence may well recommend helping someone who is suffering through some accidental misfortune, a misfortune that is not of their own making. Limited benevolence would quite likely applaud such a temporary intervention; but universal benevolence would still be concerned with the effect of such a policy upon large numbers of other persons (African cotton growers).

THE QUESTION OF VIRTUE

As I have pointed out earlier, however, for Hutcheson, morality is really a matter of virtue, of motives. Actions are morally most significant insofar as they provide us with information about an individual's motives. The true focus of moral judgment, therefore, is a person's moral character. As Hutcheson notes, we tend to approve of a person who has truly benevolent intentions, even if through accident, bad luck, or unfortunate miscalculation their action actually fails to benefit others. Even if someone performed an action that was enormously beneficial to many persons, if it was done out of self-interest, and only benefited others by mistake or mere coincidence, then we reserve our moral approval. Indeed, though the action might in fact cause a great benefit to others, if that result was a mistake and the agent was truly motivated by a selfish self-interest and had intended, in fact, to harm those other persons, then we would morally disapprove of that agent. Thus, while Hutcheson may be looking for utilitarian-like outcomes, he is by no means a utilitarian. He is, above all, a virtue theorist.

If we are to morally appraise the various agents in the cotton subsidy controversy, then we must infer something about their various motives. Why are they doing what they do? Let us first consider a "simple" politician, if such a creature exists. This politician has been elected to legislative office and solemnly believes it is her duty to act benevolently toward her constituency. Such a legislator may well think that because the subsidy would benefit the farmers in her district enormously, she ought to work to pass that piece of legislation. If that is the motivation, then I think Hutcheson might say the moral sense would render grudging and limited approval, for she is acting out of benevolence, but only from very limited benevolence. She aims to benefit her particular constituency. Hutcheson would wish that we try to open her eyes to the wider, and harmful consequences of her actions in supporting the subsidy, thus appealing to the higher standard of universal benevolence.

More likely, though, our legislator may be thinking of reelection. Who voted for her and who made all those campaign contributions? Presuming our legislator wants to be reelected, to do so she knows she must please her voting and contributing constituency. Therefore, looking to her own future, she endorses the cotton subsidies, perhaps even being aware of their potentially devastating effects in Africa. Hutcheson would argue that our moral sense would soundly disapprove of such a character. She is pursuing her own self-interest, even when she knows that it is contrary to the greater good. If we wished to make the case even morally worse, we could add that our legislator herself happens to own a large cotton farm, and thus she is a direct economic beneficiary of the policy, as well as benefiting indirectly in the sense of campaign contributions and votes. Such a person, motivated by self-interest, knowing that her actions will cause great harm to large numbers of persons, would by Hutcheson's reckoning be regarded as downright morally evil by our moral sense.

Who, then, might earn our highest moral approbation in these circumstances? Let us suppose our legislator to be coming up for reelection. Let us also suppose that she is the owner herself of a large cotton farm and that she is aware of the subsidy's enormous harmful effects in Africa. If this legislator, knowing full well that there will be enormous cost to herself, economically, politically, and even personally (for she will be reviled in her home community), still works vigorously against the subsidies out of a benevolent passion for economically challenged Africans, then our moral sense will not only approve of her character, but it will approve of her in the highest terms, recognizing that she has struggled against self-interest, that she is willing to pay a high personal cost to pursue what she believes universal benevolence demands. Self-interest here does not cooperate with benevolence; it is in sharp and cruel conflict with benevolence. The person with the moral fortitude to rise above narrow self-interest and work instead for the welfare of the many deserves our highest praise and esteem.

As Hutcheson's theory is presented, it is very much one of that family of moral theories that we may call "spectator theories." That is, the most straightforward way in which we experience morality is in the experience of observing the behavior of and then reacting to or judging the moral character of others. That does not mean that it is impossible to morally reflect upon our own selves. It simply requires a process of some internal reflection.

As we morally judge our legislators, we may reflect upon our own moral character. For whom will we vote in the upcoming election? Will we vote our narrow self-interest, casting our ballot for the politician whom we think will be most likely to pay us back by passing legislation that benefits us personally (without regard to the welfare of others)? Or will we vote for the politician whom we believe will craft and argue for legislation that we think will be of the greatest benefit to the greatest number, regardless of how it might affect us individually?

CONCLUSION

Hutcheson offers an enticing virtue theory. He strives to present a theory that grapples with humans and with morality as we actually experience them in this world. He does not deny the strong streak of self-interest that runs through us as humans, but he does rightly emphasize that we are quite capable of substantial benevolence as well. While his notion of good action looks very much like a version of utilitarianism, he has the good sense to acknowledge that as humans we in fact do not think like utilitarians, nor do we psychologically judge, as Bentham or Mill would have us believe. Rather, we focus our moral judgments upon human character.

Morality, that is, virtue, as Hutcheson acknowledges, is much easier when self-interest and benevolence coincide. If we think in terms of something like "enlightened self-interest" this is probably more often the case than we might at first imagine. However, the truly shining moral character, the person who elicits our highest esteem, is the person who manages to rise above individual self-interest and is able to put the welfare of the many at the forefront of his or her motivation. These are the people that we truly admire and, perhaps, we can aspire to be more like them.

SUGGESTIONS FOR FURTHER READING

Hutcheson's "sentiment"-based account of moral virtue has received little specific treatment in the applied ethics literature to date; however, the virtue of benevolence and related virtues of generosity and charity have often been discussed in ways Hutcheson could approve.

Richard McCarty has discussed the development of benevolence and social-responsibility-driven business practices in "Business and Benevolence," *Business and Professional Ethics Journal* 7 (1988): 63–83, a trend which continues to grow. Howard J. Curzer discusses the relative merits of treating benevolence or "care" as a central virtue of clinical ethics in "Is Care a Virtue for Health Care Professionals?" *Journal of Medicine and Philosophy* 18 (1993): 51–70. Mark Strasser looks at the role of rights in Hutcheson's theory in "Hutcheson on External Rights," *Philosophical Studies* 49 (1986): 263–269. On the possibilities of extending the virtue of benevolence to environmental concerns, see Geoffrey Frasz, "Benevolence as an Environmental Virtue," in *Environmental Virtue Ethics*, Ronald Sandler and Philip Cafaro, eds. (Lanham, MD: Rowman and Littlefield, 2005). Jeffrey Fry discusses the moral justification of encouraging athletes to suffer pain in "Coaches' Accountability for Pain and Suffering in the Athletic Body," *Professional Ethics* 9 (2001): 9–26.

Jacqueline Taylor

Humean Humanity versus Hate

Hume's emphasis on the moral sentiments and other evaluative attitudes we take toward one another makes his version of virtue ethics rich in resources both for explaining how hate toward groups is created, and for creating strategies to counter hate. His account of the emotions anticipates a great deal of contemporary social psychology insofar as it explains how we form, communicate, and sustain attitudes—such as respect and contempt—that express our sense of the social worth of individuals. In this essay, I first provide an overview of the causes and effects of hate activity, drawing on empirical research from psychologists and legal experts. I then set out Hume's explanation of how people form the biased attitudes relevant to hate activity, and what he has to say, more normatively, about the epistemological and psychological costs, both to the perpetrators of hate activity as well as to those targeted. Finally, I construct a Humean solution to the problem, drawing on the notions of sympathy and humanity, which are at the heart of Hume's virtue ethics. The active cultivation of a sense of humanity works to diminish hate activity in two ways. First, it makes people more sensitive to, and hence intolerant of, cruelty. Second, it reduces the salience of the social markers, such as race or sexual orientation, which often inflame hatred.

HATE

Let us first take a closer look at hate activity, what it consists of, its causes, and its effects on its victims. In recent years, governments around the world have begun recognizing the criminality of hate activity that targets minority and vulnerable groups. Both law enforcement and academic experts agree that hate activity is a social problem, and is not due simply to the aberrant or random behavior of a few individuals.[1] The evidence suggests that perpetrators of hate crimes believe that the majority group with which they identify sanctions their behavior. Proponents of antidiscrimination legislation for hate activity argue that laws against hate crimes are useful in providing deterrence and punishment for prejudice-driven violence. Laws also send the message that the community recognizes hate crimes as a particularly reprehensible form of violence. A widely endorsed strategy, even by many of those who find hate crime legislation problematic, consists of community education about perceived social differences. Hume's virtue ethics helps us to appreciate the value of this educational remedy to hate.

In North America, hate crimes typically target groups—or individuals perceived to be members of groups—identified by race, ethnicity, religion, sexual orientation, mental and physical disability, and in some venues, gender. Hate crimes involve physical violence toward property or persons because of membership in a targeted group. Documented violence includes assault, rape and murder of persons, and vandalism and other property damage. Verbal threats that instill a reasonable fear of physical violence are also considered hate crimes. Hate crimes constitute a criminal violation of civil rights, and the laws allow for jail time for convicted perpetrators, and for awarding actual damages to a victim who brings a lawsuit. What are known as hate incidents, including hate speech, are also expressions of prejudice, but because they do not involve physical violence, they are not criminal. In the United States, hate speech is protected by the First Amendment.

In both the United States and Canada, over half of all hate crimes target racial and ethnic minorities. Blacks encounter more hate activity than other minorities, although increasingly, people of Hispanic, Asian, or Arab descent have been the targets of hate crimes. Other targeted groups include religious minorities (particularly Jews and Muslims), sexual minorities (gay, lesbian, bisexual, and transgendered people), and the disabled. Some cases of domestic abuse and rape have been recognized and tried as hate crimes toward women. Hate activity is more likely to correlate to a recent

---

1. Facts and statistics presented here, unless otherwise noted, are compiled by the American Psychological Association; see www.apa.org/pubinfo/hate.

presence of a minority in a formerly homogeneous community, rather than to an economic slump or actual loss of jobs among the majority group. Over three-fourths of perpetrators of hate crimes are male, with many under age thirty. Most perpetrators do not belong to an organized hate group, and many have no prior criminal record.

The motive for hate acts and hate speech is prejudice. Hate acts and hate speech are driven by prejudice and a contempt for those who differ from the perpetrator in some key aspect of identity. The evidence shows that hate crimes often exhibit greater cruelty and viciousness than other violent crimes (for example, in comparison to crimes that are economically motivated). According to social psychologists, perpetrators typically have contempt for the individuals and groups they target, regarding perceived differences as indicators of inferiority. Hate crimes and other hate incidents thus send a message of extreme bias toward groups or individuals identified with a targeted group.

In addition to enduring physical violence or the destruction of their property, the victims of hate crimes suffer emotional damage. The psychological effects include feelings of vulnerability, a loss of self-esteem, anger, depression, and learning problems. Many victims exhibit signs of posttraumatic stress disorder. Fear of retaliation contributes to the underreporting of hate crimes in comparison with non-bias-motivated violent crimes. Concern that those in the legal system are themselves biased toward the targeted group is also a factor in underreporting.

I mentioned at the start of this section that community education is an important component in reducing hate activity. Those who hate others on the basis of perceived membership in a group exhibit a failure to take up or appreciate the perspective of members of the targeted group. Learning how to adopt the perspective of others, in a way that does not distort who they are, is key to diminishing hatred and prejudice. Social psychologists refer to this adoption of the point of view of others as "perspective taking," and it is often associated with empathy.[2] Hume's moral philosophy

2. On perspective taking, see B. Underwood and B. Moore, "Perspective-taking and Altruism," *Psychological Bulletin* 91 (1982): 143–173. On empathy, see C. Rogers, "Empathic: An Unappreciated Way of Being," *The Counseling Psychologist* 2 (1975): 2–10.

is notable for advocating extending our natural sympathy in order to adopt a point of view we can hold in common with others.

HUME ON MORAL KNOWLEDGE

I begin with a sketch of Hume's account of moral knowledge, which will help to establish the broader context within which he explains the social and psychological mechanisms that produce and sustain extreme prejudice, and how his version of virtue ethics suggests a successful way to counter this form of hate. Like other virtue theorists, Hume emphasizes character and the role that the emotions play in motivation, and in our sense of who we are. But there is a further feature of Hume's ethics that distinguishes it from that of a virtue theorist such as Aristotle. Aristotle focuses on the deliberative perspective of the fully virtuous agent. As someone with practical wisdom, the virtuous agent has knowledge of the right thing to do in the situations he encounters, and of the best way to live. In acting from virtue, he sets the standard for right conduct, hence the importance of Aristotle's explaining what it is to deliberate, act, and live well. In contrast, Hume focuses on the moral sentiments by which we *evaluate* character, and he pays less attention to how virtue guides our deliberation and conduct. We should understand, however, that Hume's adherence to the "experimental method" in explaining the nature of our emotions and moral sentiments leads him to advocate a quite different account of moral knowledge than that of Aristotle.

For Hume, moral knowledge is fundamentally knowledge of character and persons. The recognition and valuation of features of persons, including character, will to a large extent reflect historically and culturally variable ways of life that make some of these features more salient than others. Knowledge of what constitutes, for example, moral competence and trustworthiness on the one hand, and deviance on the other, is critical to how members of a community are educated, to the attitudes they take toward one another, and to policy decisions regarding the distribution of benefits and imposition of burdens. Hume emphasizes how the dynamic processes, such as those reflecting scientific progress or legal change, characterizing many modern societies means that social knowledge of what people are like, or what we think they ought to be like, may need to be challenged, debated, negotiated, and revised.

Despite the historical and cultural variability of what people recognize as virtuous or vicious character, Hume's sentiment-based approach holds that the character traits comprising virtues are typically ones that are useful or agreeable to the person possessed of them, or to others.[3] A trait recognized as a virtue may be both useful and agreeable to oneself and others; benevolence is a good example. Some character traits will be found in every society; Hume identifies pride, justice, and benevolence as especially important virtues, even though they may take particular cultural forms. Other virtues will be more specific to a particular time or place; a good memory, for example, may be an important intellectual virtue in societies where few are literate. Throughout time and across cultures, societies may rank the virtues differently, depending on their particular circumstances. Courage was of more importance in the ancient heroic societies, whereas justice and benevolence characterize the virtuous ideal in many modern societies. Hume also points out that some societies will advocate the more agreeable virtues, while others endorse the more useful traits. This brief overview suggests that in a Humean virtue ethics, there is no fixed conception of the virtuous character, in terms of specific traits, that will be the ideal for all times and places. Nevertheless, Hume does think we can argue that some societies are better than others. Especially in his essays, Hume pays attention to the cultural and historical variability of character, customs, and manners, and shows how particular social institutions and practices tend to produce certain kinds of characters.

Along with his interest in the relation between social institutions and the cultivation of character, Hume is also interested in the creation of prejudice and in how that leads to harmful social division. He considers the epistemological and psychological costs of prejudice, especially when it is coupled with oppression. He presents his critical remarks about prejudice toward others primarily in the context of discussing who is qualified to judge the moralities of societ-

---

3. Hume gives this definition of virtue in the *Enquiry Concerning the Principles of Morals*, Section 9. Hereafter, I will refer to the *Enquiry* as EPM and cite it parenthetically in the text, with the section number.

ies other than their own. In his essay, "Of the Standard of Taste," he writes that "a person influenced by prejudice" fails to depart from his own situation to consider that of others, "but obstinately maintains his natural position, without placing himself in that point of view" required to understand others.[4] The prejudiced person will thus "rashly condemn" what those who he perceives as different from him find valuable or admirable. In "A Dialogue," Hume observes that customs, manners, or values that are foreign to our own can become the "object of the highest contempt and ridicule, and even hatred," when they are measured by a standard unknown to those whose way of life it is.[5] He writes that such "prejudice is destructive of sound judgment," thus suggesting that the prejudiced person incurs an epistemic cost.[6] The prejudiced person holds false beliefs, beliefs that are unsubstantiated by the evidence. In not setting aside his prejudices toward others, he neglects the facts that are available to him about what others are like. Hume urges that the sentiments, as well as the understanding of the prejudiced person, are "perverted," so that he fails to appreciate properly what others are like. In keeping with a view of moral knowledge as a collectively established and shared resource, we will view the prejudiced person as lacking in credibility and authority.

HUME ON PREJUDICE AND CONTEMPT FOR OTHERS

According to Hume, we naturally love and hate others for features such as their character, their physical appearance and abilities, and their wealth and power—or lack of these. Despite our natural tendencies to show favor or disfavor toward people because of these various attributes, Hume also thinks that many of us find hatred toward others appropriate only when it is directed toward vicious character or intentional injury. A deliberate attempt to harm me

---

4. David Hume, *Essays: Moral, Political, and Literary,* Eugene F. Miller, ed. (Indianapolis: Liberty Fund, 1985), p. 239.

5. "A Dialogue" is a short work that Hume appended to the EPM, and which takes up the issues of prejudice, relativism, and universal moral sentiment. See: "A Dialogue," in *Enquiry Concerning the Principles of Morals,* J. B. Schneewind, ed. (Indianapolis: Hackett Publishing Company, 1983).

6. Hume, *Essays,* p. 240.

often shows that the person holds me in contempt, which is a reason for me to mistrust and disapprove of him. Someone's vicious character will lead her to be harmful or disagreeable to members of her community, and so we find her blameworthy. Even if a person's intentional or characteristic harmful conduct may not be fully within her control, it often is susceptible to reward or punishment or to social sanctions. The importance we attach to social cooperation makes us think of people's character and conduct as of greater significance than their appearance, wealth, or power (considered apart from their character).

Yet people are hated for things over which they have no control, such as skin color, sexual orientation, religious commitment, or gender. Or more precisely, a perceived difference, say, race or sexual orientation, gets linked to other features, such as (often misattributed) character traits or abilities, which are deemed harmful or otherwise undesirable. What accounts for the more extreme forms of hatred, for the pernicious prejudices that target people on the basis of perceived membership in a certain group? In an earlier work, *A Treatise of Human Nature*, Hume identifies the psychological processes that generate stereotypes. He shows how negative stereotypes get exacerbated through the attitude of contempt, which is produced and sustained by insidious comparisons and the creation of social distance between groups. I will briefly sketch Hume's description of these processes to make clearer how the prejudices they generate might be diminished by the cultivation of humanity and the virtues of good judgment.

When a community has some relatively settled views about which features of persons have value or the reverse, its members will tend to make generalizations about which kinds of person possess or lack the relevant features. What Hume calls "general rules" lead us to associate, often erroneously, some particular trait with people on the basis of some social category with which they are identified (making what psychologists call "dispositional inferences"). General rules account similarly for our attributions of emotions, interests, and values to others. When we generalize in this way we suppose that certain traits or commitments uniformly characterize all members within a certain group. Such generalizations are not always pernicious or erroneous. Our capacity to sort people according to social categories often helps us to navigate a complex social world. If we can quickly decide what sort of person we are dealing with, we can then pay attention to new information.

Yet our tendency to sort people in these general ways is also the source of stereotypes and prejudice. Hume shows a keen awareness that what a particular community regards as relevant about people is often not independent of assumptions its members make regarding class, gender, race, profession, religious outlook, and the other social markers relevant to hate crime. Pernicious stereotypes may arise when the majority's values ignore or deliberately exclude minority interests and values. The prejudice reflected in hate activity is a particularly virulent form of stereotyping, involving the misattribution of negative traits (e.g., associating skin color with intellectual inferiority) or stigmatizing a feature (such as sexual orientation) shared by members of a group. Empirical research in the social sciences supports Hume's point about how easily we make generalizations about a person's character, values, or abilities, on the basis of social categories such as class, gender, or race.[7]

These sorts of differences in social standing often entail differences in moral standing, in the kinds of respect people show to one another, and in how they form a conception of their own worth as persons. Hume pays special attention to how respect and contempt are produced and sustained. He describes two further psychological processes, comparison and social distancing, which exacerbate the pernicious generalizations reflected in prejudice and hate. Respect and contempt are mixed forms of love and hatred, which are generated by a comparison of oneself with others. Respect is a mixture of humility and love, produced when a person compares himself with someone he regards as superior. Conversely, contempt is a mixture of pride and hatred, arising from a comparison in which he perceives the other as inferior. People take pride in and love others for pleasant qualities related to self or other, and feel humility and hate others for disagreeable qualities. But respect and contempt are directed toward qualities of persons to which we attach a special social significance. While Hume focuses on the qualities associated with social status, such

---

7. A classic work in sociology on this topic is Erving Goffman, *Stigma: Notes on the Management of Spoiled Identity* (New York: Simon and Schuster, 1963).

as wealth or extreme poverty, other perceived features of persons, such as race or sexual orientation, if regarded as grounds for privileging or excluding people, will have a similar salience in these interpersonal comparisons.

As Hume describes them, respect and contempt are not benign attitudes. Rather, comparison with someone perceived as socially inferior activates the superior's sense of pride, and contempt "invigorates" his mind, giving a "new force" to his thoughts and actions.[8] The contemptuous person feels himself to be superior and socially more powerful. Being the object of someone's contempt, on the other hand, is humiliating and undermines the confidence of the contemned person. Hume's description lines up with contemporary psychological theory, which refers to the tendency to evaluate one's own group more favorably in comparison with another, as "in-group bias." In-group bias boosts the self-esteem of the members of the group. While it may seem ironic that high-status groups, rather than low-status groups or groups with low self-esteem, tend to exhibit the most in-group bias, this is because those in high-status groups tend to believe that they deserve their higher status, and they also have greater expectations regarding the value of the resources they possess.[9]

The attitudes of respect and contempt are intensified and sustained by the creation of social distance. Hume describes social distance as an awareness of one another's social place, which helps to ensure that people display the "appropriate" attitudes, particularly of respect or contempt, toward one another. Someone who feels herself to be superior will feel a keen uneasiness if she thinks she is affiliating with someone she regards as an inferior, since she believes she must adopt a superior attitude in order to prevent uneasiness on the part of her fellow members in the majority group. Social distancing sustains in-group identification and loyalty.

---

8. David Hume, *A Treatise of Human Nature*, David Fate Norton and Mary J. Norton, eds. (Oxford: Oxford University Press, 2000), Book 2, Part 2, Section 10.

9. For a good example, see J. Crocker and R. Luhtanen, "Collective Self-esteem and Ingroup Bias," *Journal of Personality and Social Psychology* 58 (1990): 60–67.

The psychological processes of generalizing and distancing can distort our views of one another, distortions perpetuated by insidious comparisons. Yet once generalizations are in place, and a more powerful group creates a social distance between itself and others, the resulting social categories and expectations of what others are or should be like can become pervasive and difficult to dislodge. Comparisons and distancing generate attitudes such as self-esteem or contempt, that can powerfully affect how members of both in-groups and stigmatized out-groups think about their social identity and worth.[10]

SYMPATHY AND SHARED POINTS OF VIEW

Now someone might argue that we should work to replace the hate associated with prejudice with love, or even a moderate liking, for others. Francis Hutcheson, writing a bit earlier than Hume, and a leading proponent of what is known as the moral sense school (which had a strong influence on Hume's own moral philosophy), argued that we can cultivate a universal calm benevolence that we direct toward humankind in general. Hutcheson recognized that most of our benevolent actions are "particular," that is, directed toward particular people, typically those whom we most care about, and stemming from affections such as generosity, compassion, friendship, or gratitude. Even people who seldom reflect on moral goodness have these particular benevolent affections. In contrast, universal benevolence is always a virtue, for it controls excessive partiality and directs our concern to the entire species.[11]

However, Hume insists that it is impossible to love everyone. It does not make sense, then, to think that we *ought* to love, or even

---

10. We should note that people may be perceived as belonging to more than one stigmatized group, and that there is considerable complexity among social groups; this suggests that context will be important in terms of who feels and expresses respect or contempt, and that people may experience different forms of respect and contempt in different situations. I am indebted to Katherine M. Knapp for her insight here.

11. Francis Hutcheson, *An Essay on the Nature and Conduct of the Passions and Affections, with Illustrations on the Moral Sense,* Aaron Garrett, ed. (Indianapolis: Liberty Fund, 2002).

like everyone. Recall that we love or hate people for particular qualities that they possess or that we associate with them. We form friendships with, and are kind or grateful to particular persons, because they are close to us, or they benefit us in some way, or possess some admirable quality such as wit or virtue. We can love our country, or feel affection for our society, but this public benevolence is not the same as Hutcheson's universal benevolence, which includes the entire species. Indeed, Hume thinks that we not only expect people to be partial and care for a few persons above others, but we admire someone for being, for example, a good parent, spouse, or friend. As he observes in a footnote, "it is wisely ordained by nature, that private connexions should commonly prevail over universal considerations; otherwise our affections and actions would be dissipated and lost, for want of a proper limited object" (EPM 5, pt. 2).

Nevertheless, our need to cooperate with people for whom we have no natural affection means that we must sometimes set aside our own particular interests. Hume argues that we need to make ourselves intelligible to one another when it comes to discussing the public values implemented in public policy and law, and expressed in education, sermons, or in forms of entertainment from which we also take moral lessons. Moreover, although we do not feel an active concern for the species, we are not altogether indifferent to the happiness and misery of others. Hume appeals to the principle of sympathy to explain this sense we have of our shared humanity, which makes us respond emotionally at least, if not with action, to the situations and emotional experiences of others, even complete strangers. Sympathy is subject to some natural influences of the imagination, which cause us to sympathize more with certain people, and hence can exacerbate partiality to an excessive degree. Yet our need to converse intelligibly with one another leads us to recognize and correct sympathetic bias. So let us look in more detail at how sympathy works, and at the role it may play in fomenting hate, and, when suitably corrected, in helping us to recognize and eradicate prejudice.

What is Humean sympathy? While we naturally associate the term with feelings of compassion or pity, Hume intends "sympathy" as a technical term. Sympathy is a general capacity to communicate our emotions, sentiments, and even opinions to one another. We can form beliefs about others' emotional experiences by such clues as the kinds of situation they are in (e.g., about to go under the knife in surgery), their facial expression and body language, and what they say and do. Sympathy works by enlivening a belief about another's emotion so that we feel the same emotion ourselves, or have some other emotional response to them, for example, admiration in response to someone's pride in accomplishing a difficult feat.

Sympathy explains the disinterested (i.e., not self-interested) pleasure we frequently take in the happiness of others, as well as the pain we feel at their misery and distress. It also explains the variety of passions we feel while watching theater or film, reading poetry or fiction, or listening to music. Sympathy gives us the sense of sharing feelings with fellow audience members at a play or concert, and the audience's sympathetic responses; for example, tears, laughter, or joy can further animate the actors or musicians on stage. Sympathy interests us in the good and bad news of distant strangers and nations. With respect to their bad news, we feel concern for them even if we take no action on their behalf.

Sympathy stands in contrast to the act of comparison discussed earlier. As we saw, respect and contempt typically arise when one person compares herself with someone else. However, while she directs her respect or contempt to the person with whom she compares herself, she nevertheless keeps her attention fixed on herself. In effect, she remains self-absorbed since the comparison shows her how *she* is doing relative to others. In contrast, when we sympathize with others, our attention is wholly focused on those with whom we sympathize. Sympathy takes us out of ourselves, so that "our own person is not the object of any passion, nor is there any thing that fixes our attention on ourselves"; instead we enter "deep into the opinions and affections of others."[12] So sympathy interests us in others, in their situations, feelings, and opinions. As Hume notes, we broaden the range of our own emotional experience when we sympathize with others because, by imaginatively reconstructing and responding to their situation, we participate in their experiences. Elsewhere he writes, "In general, it is certain, that, wherever we go, whatever we reflect on or converse about, every thing still presents us with the view

---

12. Hume, *Treatise*, Book 2, Part 2, Section 2, and Book 2, Part 1, Section 11.

of human happiness or misery, and excites in our breast a sympathetic movement of pleasure or uneasiness" (EPM 5). Hume appeals to sympathy to argue that we are not driven purely by self-interest, and that we are often far more concerned about the feelings, situations, and lives of others.

Nevertheless, the natural operation of sympathy may work to exacerbate partiality, and even play a role in creating or sustaining the in-group bias discussed above. Sympathy enlivens our ideas of others' emotions, and this enlivening is facilitated by certain associations that the mind naturally makes. We sympathize more easily with people who resemble us, for example, with those who share our nationality, religion, profession, or political outlook. We also tend to have a more immediate sympathy with those related to us or with those who have become familiar through long acquaintance. We naturally sympathize more easily with people who are physically close to us, since their experiences unfold right in front of us. Finally, when others' situations are especially vivid, our sympathy will be more readily engaged; for example, when we are confronted with a large-scale tragedy, or when an eloquent writer movingly depicts the triumphs and tragedies of her characters.

These natural tendencies of sympathy, together with social forces such as those of family, religion, or government, shape how we learn to sympathize with others. We usually form habits of sympathizing in highly discerning ways. If we sympathize more easily with those we recognize as like ourselves in some relevant aspect, such as sharing the same nationality or religion, then it becomes more difficult to sympathize with the feelings and opinions of those whom we perceive as different from us. When the natural operations of sympathy lead people to form habits whereby they discriminate between those who are like them and those who are different, then sympathy may block invidious comparisons only between members of those in the same group. If sympathy reinforces a group's shared values and sense of loyalty, then it becomes more difficult for the members to sympathize with those they regard as outsiders.

Hume argues that we can take steps to correct the natural biases of sympathy (such as sympathizing more easily with those who resemble us in certain ways), which make us naturally more interested in some people and less likely to sympathize with others. Correcting the natural biases will in turn help to correct the more

socially conditioned prejudicial beliefs and inappropriately negative emotions such as extreme hate. The first step to correcting
these biases is to take the perspective of others. In the case of social
prejudice, what must be adopted is the perspective of those
regarded as different in some negative way. In doing so, it is important to understand how those whose perspective is being adopted
think about themselves, and to find ways to engage in dialogue
with them. Adopting the perspective of others is in turn a step
toward forming a shared point of view. Hume appeals to the
notion of what he calls a "common point of view," a shared vantage
point for conversation and debate, characterized by a set of terms
or discourse that allows us to make ourselves intelligible to one
another. Hume thinks that some people will do a better job than
others of taking up the common point of view because they have
cultivated a sense of humanity, as well as some virtues associated
with making good judgments about themselves and others.

CORRECTING SYMPATHY AND CULTIVATING HUMANITY

Before looking at how the common point of view works and at the
virtues of good judgment, let us consider an objection. Someone
might object that those who are prejudiced and hate members of
particular groups have no incentive to try to understand the perspective of those they hate, especially if their biases reflect the outlook of the status quo. I think we can find several considerations
that militate against this objection. We have already considered one;
namely, that the prejudiced person incurs epistemic and psychological costs. In holding false beliefs about those they hate they are in
error about what other people are actually like. If they could revise
those beliefs through reflection and by getting more information,
but they do not, then they are willfully ignorant. Recall that Hume
argues that the judgments of prejudiced people "lack credibility and
authority." So learning to see what others are really like will put
one in possession of greater knowledge, and make one more likely
to be listened to by others. In addition, the prejudiced person will
not have a well-developed sense of humanity. His inhumanity causes
him to view those he hates as inferior human beings, not deserving
of the respect he shows others. According to Hume, cultivating
humanity has the overall effect of moderating the passions, and

leads us to rely more on settled internal sentiments concerning what is good or bad, rather than simply reacting to appearances.

As we noted earlier, Hume argues that we must form a shared viewpoint with others if we are to make ourselves intelligible to one another. Each person's "interest is peculiar to himself, and the aversions and desires, which result from it, cannot be supposed to affect others in a like degree" (EPM 5). We must "converse" with one another in order to become familiarized to some more general preferences "without which our conversation and discourse could scarcely be rendered intelligible to each other" (EPM 5). As Hume points out, we "often change our situation" with respect to others, depending on contingent factors such as how close someone is to us, and experience shows us that "we every day meet with persons, who are in a situation different from us, and who could never converse with us, were we to remain constantly in that position and point of view, which is peculiar to ourselves" (EPM 5).

Both our natural partiality and sympathy make it possible for us to form a common point of view with others. Hume thinks that we frequently do this without much effort. We sometimes at least see that we are giving the preference, say in terms of admiration, to the person closer to us, rather than to someone equally or perhaps more admirable, who lies far from us in time or place. However, "the judgment here corrects the inequalities of our internal emotions and perceptions; in like manner, as it preserves us from error, in the several variations of images, presented to our external senses" (EPM 5). We do not think that an object is really as small as it looks when we view it from a great distance, and easily correct the evidence of our sense perception, and analogously, we know that were we to approach the distant person, we would feel the proper admiration for her. "And, indeed, without such a correction of appearances, both in internal and external sentiment, men could never think or talk steadily on any subject" (EPM 5).

We should note that Hume sometimes uses the term "humanity" as an alternative for sympathy. When he does so, the context suggests that our sympathetic response is one that reflects our sense of a shared humanity with others (rather than a more partial sympathetic response). Hume argues that all of us have some modicum of humanity. It is "impossible for such a creature as man to be totally indifferent to the well or ill-being of his fellow creatures, and not readily, of himself, to pronounce, where nothing gives him any particular bias, that what promotes their happiness is good, what tends to their misery is evil, without any farther regard or consideration" (EPM 5). Although no one is completely indifferent to the interests of at least some part of humankind, some people will be worse than indifferent toward some others. But human beings are not by nature "absolutely malicious and spiteful" (EPM 5). Rather, "interest or revenge or envy" can pervert our sense of humanity so that we become indifferent or malicious (EPM 5). Hume suggests that cultivating our sense of humanity helps us to accurately evaluate and respond to what people and their lives are like. This natural sense of humanity gives us "the faint rudiments" of a general distinction between actions, such as those that harm and those that benefit others (EPM 5). As the proportion of someone's humanity increases, "his connexion with those who are injured or benefited, and his lively conception of their misery or happiness," invigorate his sense of morality and sentiments or blame or praise (EPM 5).

In addition to cultivating our sense of humanity, Hume argues that we must also cultivate certain intellectual virtues if we are to assess accurately what other people are like. These virtues, by means of which we reason well, will help us to exercise our sense of humanity appropriately, and to be properly responsive to people. In the first section of EPM, Hume notes, "some species of beauty command our affection and approbation," but "it is impossible for any reasoning to redress their influence." That is, there are some things to which we just are attracted, and others to which we are averse. It is difficult, if not impossible, for example, to try to reason someone into liking broccoli if they simply dislike the taste of it. But our sense of the beauty or deformity of people's character or person is not only influenced by such argument and reasoning, but actually requires the exercise of intellect. To evaluate properly one another's character, Hume argues "it is requisite to employ much reasoning, in order to feel the proper sentiment." The actual beauty or deformity of someone's character "demands the assistance of our intellectual faculties, in order to give it a suitable influence on the human mind." To have "a proper discernment" of what someone is like "we find, that much reasoning should precede, that nice distinctions be made, just conclusions drawn, distant comparisons formed, complicated relations examined, and general facts fixed and ascertained."[13] In the first appendix of EPM, Hume argues that we must rely on reason to learn which character traits and actions tend to benefit society and which harm it. However, while reason instructs us regarding the beneficial or harmful tendencies of traits, only our sense of humanity can accord favor to what is beneficial, and disfavor to what is harmful. So both reason and humanity must work together.

In his essay on the standard of taste with regard to works of art, Hume urges that reasoning well and cultivating a sense of humanity actually comprise a set of virtues, and that only someone in possession of such virtues can say with authority whether something really merits our approval or disapproval. The person with good taste or judgment exhibits "strong sense, united to delicate sentiment, improved by practice, perfected by comparison, and cleared of all prejudice."[14] Let us see how these virtues help us to assess what someone is like, in terms of their character or person. Someone must acquire a competence in judging well, and this will require practice; for example, we may need experience of several instances of generosity to discern what makes someone generous. Does receiving a benefit from someone make the giver generous? Or does motive or attitude also count? Over time, we all gain experience of judging others as untrustworthy, duplicitous, or cowardly, or of having ourselves judged as such by others; and of admiring others for their kindness, courage, sense of parental obligations, or overall good character. Comparison of different cases can help us see what is similar or different between two persons, actions, or situations. Comparison will thus be useful in bringing the physically distant case closer, and help us to see that, for example, what we feel less strongly about because it is remote is just as worthy as what is close to us. Or in the case of cultural difference, comparison may help us see what is common in, for example, parental concern, loyalty, or honor, even if these values are expressed in different actions. We saw above that with respect to our assessment of persons, delicate feeling or sentiment belongs to the person

---

13. These quotations are from Section 1, "Of the General Principles of Morals," not reprinted in this volume.

14. Hume, *Essays*, p. 241.

who has a cultivated sense of humanity and "a warm concern for the species"; she is more likely to notice the particular features of individual cases, and to sort through and respond to their complexities. To avoid prejudice, as we also saw above, we must put aside our particular interests and our biases and take people or situations on their own terms. Hume says that "it belongs to good sense to check" the influence of prejudice before it perverts the operations of our intellectual faculties or our sentiment.[15]

Above I noted that we often naturally adopt a common point of view, from which we consider the perspectives of the relevant parties. Yet the discussion of the cultivation of humanity and the virtues of good judgment suggests that taking up a shared perspective with others is not automatic, and not always easy. Indeed, we may often find it easier to pass judgment even when we do not have all the facts, have not formed the proper comparisons, or put aside our prejudices, since such judgments conform naturally to our habitual opinions or feelings. The connection Hume draws between the virtues of judging well with the authority of our judgments emphasizes his point that not all judgments, including evaluations grounded in feeling or sentiment, are equal.

LANGUAGE AS THE REFLECTION OF OUR SHARED SENSE OF HUMANITY

As I have noted, the shared or common point of view is one characterized by a discourse that makes us intelligible to one another. Hume famously distinguishes between the language of self-love, which reflects a person's private interests, and the more public language of morality:

> When a man denominates another his *enemy*, his *rival*, his *antagonist*, his *adversary*, he is understood to speak the language of self-love, and to express sentiments, peculiar to himself, and arising from his particular circumstances and situation. But when he bestows on any man the epithets of *vicious* or *odious* or *depraved*, he then speaks another language, and

---

15. Hume, Essays, p. 240.

expresses sentiments, in which, he expects, all his
audience are to concur with him. He must here, therefore, depart from his private and particular situation,
and must choose a point of view, common to him with
others (EPM 9).

We might note that prejudice and extreme hate are also usually
betrayed in our language. So the common point of view will also
disqualify sexist, religious, ethnic, and racist epithets, as well as
those that denigrate others on the basis of sexual orientation. If we
expect others to concur with our sentiments, then we must use the
more publicly acceptable language that accurately describes character or expresses a more objective sense of what makes others
good or bad people, rather than the particular terminology of self-
interest or prejudice. This public language will reflect public dialogue, in which we aim to arrive at more general preferences about
what benefits or harms our community, and puts us on common
ground. This social "intercourse of sentiments, therefore, in society
and conversations, makes us form some general unalterable standard, by which we may approve or disapprove" of one another's
characters, actions, and ways of living (EPM 5). Hume is well aware
that people may abuse the language of morality and use it to express
self-interest or prejudice in a more underhanded way. He notes that
"we commonly pervert our adversary's conduct, by imputing malice or injustice to him, in order to give vent to those passions,
which arise from . . . private interest. When the heart is full of rage,
it never wants pretenses of this nature" (EPM 9, n. 57). It is here
that the virtues of good judgment and a more delicate sympathy
will be particularly useful in helping us to assess the intentions
behind the expression.

The language used when we take up the common point of view
is important for another reason. While even the prejudiced may
sometimes take up a common point of view, and the virtuous frequently do so as well, people may often struggle with giving up
their prejudicial beliefs and feelings. In particular, it may not be
easy to eradicate bias at the emotional level. Hume stresses that in
cases where one cannot put aside prejudice or self-interest, we can
still verbally express the appropriate judgment. "Though the heart
takes not part entirely with those general notions, nor regulates all

its love and hatred, by [them] . . . yet have these moral differences a considerable influence, and being sufficient, at least, for discourse, serve all our purposes in company, in the pulpit, on the theater, and in the schools" (EPM 5). While the language of morality and humanity is grounded in the properly cultivated sentiments of those who judge well, others may learn to become competent in this language and thereby themselves acquire the virtues of good judgment and sense of humanity that will lead them to appreciate what people are really like as valuable or harmful members of society. We may recall here my earlier claim that on the Humean view, moral knowledge is a resource that we establish collectively. When we become competent at moral evaluation, we have an authority with others, and our collectively authoritative judgments have a practical effect on society.

Those not the targets of hate and bias might take various active steps to understand the values and commitments of people who are stigmatized because they are perceived as different. Listening directly to them, for example, to their testimony or protest, is one way. People might make an effort to become familiar with the history and literature of a group, and of the narratives through which they have formed their own sense of their identity. As Hume urges, despite some historical and cultural variability of values, there is an underlying commonality that human beings share, and most of us value friendship, honor, courage, justice, and so forth, although these may take culturally variable shapes.

Finally, it is important to realize that the common point of view, that shared vantage point where we find common ground through language to negotiate judgments and evaluations of one another, is not necessarily a perspective that will provide us with full agreement with one another, even if agreement may be the goal at which we aim. The common point of view provides us with the terms for broader moral and political inclusion in shared dialogue. That dialogue may take the form of debate and challenge, especially to preconceived notions of what people are like. It may take the form of negotiation, and of revision or elimination of our social categories as people work to establish the evidence for more reflective judgments about the values we can share. In addition to relying on a common language of morality or humanity, Hume holds out the hope for our cultivating a universal sentiment concerning which kinds of people are good for society and which are harmful, based on an objective assessment of character rather than on stereotypical generalizations. By adopting a more inclusive perspective, people extend their sympathetic concern to others, which thereby introduces an affective quality—a felt sentiment—to how they regard one another. As Hume notes, those committed to cultivating a sense of our shared humanity will thus form the "party of humankind against vice or disorder, its common enemy" (EPM 9).

Suggestions for Further Reading

Hume was viewed as a moral skeptic for the first two centuries after his death and it is only fairly recently that scholars have begun to take his positive account of the virtues seriously. Hitherto the best place to look for ideas about how to apply Hume's virtue theory was to Hume himself, in particular to his short essays (see his *Essays: Moral, Political, and Literary*, 2nd ed., E. F. Miller, ed. (Indianapolis: Liberty Classics, 1987). There is now in addition a small but growing body of secondary literature applying Hume's virtue theory to practical matters.

An entire issue of the *Journal of Medicine and Philosophy* has been devoted to the subject of "Hume, Bioethics, and the Philosophy of Medicine," with articles on topics such as Hume's influence on the development of clinical ethics, and the applicability of his views to topics such as sympathy, suicide, and justice in health-care allocation. See the *Journal of Medicine and Philosophy*, 24 (1999).

The implications of Hume's views for our conduct toward animals is discussed by Annette Baier in "Knowing our Place in the Animal World," in her *Postures of the Mind* (Minneapolis: University of Minnesota Press, 1985) and more recently by Tom Beauchamp in "Hume on the Nonhuman Animal" in the *Journal of Medicine and Philosophy* 24 (1999): 322–335.

Earl W. Spurgin takes a Humean approach to the problem of business ethics, in "Looking for Answers in All the Wrong Places," *Business Ethics Quarterly* 14 (2004): 293–313. For a treatment of the "last man" problem in environmental ethics, in keeping with Humean sensibilities, see Jennifer Welchman, "The Virtues of Stewardship," *Environmental Ethics* 21 (1999): 411–423. On moral education for children, see Edmund Pincoffs, "On Becoming the Right

Sort," in *Quandaries and Virtues: Against Reductivism in Ethics* (Lawrence: University of Kansas Press, 1986). Annette Baier compares Hume's approach to punishment with Kant's in "Moralism and Cruelty: Reflections on Hume and Kant," *Ethics* 103 (1993): 436–457.

Clancy W. Martin

Nietzsche's Virtues
and the Virtues of Business[1]

1.

What does Friedrich Nietzsche have to say to a successful twenty-first-century businessperson, or to someone who plans to become one? At first it sounds like an unlikely and fruitless question. Nietzsche lived most of his life in poverty. He never engaged in business. Moreover, he was deeply suspicious of capitalism and of what he believed would be its likely effects on Western civilization. He worried that capitalism and its political partner-in-crime—democracy—would encourage what he called the *leveling* of Western culture. Because the market rewards mass appeal, he thought that it would inevitably drag our culture down to the lowest common denominator of human interest. Easily produced material goods and comforts, with their immediate pleasures, would replace the rarer and more labor-intensive products of the fine arts and the spiritual life. Mankind would come to measure itself by popular applause rather than by reflective critical standards. To be fair, in many respects, Nietzsche did not miss the mark.

Nevertheless, the business world of today, in its best examples, is something Nietzsche would (mostly) have admired. The most successful businesspersons today, whether they know it or not, tend to be Nietzscheans in their morality, at least in business contexts. This is because Nietzsche's virtue ethics and the best contemporary businesspeople operate with the same fundamental guiding principle: excellence.

---

1. My thanks to Jennifer Welchman for her extensive editing, and contribution of arguments, to this essay.

What does it mean to excel? Notice that it is a very different sort of question than "What does it mean to be good?" Following the Judeo-Christian tradition, many of us might say, for example, that it is good to be humble, but it seems odd to say that to be humble is to excel. Humility is a plausible example of goodness on this view, but it jars as an example of excellence. There is in fact an interesting tension between humility and excellence: those who truly excel often are not particularly humble and, we might add, for good reason. David Hume famously remarked that it was unhealthy and dishonest for a person who was clearly superior to those around herself to pretend—either to herself or to others—that she was not. In the early days of Microsoft, Bill Gates "motivated" his programmers by telling them that he could have written in a weekend programs that had taken them months to complete. There is little doubt about the *excellence* of David Hume and Bill Gates, but in neither was excellence expressed as *humility*.

For Nietzsche, Western civilization went perilously astray when it exchanged an older ethic of excellence for the new, Judeo-Christian ethic of goodness. It is not "goodness" in general that Nietzsche wants to indict, rather a particular kind of goodness, the goodness that he thinks was invented by the Judeo-Christian tradition. We should not suppose that Nietzsche is advocating a return to the ethics of the ancient Greeks or any other pre-Christian morality. Nietzsche is not saying that what counted as excellence among ancient Athenians should count in the same way for us today. The historical and ethical position we find ourselves in, he insists, requires a new approach to morality, but one that is nevertheless informed by this antique ideal of excellence.

Perhaps the most basic change that Nietzsche calls for in his list of revaluations of our present values is the difficult and in some ways dangerous shift from seeing actions as right or wrong to seeing persons as good or bad. As he once wrote in a notebook: "One must free oneself from the question, 'What is good? What is compassionate?' and ask instead 'What is the good *human*, the compassionate human?'"[2] For Nietzsche, actions are only morally interesting insofar as they reveal the moral character of the persons who perform those actions. Yet when we move into the strictly

---

2. Notebook 35, Number 19, May–July 1885. Translated by the author.

moral context we may be reluctant to say, "It isn't just that he acted badly, he's a bad person," or "It isn't just that her deceptions were harmful, she's malicious." That hesitation, Nietzsche argues, is a symptom of our moral sickness.

2.

Nietzsche sees two basic kinds of morality at struggle in the history of the West (sometimes he even suggests that these two moralities are basic to all the world's ethical history). He calls these moralities *master morality* and *slave morality*. These two moralities develop from opposed contexts of relative power. Master morality arises in the class of those persons in a society who hold power. Slave morality arises among the class of those persons who are, relatively speaking, powerless.

Master morality operates with a conceptual value pair called "good" and "bad." "Good" is whatever is deemed valuable to the class of persons who call a thing "good." Quite naturally, the things that a class of persons designates as good turn out to be things that please or benefit that class. Health, food, property, sex, strength, pride: all these things are, Nietzsche argues, naturally pleasing to the human animal and so are called "goods" by the master class. What is displeasing is called "bad": sickness, poverty, hunger, chastity—these are all easy examples. "Good" and "bad" apply not only to things, but also people. "Good" people, from the point of view of those who create and live master morality, are "people like us": the friends, peers, and equals (including equal enemies) of the "masters" themselves. "Bad" people, on the other hand, are not so much harmful from the point of view of masters as they are contemptible. They are bad because they are not equal to the masters (hence their designation as "slaves," i.e., subordinates.)

It would be a mistake to say that master morality is a straightforward form of egoism (the moral system that asserts that what is valuable in itself is that which is valuable for me). It more closely resembles a blend of egoism and a kind of social naturalism, in which what is valuable is so because it is valuable for "me and people like me" and contributes to "our" well-being. What is good is what is naturally good for "us."

Slave morality operates in a very different way. Slaves find themselves in a society where they do not possess power or its advantages. However, Nietzsche argues, the drive to gain power—what Nietzsche calls "the will to power"—is fundamental to all life. Slaves cannot escape their need for power, despite the fact that they are powerless. So, Nietzsche says, the most cunning and in some ways the most creative moment in all human history occurs: the slave class creates a new table of values in order to invert the existing power structure. The slaves (i.e., the oppressed) realize that the significance of their lack of power is a function of the value structure the master class has created. Wealth is good because the masters say it is good; strength is good for the same reason; and because slaves are denied these things, they lack value or status (itself a kind of power). Suppose wealth were not good, but evil? Suppose strength were evil and weakness the true good? Suppose that true goodness lay not in the appearance of power and happiness in this life, but in the reward of enormous power and happiness in the next?

Slave morality turns master morality on its head for the purpose of taking power away from the masters. The things that masters despise are revalued as goods; the goods masters appreciate are revalued, not as "bad" (lacking goodness) but as "evils" (opposites to good). Slave morality's new conceptual pair, "good and evil," is necessary to its refusal to accept its own powerlessness as a sign of inferiority. Thus, slaves must take the position that the material and social power they lack are merely apparent goods. True goodness must be something for which material power is irrelevant, say "the next world," nirvana, or what have you. To the extent material power distracts one from "true goodness," it is a temptation opposed to good—an "evil." According to the new table of values, wealth becomes an evil and poverty a good; strength an evil and weakness a good; pride an evil and humility a good; sex an evil and chastity a good; the body itself an evil and asceticism a good. The marvelous thing about slave morality is not just its ingenuity, but that it *works*. In time the master class accepts the moral revaluation of the slaves. The old master morality withers, and Judeo-Christianity, the embodiment of the new slave morality, flourishes, and takes over.

However, there is something wrong with slave morality. We should not say that there is something *morally* wrong with it, because precisely what we are describing is a shift in moralities and a new concept of moral right and wrong. Rather, the wrongness is a sickness: there is something *unhealthy* about slave morality.

The unhealthiness of slave morality is a consequence of its motivational structure. Nietzsche believes that basic human drives demand expression in some form. If they cannot *discharge* themselves outwardly, they will do so inwardly, but discharging themselves inwardly means they never discharge themselves fully or without residue. Thus they make us sick (this is sometimes called a *hydraulic* view of human nature). The motivational structure of master morality is healthy, Nietzsche argues, because it allows our drives to discharge themselves fully. The motivational structure of slave morality is more complex. The slave's self-repression is a source of ongoing dissatisfaction, giving rise to an attitude that Nietzsche calls *ressentiment.*

Ressentiment is more than ordinary "resentment" for particular objects or persons, but rather a much more generalized attitude toward one's world. In *ressentiment,* the slave feels driven to pursue what the master class values, but cannot endorse it without endorsing his or her own powerlessness. So the slave must alienate him or herself from the drive, condemning it as evil. Of course this doesn't make the drive go away, but it does provide it with a new object—power over one's self and one's own drives. The drive is expressed as a denial of itself. Spiritual or moral power is sought through the denial of the drive to own and enjoy wealth and acceptance of a life of "poverty and good works," but the strategy ultimately fails because the slave can never eradicate the drive to power by repressing it. The slave's inability to overcome this inner "evil" is "the bite of conscience." Unlike masters, slaves come to feel, as Nietzsche says, *guilty.*

Fascinating though it may be, why are we worried about this diagnosis of a historical (or merely hypothetical—Nietzsche may only be telling us a kind of "state of nature" story) change in moralities? Because, for Nietzsche, not only is the popular Judeo-Christian morality an expression of slave morality, so also are the two great ethical theories of his own day: utilitarianism and deontology. How Nietzsche attempts to demonstrate this is too long a story to retell here but the fundamental thrust of his attack is not difficult to understand. Both kinds of theories are intended to provide a philosophical foundation for the moral intuitions that are already in place, not to bring about a revolution in the values of their societies. Both thought that the average "man in the street" had a pretty good idea of what was right and what was wrong.

The theoretical disagreement between the two took place at the level of properly analyzing and describing those mostly reliable popular moral intuitions.

For Nietzsche, however, the popular moral intuitions of our society are themselves the problem. Whatever their philosophical articulation, when we believe that some actions are "good" and others are "evil," we are accepting the perspective of slave morality and we are thus undermining our own flourishing. We are endorsing values that, rather than contributing to our psychological and cultural health, are in fact making us *sick*.

One grave symptom of this sickness is slave morality's insistence on dividing persons from their actions. In master morality, a person is judged by her position in life, her friends, the goods she has acquired, the accomplishments she has achieved, and so forth. Collectively, they reflect her moral worth as a person. The good person has on the whole succeeded in her efforts: she excels, she has, so to speak, proven her worth. The bad person, on the other hand, is a failure: collectively the failure of her actions reflects her overall failure as a person, her "badness." Master morality presumes that one acts the way one does because of the person one is; the kind of people we are is revealed by our actions. Who we are and what we do is continuous, one with the other.

Slave morality, on the other hand, originating from a position of weakness, refuses to treat the moral worth of a person as a function of his or her outward success or failure. Appealing to its own value pair—good and evil—slave morality insists that the goodness or badness of a person's conduct does not directly entail a judgment about the good or evil of the person acting. A person may fail to act well without being evil, and vice versa. Moreover, a person whose acts turn out well, if undertaken for evil purposes, will actually suffer because of her success—she will be (or should be) wracked with guilt. As Nietzsche points out, the outcome would be laughable if not so tragic. The better we are morally, and thus the more sensitive to our failings, the more miserable and guilt-ridden our lives will be.

3.

As we have seen, Nietzsche takes from his analysis of master and slave morality the idea that we should not distinguish sharply between persons and their actions. However, when we take this more holistic view of persons, they do not all turn out to be "moral equals." Since a person's worth is partly a function of his or her success or failure in life, some people are *superior* to others. The suggestion that there are ethically significant differences between persons may ring harshly in democratic and egalitarian ears. We like to insist that all persons, at least ethically speaking, are equal. Today we often go on to insist that all persons are, or ought to be, equal politically, legally, and perhaps in many other ways. The notion that all persons are, or ought to be, considered equal is relatively new in human history; and, Nietzsche insists, this notion is both mistaken and unhealthy. For Nietzsche, the human need to value, and especially the need to create and impose moralities, is an expression of the historically obvious fact that there are differences among persons and classes of persons.

Nietzsche characterizes evaluative differences as *orders of rank*. When we value anything, he argues, we impose an order of rank upon it. When we say that this Mondrian is a good painting and that this Klimt is a poor one, what we are expressing is a ranking among paintings: this Mondrian is better than many other Mondrians and indeed many other paintings. When we say that this sushi restaurant is excellent and that one down the street is lousy, we are (very reasonably) acting just like food critics who rank sushi restaurants from best to worst. Similarly, when we call persons "good" or "bad," Nietzsche thinks, we are expressing the idea that this person stands *above* that other person.

It's one thing to rank the products of acts, like paintings. It's quite another to try to rank actions themselves—it seems bizarre to create a scale on which lying is a lower action than, say, stealing, or similarly, an act of generosity is higher than an act of friendship. If we are honest, however, we will admit that we do in fact rank *people* all the time. When we do so, we see that we rank them in terms of the functional roles that people occupy, and these functional roles are naturally defined in terms of the groups in which those functional roles operate. When we say of a person that she is "good" what we really mean is that she is a good friend, or a good writer, a good computer programmer, or a good citizen—or perhaps all of those things. We do not have a standard of her goodness in any of those roles independent of the group in which the role operates. So when we say that she is a good programmer, what we mean is that she is better than many programmers, at a par with some others, and not quite as good as those we would characterize as the very best programmers.

For Nietzsche, our recognition that to value is to rank has further moral (or what we might better call meta-moral) consequences. As he writes in *Beyond Good and Evil* (221): "One must force moralities to bow down first of all before the *order of rank*, one must shove their presumption before their consciences—until at last they come to agree that it is *immoral* to say: 'what is right for one is fair for another.'" This perhaps shocking remark stands at the very heart of Nietzsche's ethics. His idea is that once we recognize that there are orders of rank among persons we can see the attitudes that are appropriate and inappropriate between those ranks, and see still different attitudes appropriate to members of a particular rank. The (moral) attitude and responsibilities of a member of a higher rank toward a lower rank is, or ought to be, different than the attitude and responsibilities that person would have to her own rank, and different again than the attitude and responsibilities she would have to a member of a superior rank.

An example is helpful here. Suppose you are a middle manager in advertising sales at a Web-services company like MSN or Google. To succeed, you must negotiate a range of different attitudes and responsibilities. You must be a mentor to the junior salespeople on your team but also, when necessary, a disciplinarian. You must be a deferential understudy to your boss but also willing to stand your ground and speak your mind. You must be a helpful colleague to the other middle managers. You must also be friendly, devoted, and helpful to clients while remaining a cagey and self-interested representative of your company and you must take care to be a fierce but respectful competitor to your peers at other Web-service companies. All of these various relationships embody differences in rank that bring with them different "moral" demands. Being truthful with your boss, for example, will be very different than being truthful with your employees, or with your peers, your customers, and your competitors. To say that everyone here should be treated equally, Nietzsche argues, is not only naïve and self-destructive, it is also immoral, because it would inevitably force you to treat some people in ways they did not deserve. Treating your employees with the deference you reserve for your boss would confuse them. Giving your boss orders would have very unhappy consequences for you.

What Nietzsche does *not* mean to imply here (at least in the passage I quoted above) is that it is defensible for the strong to mis-
handle the weak, or for the powerful to trample upon the
powerless, or for the ruling majority to oppress the ruled minority.
On the contrary, if in the interest of supposed "fairness" the powerful make the same demands on those without power that it
makes on its own class, this supposed "equal treatment" would,
Nietzsche thinks, create oppression. It is oppressive to demand
from a person or a class of people what that person or class does
not have the power to provide.

In *Beyond Good and Evil* (272), Nietzsche describes the awareness of the moral significance of orders of rank as a "sign of nobility": "never to consider lowering our duties to duties for everybody,
not to want to hand over, nor to share, one's own responsibility;
to reckon our privileges and their exercise among one's *duties.*"
This almost sounds like a short laundry list of the virtues of a
good businessperson. (A businessperson might respond to this list:
what about delegating? But to delegate is not "to share one's *own*
duties": depending upon one's position in an organization, delegating certain responsibilities may in fact be an example of "one's
own duty" or "one's own responsibility.") The point here, both
for Nietzsche's noble human who is aware of her order of rank
and for a good businessperson, is that one's duties, responsibilities, and privileges are precisely those things that create, demonstrate, and reinforce the rank one enjoys. The space here being
described is explicitly a moral space: Nietzsche uses the language
of duty, responsibility, and privilege advisedly. Yet it is a moral
space inhabited gladly by the person aware of her order of rank
because, unlike the constraining limits of the space inhabited by a
person operating in traditional morality, the moral space of the
order of rank itself creates the possibility of desirable action. The
actions the noble person may choose are the expression of the
order of rank she occupies. For this reason the person who understands morality in this way does not desire freedom, because her
morality in no way restricts her action (quite the opposite). For
the person who does not understand morality in this way, however (typically, a person of slave morality), there is nothing he will
crave more fiercely than freedom, because he experiences his
morality as constantly opposing actions that he would otherwise
be able to perform.

It should be admitted that this is an ethic developed precisely for the exception and against the rule. One commentator aptly summed up Nietzsche's philosophy as "aristocratic radicalism." The higher one ascends the "order of rank," the more noble one appears to be, and the further behind one leaves the "common man," "the public," and what Nietzsche in his most derisive moments calls "the herd." Of course, to endorse an ethic of excellence of this kind is to accept the consequence (or more, to affirm the fact) that not everyone is or can be excellent (at least, not in the same ways). We should be careful not to cheapen the ideal of the excellent exception by supposing that it should be applied only to those who are exceptional in strength or other forms of "material" power. In fact, Nietzsche's most common examples of the truly excellent are not kings, generals, or politicians, but artists.

Fascinatingly, the attitude most characteristic of the noble person who is conscious of her rank and excellence is not that of arrogance (as we might worry) but its contrary, reverence: "the art and enthusiasm in reverence, in devotion are the regular symptoms of an aristocratic manner in thinking and evaluating" (*Beyond Good and Evil* 260). Nietzsche does not explain why this is so, but he also remarks that a mean-spirited disrespect for all rare and lofty things is characteristic of those persons who are ignorant of rank or who resentfully regard the higher rank of others from below. From this we might conclude that the person who regards order of rank as a necessary and desirable part of human life respects not only her order in the rank, but also those people and things ranked above her. She is reverent because she considers herself good but does not suppose she is best, and she reveres those persons and things that contribute to her own goodness.

A particularly nice passage contrasts the high order of rank of the reverent with the low order of the resentful:

> Anyone to whose task and practice it belongs to investigate souls will employ precisely this art in many forms in order to ascertain the ultimate value of a soul and the immutable, inborn order of rank to which it belongs: he will test it for its *instinct of reverence. Difference engender haine* [difference engenders hatred]: the callowness of many natures sprays out suddenly like dirty water if some holy vessel, some treasure from a sealed shrine,

some book with the mark of a great destiny is carried
by; and on the other hand there is an involuntary
silence, a hesitation of the eye, a cessation of all gestures
that express how a soul *feels* the nearness of the most
venerable." (*Beyond Good and Evil* 263)

Arrogance, again, is expressed by precisely those who do not
appreciate what is deserving of respect, those who fail to recognize
the things which stand in a high rank above themselves; while
those who can discern where they fall in the order of rank, and
what lies above them, are suitably deferential, even hesitant. Thus
Nietzsche finds virtue even in a kind of tentativeness, so long as
that timidity is directed toward the appropriately valuable object
(for this same reason he claims that those aware of value as order
of rank invented love as a passion—they saw the importance of
elevating the beloved to an object of not merely sexual attraction,
but almost religious reverence).

In a business context this virtue of reverence is surprisingly helpful. We do not normally think of good businesspeople as *reverent*
but perhaps we should. Consider, for example, the gross presumption—even *hubris*—of a recent case like Dennis Kozlowski of Tyco.
While Kozlowski was building his enormously successful company,
he treated it with the kind of gentle reverence that reminds us of a
parent caring for a child. Indeed, when you talk to entrepreneurs
who are building their young businesses, this is precisely the sort of
language they use: the business is " a baby," "in its infancy," "still
just growing," and so on. However, once Kozlowski had grown the
business to adulthood and taken it public he began treating it with
the now-infamous arrogance that eventually destroyed it: throwing
multimillion-dollar parties on the company tab, borrowing huge
sums from the business at no interest and without approval from
the board of directors, bullying the board when he troubled to consult them at all, and so on. Even had there been no harm done and
no secrecy in all of this outrageous behavior, we would nonetheless
be morally offended because of the disrespect, the utter lack of reverence it shows for the business that made Kozlowski's success possible. When we contrast Kozlowski with a figure like Bill Gates,
who speaks of Microsoft and its role in world affairs in almost
messianic terms (and who has used his Microsoft wealth to become
the single largest philanthropist in history), the importance of respect

even among the most powerful for what has created that power is cast in especially dramatic light.

This is not to suggest that businesspeople are to "worship mammon" or revere the accumulation of wealth. What they should revere is the excellence in their own achievements as artists revere the aesthetic beauty their work sometimes achieves and resist, as artists do, the temptation to cheapen their achievements and so also themselves.

4.

What are the virtues for Nietzsche? Business ethicist and Nietzsche scholar Robert C. Solomon counts as many as fifteen different virtues offered by Nietzsche, and Nietzsche himself writes up several different lists.[3] My favorite list is from his early work *Daybreak*:

> *The good four.* Honest with ourselves and whatever is friend to us; courageous toward the enemy; generous toward the vanquished; polite—always; that is how the four cardinal virtues want us.

For Nietzsche, "honesty" or what he later comes to call "truthfulness," is preeminent among the virtues. Honesty here is not to be understood in the sense of sincerity or "speaking one's mind." Rather, the ideal is that attitude which seeks the truth and, having found the truth (or what it believes to be true) refuses to hide, counterfeit, or betray that truth. In this context Nietzsche often mentions the spiritual rigor of the scientist. A scientist is not content with the results of her first experiment: she must test and retest, and see her results repeatedly confirmed; she must vet her conclusions with other scientists; her results must cohere with the best science of her day. Her respect for truth is not merely an acknowledgment of its importance, it is also the discipline of a method, and a suspicion of any "truths" that are insufficiently investigated, less than demonstrated, or won too easily.

For Nietzsche the rigor of truthfulness extends into our relations with our work, our values, our lifestyles, and ultimately to

---

3. Robert C. Solomon, *Living with Nietzsche* (New York: Oxford University Press, 2003), pp. 137–174.

our relationships with ourselves. We should not merely accept the things we suppose to be true, whether on the basis of tradition, the teaching of others, experience, or deeply held belief. We must rather constantly interrogate ourselves and ask, for example, "*Why* do I believe this? Is it for good reasons or bad? Do I simply believe it because I *want* to believe it? Or do I believe it because, of the various options, it seems to me to most closely approximate the truth?" We must always beware of the ticklish sensation of self-deception.[4]

Truthfulness also matters to Nietzsche because it reveals and reinforces something about the motivations of the person who speaks the truth. Nietzsche argues that lies are a sign of weakness or fear. A lie is a kind of evasive strategy employed by the liar because he lacks better means of gaining his ends. The truthful person speaks the truth with contempt for any negative consequences of her truthful speech. She speaks the truth because she is powerful enough to do so, and she refuses to use a lie to procure an advantage that she could gain by other means.[5] For her, truthfulness is not so much a discipline as it is a mark of self-respect.

Nietzsche is careful, however, to distinguish to whom one owes the truth: to oneself and one's friends. This is certainly not the unconditional "never tell a lie!" insisted upon by Kant in particular and by Judeo-Christian morality in general (Kant famously or infamously argued that it is morally wrong to tell a lie even in the attempt to save a human life). We owe the truth to ourselves and to our friends because, presumably, falsehood could harm us and those we care for (the truth is often, if not always, an instrumental good)—to the extent that they share in our projects. We do not owe truth to those who are not, or who will trivialize or misuse the truth. Nor do we owe it to those who are not stakeholders in our

---

4. Nietzsche also has several fascinating arguments on the goods that may be provided by self-deception, but examining those would take us beyond the scope of our discussion here. Cf. my "Nietzsche and the Tell-Tale Boxers," *International Studies in Philosophy* 36(3) (2005): 221–245.

5. There are some advantages, however, that can only be gained by lying, and Nietzsche is more ambivalent about these cases. For example he condones the lies told by Odysseus in *The Odyssey* and *The Iliad*. Cf. my "Nietzsche's Homeric Lies" forthcoming in *The Journal of Nietzsche Studies*.

endeavors. The claims of such persons have no hold upon us; the claims of enemies still less. With regard to the truth, at least, they are on their own.

For businesspeople, this virtue of truthfulness is of the greatest interest in the sense of "being tough on oneself." (Nietzsche sometimes also calls this virtue "wakefulness," a helpful metaphor.) A common mistake in business is what we might call "the glass-half-full mentality"; that is, because of the importance of optimism for success in almost any business context, there is a tendency for businesspeople to try to look on the bright side of most business situations (however dark it may, in reality, be). Just as important as conveying a sense of optimism even when things are gloomy is having the self-discipline to look at the hard facts of the business problems one is confronting. If your profit-and-loss statements show a steady decline in earnings and inventory month after month, it is true yet dishonest (or failing to display the virtue of truthfulness) to say: "Well, we are still making money."

Nietzsche's virtue of truthfulness does not require people to be truthful with competitors or other interests wholly exterior to those of the business, but notice that it does require truthfulness with vendors, customers, and colleagues within the company, to the extent that they share one's enterprise. Falsehood practiced with any of these could cause harm, and ultimately the business itself will suffer harm if it loses customers, vendors, or good fellow employees. This of course doesn't mean we must be truthful in the same degree to each. For example, it would not be in the interests of the business or the vendors, probably, if customers knew the pricing structures of suppliers. However, in every case we must be truthful in such ways that will promote the prosperity of the friendly parties concerned.

Perhaps the most common test of truthfulness discussed in business ethics is that of "the whistleblower." The reason whistleblower cases are so difficult is that the whistleblower generally acts both against her company's interest and her own interest in the service of some larger good that, she believes, is more important than her company or herself. You may have seen the movie *The Insider*, in which the hero, a chemist for a big tobacco company, loses his job, his family, and very nearly his life because he is concerned to expose the deliberate and deadly addictions promoted by cigarette manufacturers. What, we may ask, would Nietzsche say about a case like this? It looks like a tough case. Shouldn't the chemist consider what he owes himself, his family, and his company, before he considers humanity at large?

When we are thinking about virtues we should remember that their range is determined by the kind of functional roles one is positioned within. The businessperson may also be a friend, a parent, a child, a religious communicant, a member of a club, and/or citizen of a political community. These enterprises make the good of most, if not all, of the society around us important to us in some respects. A threat to the basic health of a large percentage of this community can override a narrower threat to our business career. In such an instance, then, it may well be that all those at risk count in a broad sense as "friends."

As we have said, in the world as Nietzsche sees it, while it is virtuous to be truthful with our friends—who have only our best interest at heart, as we do theirs—it would be folly at best and a vice at worst to be truthful to our enemies, who could use it against us. In the competitive world of business today this not only makes good sense, it is established practice. Daimler-Chrysler does not think it owes the truth to Honda about its development of competing fuel technologies, and indeed either company will doubtless mislead the other if it has the opportunity to do so.

We should notice, however, that one's competitors are not necessarily one's enemies. In the retail jewelry business, for example, it is quite common for competing jewelers to swap inventory back and forth, share watches and diamonds, run coordinated promotions, and so on; this is true in nearly every industry. There is such a thing as *friendly* competition, and in such circumstances businesspersons and companies owe one another the truth in precisely the way they would owe the truth to some noncompeting friend, such as a supplier. The point is that friends trust one another and so that trust must be sustained by truthfulness; enemies, however, do not expect the truth from one another: the rules of the game are different, and so it is a different kind of play (employing different skills or virtues).

In any list of the virtues Nietzsche would write, truthfulness is the first among equals, but if Nietzsche had a favorite virtue it would be courage. Of course for Nietzsche, as for us today, courage rarely if ever meant physical courage. Courage for Nietzsche—as for today's businessperson—means: to take risks and to confront one's fears.

Courage is the defining virtue of the "free spirits" we discussed above and if there is any virtue that Nietzsche himself especially exemplified, it was courage. Nietzsche lived a short, unhappy life, plagued with recurrent sickness and terrible physical suffering, always effectively homeless, usually alone, wandering in poverty and obscurity from place to place. Yet he never stopped working, he never gave up, and he always maintained an invincible spirit of optimism. This refusal to give up is Nietzsche's ideal of courage.

The best display of courage, for Nietzsche, is the attitude of *cheerfulness*. Like his early influence, Schopenhauer, Nietzsche believes that most lives are at least as full of suffering as happiness. For this reason Schopenhauer became a gloomy pessimist and denied the value of life. Nietzsche, on the other hand, saw that suffering was as necessary to life as happiness, and responded to it by demanding that we strive to remain cheerful.

For the businessperson, most of the advantages of courage are obvious and we need not linger on them here. It is a staple of pop-psychology books on business that no one ever succeeds in business without bravely taking some risks and persevering where others have failed. What we should particularly note here is the importance of courage in the face of suffering, the importance of cheerfulness in the face of business failure. Most great businesspeople have failed once or more than once (in Silicon Valley in the late 1990s it was considered a weakness in your resume, a sign of timidity and lack of experience, if you had not taken at least one venture through bankruptcy). What distinguishes the great businesspeople is the attitude that goes along with perseverance. It is easy to be cheerful when you have a million dollars in the bank; it is something quite different, and inspiring, when you continue to be cheerful when flat broke and signing a second mortgage on your home to get your latest idea off the ground.

Like truthfulness and courage, generosity is a virtue Aristotle included in his list of the virtues in *Nicomachean Ethics*. Businesspeople can and should be "generous" in many of the ordinary senses of the term. They should be willing to help associates, to mentor junior colleagues, to work to generate goodwill in the workforce and in the surrounding community. Doing so benefits the enterprise and those who we recognize as stakeholders within it. However, for Nietzsche, "generosity" in this ordinary sense is not generosity in the most important sense. Nietzsche is specifically concerned with "generosity to the vanquished"; that is, generosity to those beaten in competition. Nietzsche places tremendous value in the notion of what the Greeks called the *agon* or competition. Competition calls us to greater accomplishments than we could ever have attained on our own; it strengthens and emboldens us; it makes us call on resources that, were we not in competition, we may not even have been aware of; but competition requires equal competitors (no game is any fun when there is "no competition"). So the defeated competitor should not be crushed, but encouraged, so that she can provide competition again.

Similarly, it is unhealthy for any business to exist without competition. In the end monopolies are harmful not only to markets, but to themselves, because they lack the self-discipline that is found in the struggle to compete. Thus—though it sounds a bit strange to our ears—good competitors, while any company will of course strive to outperform them, are necessary to the long-term flourishing of companies. The businessperson will be generous in victory, not because she hopes to enjoy the same generosity should she ever find herself vanquished (such a fearful motivation would be an expression of slave morality), but rather because she wants to guarantee herself the health that comes from competition.

Let us conclude our discussion of Nietzsche's "virtue business ethics" by looking at the virtue of politeness. Because politeness is so deeply woven into the fabric of our ordinary lives we may tend to underestimate its importance as a virtue (at least, until we encounter someone who is truly *rude*). Politeness is much more than nodding to a colleague when you pass one another in the hallway or responding to the question "How are you?" with the perfunctory (and often deceptive) "Just fine, thanks for asking." The virtue of politeness is an expression of the human value of proper comportment, deference, and respect. In this sense it is the virtue that best captures the awareness of the *order of rank* that we saw as so crucial to Nietzsche's ethics in Section 3. Furthermore, we should observe that politeness does not extend only to those who we consider to be our superiors. On the contrary, politeness is perhaps even more important with those who are in positions inferior or subordinate to our own. While politeness does not require that we shift our power relations with other people, it does demand that we exercise our powers in a way that acknowledges the sense of self-worth of others.

Politeness is the grease of business—so much so that, at the end of a long day at the office, you might sometimes feel a bit greasy. (Perhaps for this reason, in *Beyond Good and Evil* Nietzsche describes politeness as a vice, but as a vice that we should nevertheless cultivate.) In the competitive world of business, where businesspeople often find themselves seated at the same table with a person who is trying to buy their company (and perhaps take their job), trying to steal their customers, or holding out for a price less than their products are worth, there is in many ways no virtue more important than politeness in order to sustain the business relationship. If in business we always said what we thought about our customers or our vendors or our competition or our colleagues (much less our bosses and employees), business simply could not be done. Everyone would be at everyone else's throats. However, because politeness is maintained, even an excess of politeness (think of the almost too-sweet friendliness of the "good old boy," for example), people continue to operate well even in the most adversarial situations. Anyone who has ever lost his temper during a business deal and abandoned politeness will tell you what an expensive lesson they learned. Politeness may not always gain you an advantage in business, but rudeness will always lose the advantage.

5.

The perspective on value offered by slave morality is anathema to many businesspeople. It is tough to persuade them that they should scorn the rewards of this life because they will find salvation in the next. It is tougher still to persuade them that a "good" businessperson is not necessarily a "successful" businessperson, and it is nigh on impossible to convince them to stop ranking themselves and one another. (Witness "The Fortune 500," "America's 100 Best Companies to Work For," "The Top Twenty-Five MBA Programs," "America's Fifty Leading Executives"—and note that all these rankings guarantee best-selling issues and highest advertising prices for the magazines that offer them.) Master morality, as we have sketched it, with its emphasis on the order of rank and the virtue of reverence, looks like a much better candidate for a "business morality" than slave morality.

People often joke that "business ethics" is a misnomer because there is no ethics in business. However, using Nietzsche's analysis we can explain both why there is an ethics of business and why it sometimes puzzles us. The ethic of business, at least of those who take it seriously as an enterprise and aim for excellence within it, is an ethic of virtue. As such, it operates at odds with the rule-based ethics of deontological and consequentialist moralities. Moreover, to the extent that business ethics incorporates a Nietzschean understanding of the virtues, at least within its own domain, it is a virtue theory at odds with other theories that have contributed to Western moral thought.

May the best businesspeople conclude that they are the best people morally speaking? Not if we pay attention to the way Nietzsche understands moral value and evaluation. The best businessperson is the person who has best lived up to the demands of his or her role in his or her character and conduct. However, to say that he or she is also the best sort of person would be to ignore the many other functional roles each plays in his or her community. Success or failure in these other roles must also be taken into account in coming to an overall assessment of a given person.

Is this relativism? It is not relativism in the usual sense of the word. Nietzsche is not suggesting that we simply evaluate people relative to cultural standards or customs. Rather, evaluation is relative to the goal of the roles or practices in which an individual engages, its distinct good. Because most of us adopt many roles, committing ourselves to the pursuit of many goods, we can be subject to and evaluated in terms of many moralities. The best businesspeople are people best in respect to a particular role. It remains an open question whether they are also good tennis partners, neighbors, citizens, or spouses. If so, their success will probably be due in part to virtues displayed in their business practices. Given the number and range of virtues Nietzsche acknowledges in his work, it seems reasonable to suppose other roles could require other virtues.

Nietzsche's virtue theory differs importantly from the virtue theories that preceded his own. Nietzsche's virtues are not Hutcheson's or Hume's, both of whom partake too much of "slave morality" for Nietzsche's tastes. Nor are Nietzsche's virtues Aristotle's or Seneca's, though they have important affinities. The centrality of the pursuit of personal excellence is common to Nietzsche and the classical theorists he admired. Nietzsche's approach is far more pluralistic; the avenues by which excellence is open to be pursued are limited only by our creativity in spotting opportunities, courage in the face of risks, cheerfulness in adversity, and truthfulness, especially with ourselves, about ourselves, and our world. Thus from a Nietzschean perspective, business ethics is by no means a misnomer. Nor is the distinct set of virtues it develops problematic as moral virtues. They are among the virtues any one of us has reason to value, whether or not we think of ourselves as businesspeople (although of course to a certain extent we are all "in business"). Business, and those who make their careers within it, will always be central to the life of our communities. Thus it is in all our interests that its practitioners cultivate the virtues of their calling.

SUGGESTIONS FOR FURTHER READING

Nietzsche's conception of good character was importantly influenced by Aristotle, but differs in key respects. Joseph H. Kupfer discusses similarities and contrast in their respective views of generosity in "Nietzsche and Aristotle Generosity of Spirit," *Journal of Value Inquiry* 32 (1998): 357–368. Susan S. Stocker looks at the differing ways their respective views can be empowering for individuals facing disabilities in "Facing Disability with Resources from Aristotle and Nietzsche," *Medicine, Health Care and Philosophy: A European Journal* 5 (2002): 137–146. John Paley discusses the significance of Nietzsche's master/slave dichotomy for caring professions in "Caring as a Slave Morality: Nietzschean Themes in Nursing Ethics," *Journal of Advanced Nursing* 40 (2002): 25–35. Nietzschean views on the environment are discussed in Martin Drenthen, "The Paradox of Environmental Ethics: Nietzsche's View of Nature and the Wild," *Environmental Ethics* 21 (1999): 163–175, and Wilhelm Schmid, "Did He Not Kiss the Horse? Nietzsche as Ecological Philosopher," Lanei M. Rodemeyer and Aaron Smith, trans., *New Nietzsche Studies* 5 (2002): 1–11.

The question of whether, or how, Nietzsche's noble morality can be viewed as compatible with liberal democratic institutions has been a subject of controversy. Lester H. Hunt offers a case against in "Why Democracy Is an Enemy of Virtue," *International Studies in Philosophy* 30 (1998): 13–21. Arguments for compatibility are offered by Lawrence J. Hatab in *A Nietzschean Defense of Democracy: An Experiment in Postmodern Politics* (Peru: Open Court,

1995) and more recently in "Why We Can Still Be Nietzscheans," *The Journal of Nietzsche Studies* 24 (2002): 132–147. On the same topic, see David Owen, "Equality, Democracy, and Self-respect: Reflections on Nietzsche's Agonal Perfectionism," *The Journal of Nietzsche Studies* 24 (2002): 113–131.

On Nietzsche's lessons for education, see Stefan Ramaeker, "Teaching to Lie and Obey: Nietzsche on Education," *Journal of Philosophy of Education* 35 (2001): 255–268; and Aharon Aviram, "Nietzsche as an Educator?," *Journal of Philosophy of Education* 25 (1991): 219–134.